COURTS OF REFLECTION

A MEMOIR

I0461432

By Michael K. Semiao

And maybe, just maybe, someone was waiting for me…

A young girl who found me and later made herself visible so I could find her too.

To my loving wife Rita, who has weathered my storms and continued to love me through them.

Thank you.

"Perhaps everything terrible is, in its deepest being, something that needs our love."
Rainer Maria Rilke

A Note on Structure

Throughout the memoir you will see the symbol ◇ ◆ ◇.

These moments reflect a shift in perspective, insights, memories, or understandings that rise above the action of the scene. They represent the voice of reflection, the place where experience becomes meaning.

Table of Contents

Preface

There are stories we tell to survive. And then there are stories we tell when we are finally ready to understand. This is one of the latter.

Phil Jackson's principle, *one breath = one mind*, has always stayed with me. It mirrors something I later found in the Army's Holistic Health and Fitness manual: that mindfulness, true presence, is essential not only to performance, but to healing. The connection between breath, clarity, and being fully here became a guiding force for this work.

When Jerry West, in *My Charmed, Tormented Life*, referenced Joan Didion's famous line, *"We tell ourselves stories in order to live,"* it resonated. That was the point. This was not just about telling stories from my youth. It was about reclaiming meaning.

The line from James Patterson. "I want to tell you stories...the way I remember them, anyway," resonates with me.

The more dramatic prose: Dostoevsky, from Crime and Punishment, "Your worst sin is that you have destroyed and betrayed yourself for nothing."

Netochka Nezvanova: "You sensed you should follow a different path, a more ambitious one, you felt you were destined for other things, but you did not know how to achieve them, and, in your misery, you began to hate everything around you."

The temptation to stick to basketball memories, the wins and losses, the stats, and headlines was strong. They are easier to tell apart. More accepted. But I knew a deeper story lived beneath them. Not a better story, just a more honest one.

This book is not about explaining everything. It is about acknowledging what I once could not name: anxiety masked as composure, silence mistaken for strength, success achieved at the expense of connection. The emotional cost of ambition. The toll of being seen but not known.

So why tell my story?

Because I know I am not the only one. Families, even the loving ones, carry unspoken tensions, and silence, when left too long, becomes its own kind of scar.

I do not write about parenting, relationships, or professional pressures directly. But if you have lived through them, you will see the shadows of those struggles in mine.

Writing this came with risk. The risk of not being understood. The risk of not saying what I meant. But the act of telling it truthfully felt like a kind of victory.

I came to understand that failure is never final. It is often just a place to pause, reset, and begin again. That insight did not come all at once. It revealed itself slowly, after years of chasing validation and wondering why the game I loved left me feeling so alone.

Looking back now, I see patterns. I see how deeply I craved recognition while keeping myself hidden. I feared misunderstanding while keeping others distant. These were not signs of weakness. They were signs I was still learning how to live in a world that only saw what I wanted them to see.

And that is why I wrote this:

To step out from behind the performance, to give the younger version of myself a voice and to remind anyone out there who is still carrying silence: you are not alone.

Michael K. Semiao

Introduction

Anxiety had a strange way of shaping reality. It didn't always feel like fear. The racing heart or sweaty palms the physical symptoms people usually associate with this hormonal response were not always present. For me, instead it built a world that felt safe, even comforting, because I did not yet know what existed beyond it. Success gave me structure. Expectations gave me direction. I built my world inside the walls of discipline and repetition, where there was no room for doubt or distraction. For a while, this seemed like enough. I was succeeding. The headlines, the points I scored, each felt like evidence I was doing what I was supposed to do. But something was missing. I kept telling myself that fulfillment would come after the next win, the next milestone. But "later" never arrived. People nodded with approval, but no one, me included, ever celebrated long enough for it to feel real. Everyone expected success. And with expectation came dismissal. People acknowledged achievements and then forgot them. There was no pause. No breath.

I didn't understand why the joy I thought I should feel never came. I did not have the words to explain the quiet loneliness of achievement, the hollowness that lingered where fulfillment was supposed to live. But now, looking back, I see it clearly. Psychologists call it the hedonic treadmill, the relentless pursuit of goals that raise the bar but never satisfies. Ancient traditions warned us long before that external rewards could never bring lasting peace. But I was not thinking about philosophy back then. I was just a kid trying to figure out why the game I loved, the one place I felt safe and seen, also made me feel so alone. I learned earlier that a scoreboard doesn't show happiness. Points and trophies could not measure it. But when you are young, no one tells you that. No one tells you that winning can be isolating. That the thing that sets you apart can also leave you standing alone.

If I could speak to that younger version of myself, I would tell him this: Your achievements do not define you. You will not find joy in applause alone. It will not come with the next win or the next milestone. It comes from within. Learn to embrace yourself even in silence, even after the cheers have faded.

Introduction

This memoir is about that journey. The struggle of a young athlete trying to navigate expectations, success, and self-worth. It is about the emotions we hide, the questions we are afraid to ask, and the crushing weight of victories that feel more like burdens.

Prologue

My story starts at the end.

I lie on the trainer's table at Bryant College in the fall of 1983. The trainer hovers over me, assessing my injury. His whisper cuts through the fog: "Why didn't you say something sooner?"

Acknowledges the unspoken accusation as it hangs in the air.

The chance to prove myself was too tempting to pass up, no matter the cost. Now, facing the real possibility of losing the entire season, brutal questions appear: Was it worth it? What did you prove in the end?

Awareness arrives in pieces. Memories rush in, scattered, urgent, revealing moments that shaped me. My first game at Bryant College as a freshman felt monumental. Every play, every moment, seemed important. I remember facing ranked Cheney State at the Providence Civic Center. That night at AIC, unprepared but thrown into the game, I found the resilience of leading a comeback. The last-second shot at WNEC felt like the culmination of every play I had ever made.

Darker memories surface. Sitting alone in our locker room where I strategized how to keep my scholarship while not playing basketball, which was unthinkable. I remember the heated altercation with one of the co-captains. I had called him out for his lack of hustle during a scrimmage. His response, fueled by a conversation with his girlfriend who admired my play. This sparked a jealous, familiar response. "He thinks he's better than he is."

Or in the evening in someone's dorm suite, four of us, my teammates and I, sat around talking when, surprisingly, player evaluations became the topic of discussion. Bracing for the inevitable, my reaction during this period unfortunately was like a beaten animal, flinching at this topic and discussion. Suddenly, hearing someone say, "Semiao is the best all-around guard we have on our team and maybe the best all-around guard in our conference." Those words, washed away by sentiments unknown to you, abruptly awakened me. Where I now contemplate and measure the game and my own experiences as these memories swirl like a kaleidoscope.

The first game on our schedule is against New Hampshire College at our gym. My experience tells me the first game of the season usually goes two ways: your team comes out strong and burns itself out during the game or you come out tight. My team is suffering through the latter. We are playing tight, cautious, and timid. Sensing the need for a spark, our coach put me in just three minutes into the game. The scouting report on New Hampshire College: the athleticism of New Hampshire allows them to apply full and half-court pressure throughout the game.

During my first possession, I read the defense while advancing the ball toward half-court. Crossing half court, I recognized New Hampshire half-court press, a trap they were eager to set. The New Hampshire head coach hoped I was cold coming off the bench, hoping I would not see the trap forming. I kept my dribble steady, letting the press close in. As they converged, I spotted a gap and exploded through it, splitting the trap with precision.

In the summer of 1979, at the All-New England Basketball Camp in Hartford, Connecticut, I experienced a defining moment. On the second-to-last day, former University of Connecticut basketball coach Dee Rowe prepared to lecture on the fast break. Before starting, he turned to the coaches and asked, "Who is the best team in camp? Without hesitation, they answered in unison: The Braves. My team. Coach Rowe nodded, then scanned our group. His next question was even bigger. Who is the best player at the camp this week? A collective response rang out: "Semiao."

My legs buckled at that acknowledgement. Coach Rowe approached me, extending a firm handshake and placing a hand on my shoulder. Looking into my eyes: "Don't you ever forget this moment." Coach Rowe introduced a fast-break drill. We lined up ready to run.

I caught the outlet pass on the right wing after a missed shot. With a quick left-hand dribble, I cut to the center, pushed the ball ahead, and sprinted after it. I saw a teammate further up the court. One pass later, we had a smooth transition and an easy layup.

After the drill, Coach Rowe approached me. "Why did you dribble like that?" he asked. I explained my strategy. Running without dribbling allowed me to move faster. It maximized our numerical advantage and created a more efficient scoring opportunity.

Coach Rowe grabbed my arm and led me toward the campers. The gym fell silent. Undeterred, he bellowed, "Why did I push the ball ahead and chase it instead of dribbling?" My response in moving the ball forward increases speed and maximizes the fast break's advantage. He pressed further. Why did I pass to my teammate instead of dribbling up the court? My answer was direct; my teammate was open. Passing moves the ball up the court faster than dribbling, and we had a numerical advantage. I wanted to secure an easy basket.

Coach Rowe seemed delighted with my responses. He turned to the campers, asking if they understood what they had just heard. The core principle when I thought about it again was surprisingly straightforward: exploit the fast break mismatch.

Coach Rowe turned to my teammate, the one who had scored. "Why did you run so hard up the floor?" Without hesitation, my teammate answered, if he sprinted up the court and got open, he knew I would find him in the best spot to score. Coach Rowe paused. "How long have you two been teammates?" My teammates response, "Just this week at camp."

The coach looked between us; his voice filled with surprise and admiration. "You built that level of trust with Semiao in one week?" My teammate nodded. "Semiao is easy to play with and a strong leader on the court."

I stood there, absorbing the moment. All the practice, all the effort, had led to this.

I had experienced success before, but never had a teammate spoken about me this way. Something shifted inside me. This moment meant more than any individual achievement.

Coach Rowe thanked my team for helping with his lecture. I walked off the court in a daze, still processing what had just happened. Coach Rowe approached me, extending his hand, and he smiled. "Quite an afternoon for you, huh?" he said, thanking me for my input.

In the next two days, my team will win the camp championship. They will name me Most Valuable Player of both the all-star game and the entire week, an unprecedented achievement. This moment marked a turning point, a transformation I never saw coming.

A Teammate's Point of View

I had not known him before this week, but I had heard about him. His name carried weight, the kind that followed a player into every gym, every camp, every game. I had watched him all week, how he moved, how he saw the floor before anyone else, how he never let a moment get too big for him.

But what stood out most was not the talent. It was all of us who took their cues from him. Without saying much, he set the tone. When things got tough, we looked at him, not just for the ball, but for something more, something unspoken. Confidence. Belief. A reason to push harder.

So, when they asked about leadership, the answer felt obvious.

He was the one we all looked to. The way he played, the way he carried himself, made us believe we could win. That is leadership.

I saw his reaction. The way his body tensed, the way his balance shifted just slightly, like I had said something unexpected. It caught me off guard. Didn't he know?

Didn't he see the way we had followed him? The way he had pulled us all together made us better just by being there?

Maybe not.

I watched as he nodded silently, as if he were trying to hold on to something that might slip away.

That is when I understood. He had never really seen himself the way we did.

Moving toward the lane. Three New Hampshire players hesitated. The defense collapsed. I pulled up at the foul line; a shot I had practiced thousands of times in my driveway. But I was moving too fast. My sneakers squeaked as I came to a sudden stop.

Something feels off. The speed, the height of my jump. I released the shot hoping for the best.

Swish.

I landed, and my left foot collapsed, and my ankle rolled. Adrenaline masked the pain as my pulse thundered in my temples, drowning out all sound. Tears welled up in my eyes, blurring my vision. I tried to stand, and limp to the sideline. Frustration and pain were now competing for dominance.

Following an old, learned behavior, I tightened my sneaker to control the swelling. I noticed my hands shaking, my breathing becoming erratic, and my pulse continuing its relentless pounding.

I had dealt with injuries before, but this injury felt different. With my back to our bench, I faced the visitors' section, noticing people pointing and talking. Each person was visibly concerned. I could not hear their words over the roar in my ears. I bent to tighten my sneaker laces, my hand hitting the floor first, steadying me before pulling them taut.

As I rose and turned to my bench, our coach waved to me. As if on autopilot, I limped toward him. He wrapped an arm around my waist, speaking words I could not hear. I gave a silent nod.

Together, we moved toward the scorer's table. Without hesitation, I signaled to check back into the game. As I reentered, my head felt foggy. Pain pulsed through my foot and ankle with every step.

As I dribble up the court, I notice New Hampshire has abandoned the half-court trap for a man-to-man defense. My teammates recognized the change in strategy. We adjusted, running a pick-and-roll between the forward and the point guard, me. I shifted left, creating space as the forward set up at the top of the key. Spinning back to the right, I drove my defender down the lane, steering him into my teammate's screen. As he reached for the ball, he committed a foul. The sudden stop sent a sharp pain up my leg.

Disoriented, I stepped to the foul line for a one-and-one. My muscle memory took over. I sank both shots, my last points of the game.

During the timeout, I realized I was sweating heavily, a sign of my racing pulse. The coaches' voices blurred into white noise. I barely registered their instructions, recognizing our switch to man-to-man defense only through my teammates' movements.

My injury weakened my defense. To keep my man in front of me, I had to give him space. Challenging passing lanes or providing help defense was out of the question. I felt isolated, sensing I was a liability on defense. My only choice was to bluff, hoping to keep my opponent from taking advantage of my limited mobility.

In past games, I had learned to compartmentalize pain. Injury was just another obstacle to push through. Emotional detachment had always been my defense. Now, I relied on it again, searching for that mental space where pain faded into the background.

As the game progressed, my pain tolerance grew. I forced two steals by deflecting passes, set up plays for my teammates, and drew offensive charges. With each possession, contributing, despite the pain.

One play stood out. I ran the offense, moving left through the top of the key. The defense shifted with me. Then, I spotted my teammate in the right corner, cutting to the basket.

Without hesitation, I fired a two-hand overhead no-look pass. A perfect assist. An easy layup.

The bench erupted. Their excitement burst through the gym.

Years earlier, the Fairhaven Blue Devils played in the MIAA 1978 South Final at Brockton High School. Our opponent, Rockland High School, came from the Old Colony League.

From the opening whistle, we took control. Our quickness overwhelmed them, and we sprinted ahead in the first half.

As the second quarter was quickly ending, our coach called for our four-to-score offense from the four-corner set. It was not just a delay tactic. We spread out across the floor, searching for openings.

I positioned myself in the middle, probing the Rockland defense. My head stayed up, scanning for a teammate breaking free through a screen or backdoor cut.

Moving to my left, I spotted a teammate flashing to the basket. Instinct took over. I fired a two-handed overhead no-look pass. It was crisp, sharp, perfect. But the play drew a foul.

As I walked to half-court, my coach's voice cut through the noise. "Nice pass, but we did not need it."

On one play, I lost my defender with a simple crossover. It surprised even me. Moving from left to right, then back to my left hand, I drove into the lane. I spotted a teammate cutting to the basket. A quick left-handed bounce pass. An easy layup.

The game remained tight. Somehow, I played without further aggravating my ankle, doing whatever I could to help the team.

With one minute left, the score stood at 66. I moved to the right wing. After a ball exchange, my teammates swung the ball back to me. Following our coach's strategy, I looked inside. Our forward flashed through the lane, and I prepared to feed the low post.

I spotted a mismatch in the post, but the passing lane was not there. Dribbling toward the corner, I created space, expecting New Hampshire to trap. My teammate saw my move. He held his position, extending his left hand, a perfect target.

The trap came fast. Three defenders, all around six-foot-five, with wingspans of roughly eighty inches, swarmed me. I extended my arms and lofted a lob pass. My teammate leaped, catching it in one motion. He rose above the defense and released a smooth jump hook.

The ball dropped in. We were now ahead 68-66.

New Hampshire called a timeout. With six seconds remaining in the game.

In the huddle, our coaches were clear: keep the opponent in front of you, hold your position, and do not foul.

A quick internal dialogue played out in my head: one more play… one more play… one more play.

Positioning myself at three-quarter court, I watched New Hampshire inbound the ball to their point guard, John Burris. I met John at the All-New England Basketball Camp during the summer of 1979. John sprinted up the left side of the court, streaking past our bench. Through my experience, I expected his play. Positioning myself to shadow him while using the sideline as an added defensive aid.

Attempting to move toward the court's center, I blocked his path. He pulled up thirty-five feet out. We rose, suspended in an almost balletic moment, balanced, frozen in midair. There was sufficient distance between us to prevent any contact or foul.

I landed as the shot came off the backboard. The buzzer sounded.

Catching my breath, I exchanged a quick handshake with John. I offered a brief "Nice game" before we parted ways.

We fought hard and deserved this victory. Bryant College had defeated New Hampshire College 68-66, launching our season with a hard-earned win.

A Teammate's Point of View

The first game of the season always carried extra weight. The anticipation, the nerves, the energy in the gym, it all felt amplified. We had put in the work during the preseason, but now it was real. And as soon as we stepped onto the court against New Hampshire, it was clear this would not be an easy night.

Three minutes in, Coach made the call. He sent him in, and from the moment he checked in, the pace of the game shifted. New Hampshire was aggressive, pressing at half court, but he did not hesitate. I watched as he sliced through their trap like he had seen it coming a mile away. By the time he reached the foul line, I knew he was pulling up. That was his shot. We had all seen him hit it in practice. He is the best straight-up shooter I have ever seen. But as soon as the ball left his hands, something looked off. He was moving too fast.

Swish.

Then he went down.

At first, it seemed like just another hard landing. Nothing unusual. But when he grabbed his ankle and did not bounce back up right away, I knew it was bad. He barely made it to the sideline, limping, face tight with pain. I thought his night was over. We all did. But then, just minutes later, he was signaling to check back in.

I do not know how he convinced Coach, but there he was, back on the court like nothing had happened.

At first, it was clear he was not himself. He had to adjust, giving his man more space, bluffing on defense instead of stepping up to challenge shots. But then, little by little, he contributed. A deflection occurs here; a stealthy theft happens there. The plays that do not always show up in the box score but change the momentum of a game. And then there was that pass.

I was on the opposite wing, watching as he drew the defenders to him. They were closing in fast. It should have been a turnover, but somehow, in one motion, he flicked a perfect no-look pass over their outstretched arms, hitting our forward in stride for an easy layup. The bench exploded.

That was the moment I realized just how locked in he was. Even injured, he was seeing the game at a different level.

The game stayed tight, possession for possession. Somehow, he kept going, making plays, setting up teammates, making an impact despite barely being able to move the way he normally did.

With a minute left, the score was 66-66.

He found himself trapped in the corner again, this time with three defenders all over him. Most players panic in that situation. But not him. He stayed patient, reading the defense, waiting for the moment to make his move. And then, with perfect touch, he lofted a pass inside. Our forward went up, caught it clean, and finished over the defense, 68-66.

New Hampshire had one last possession. We just needed one stop.

They inbounded to their point guard, John Burris, a guy who could create his own shot from anywhere. He sprinted up the sideline, looking to turn toward the middle. But there he was, cutting him off, forcing him wide.

John had no choice; he pulled up from way beyond his comfort level. It was a prayer. The shot hit the backboard. The buzzer sounded. Game over.

We won. And he, our teammate, the one who should have been in the locker room with us celebrating our win. He had played a crucial role in getting us our win.

After the game, I saw him on the trainer's table, his ankle swollen, his expression distant. The trainer muttered something about why he had not spoken up sooner, but we all knew the answer. He would not sit this one out.

That night, I realized something about him. Certain individuals derive pleasure from the activity. He played because, in his view, to him, there was no other choice. No matter the pain, no matter the risk, when the game was on the line, he was going to be out there.

And that is why, even though his body paid the price, we all knew we could count on him when it mattered most.

Chapter One

B efore basketball became the center of my life, there was a place: southeastern Massachusetts, a landscape of small towns, fading mill cities, and quiet back roads where my childhood unfolded.

Southeastern Massachusetts includes fifty-two cities and towns from Bristol, Plymouth and Norfolk Counties. Massachusetts Bay, Buzzards Bay, the Taunton River watershed, and its location relative to Boston, Rhode Island and Cape Cod geographically define the region. Bristol County, Massachusetts, and Bristol County, Rhode Island, are contiguous and are the only counties in the nation where Portuguese Americans make up the plurality of the population. This is because of the Portuguese American, Portuguese Brazilian and the Portuguese-Cape Verdean population that came to Southern New England in the 19th century to do the much-needed whaling work.

The Wampanoag sold Acushnet in 1652. Throughout its history, three separate towns included it. It was formerly the northeastern section of the town, Dartmouth, as well as Old Dartmouth, which included the towns of Westport, New Bedford and Fairhaven.

In 1787, New Bedford separated from Dartmouth, bringing Fairhaven and Acushnet along. Incorporating Fairhaven in 1812 shifted the boundaries again. In 1860, Acushnet gained independence.

Initially, Native Wampanoag people named this land "peaceful resting place near water." These original inhabitants later sold their land to Puritan settlers, forever changing the landscape.

Founded in 1910, manufacturing by the Acushnet Process Company spurred the town's economic growth. Unlike diverse New Bedford, Acushnet remained white, shaping social boundaries in daily life.

During this period, by the 1970s, Acushnet's quiet roads filled with new homes; its population jumped from 7,700 to 8,700 within a decade. Our first home in Williams Park development reflected this expansion. The small three-bedroom ranch housed our family for two and a half years. It finally felt like home. From 1971 through 1982, my family lived in Acushnet.

Until our family moved there, Acushnet was a place that existed beyond my childhood imagination. Rural landscapes stretched before my eyes. A dairy farm with grazing cows appeared off the main road, and apple orchards surrounded our neighborhood. My earliest impression of our new home was the silence. No more ambulance sirens wailing toward St. Luke's Hospital. At night, instead of sirens, I heard crickets ticking in the weeds.

In this pastoral setting, I watched my adolescent and teenage years unfold. My parents, younger and more economically mobile, stood for a new generation in our neighborhood and town. It seemed every week another foundation appeared. New driveways carved through old fields, construction trucks rattling through our neighborhood.

Our education changed because of the town's small-school approach. Grammar schools dotted the landscape, complemented by a dedicated building for fifth and sixth graders and a junior high school. My sister and I attended Marie S. Howard Elementary School on Middle Road, a modest four-classroom building that somehow held an entire world of learning.

The school sponsored a book club, hoping to encourage reading. This club opened unexpected doors for me. The book, *Basketball Magician,* is just a basketball book, so I thought, but this one, about Pete Maravich, was the prize. I devoured each page, tracing the path of his records, the achievements listed like impossible feats. How had a player like this escaped my notice? His name, his face, the stories, they were a world I had never known, but one I knew, even then, would chart the course of my life.

Months later, fate deepened this connection. Visiting family friends one wintery afternoon, on their television, the sound of a basketball game and the name Pete Maravich caught my attention. Magically pulling me toward their empty living room. I sat cross-legged on the shag carpet, eyes inches from the screen, while behind me adults murmured over coffee. There, a slim figure with floppy hair commanded the screen, his movements hypnotic. During a fast break, Maravich executed a behind-the-back dribble at full speed. The moment seared into my memory. Basketball. I had never seen it played this way. His speed and casual mastery replayed in my mind in slow motion, each viewing drawing me deeper into the game's possibilities.

During Marie S. Howard's recess periods, my competitive instincts appeared each day. Testing that vision daily, mixed with other sports, was where I discovered my natural coordination. My ability to excel in running, catching, and throwing, I thought, set me apart from my classmates. Whispers about a local basketball league caught my attention, sparking dreams of measuring my raw talent against my peers.

Athletic excellence was absent from our family's history. Yet my father's genuine gift was not his swing or his backhand; it was his mind. For example: my father mentioned distance running to build a well of endurance. My father sensed my ambition. Instead of pushing me, he would talk about the great local high school players, dropping names and stories into our casual conversations. My father understood that those simple tales would be enough to keep me motivated, not just to improve at basketball, but to improve as an athlete.

Although there was little encouragement for women's sports in her time, my mother excelled at swimming and tennis, exceeding expectations. My sister inhabited a different athletic realm. Natural talent flowed through her movements, whether picking up a tennis racket after months away from the sport or dominating the field hockey pitch. Basketball became an afterthought for her, played with casual brilliance.

Over time, my path took a different route. Through sheer determination, I became what players call a gym rat, constantly striving for improvement. Simple logic guided my approach: more practice meant better performance. Yet, time revealed a deeper truth. Success demanded more than endless hours of repetition. It required strategic and purposeful effort. What began as repetition became ritual, the engine that would carry me for years.

Repetitive actions soothed my racing mind and became my haven. Yet this comfort led to impossible self-expectations. My coaches often saw this struggle, watching me battle with visible frustration over missed shots. "Semiao, you can't make them all." These words penetrated my self-imposed standards.

When Acushnet merged its grammar schools, the new elementary school changed its educational landscape. Students from across the town converged for the first time, revealing the true scale of our community. Also, to prepare students for junior high, the school implemented a structured lunch program, organized gym classes for fifth and sixth graders, and set up class rotations.

Gym class reintroduced structured athletic competition, reminding me of summers at *Camp Massasoit*. While other students struggled with organized physical activities, I found my element. Physical measurements showed nothing out of the ordinary. Yet endurance, speed, and throwing accuracy set me apart, hinting at untapped potential. The traditional familiar sound of sneakers squeaking across the gym floor was comforting to me. Hearing my classmates gasp for breath and watching them struggle physically was also comforting, but for entirely distinct reasons. Those sounds and touches empowered me to state my case as a developing athlete. No words, just effort.

For six summers, the YMCA-sponsored Camp Massasoit became the mainstay of our summers. My family invested time and resources to ensure this experience shaped our development. The camp's blend of sports, swimming, arts, and sciences created a complete world. My sister and I transformed into confident swimmers with our family's encouragement. Swimming lessons during the fall at the YMCA introduced stroke refinement and lifeguard-saving techniques. Watching our peers struggle with coordination and the physical nature of what was asked of us created a hierarchy of sorts in our peer group. I can remember willingly accepting the leadership during our endurance swim. Somehow the water in the pool became less of a barrier for me when I tried to process my body image issues. Physically, I was quickly maturing. Hair appeared in areas on my body that were not shared by my peer group. I was average in size, but I knew my physical size had changed in the last year. It was odd to acknowledge; I did not have the physical characteristics of a young boy any longer; I was more closely identified as a young man. With that, my body image issues were raging.

Tennis entered my life by accident, then it tried to teach me purpose. Unlike any sport I had tried before, tennis drew me in with its geometry and quiet precision. The first thing that captivated me was the sound, the clean, sharp pop when the ball met the center of the racquet. For a split second, it felt as though the ball stayed there, suspended in my control, before being released across the net. That illusion, the catch and release, became addictive. The pop of the ball off the strings was tennis itself. Every player I would later meet chased that same sound and feeling for as long as they played.

Tennis was unlike anything I had tried before. The court's layout and the elegance of the game intrigued me. The lessons introduced by my parents refined my raw ability. During this period, I discovered joy in the sport through sheer will and the challenge of movement. It became an opportunity to stand out in a setting where none of my friends played.

However, what started as a source of enjoyment soon became overwhelming. I began playing tennis in the summer of 1972. My family had been vacationing in the White Mountains of New Hampshire. On the way home, we stopped at a resort for lunch, and in the distance, I saw four tennis courts. Their surface, bright green with crisp white lines, looked impossibly perfect, like something out of another world.

My father noticed me watching the courts. He surprised me when he said, "You know, we could play when we get home." I still remember the first time I went onto the court with him. The quietness of the surroundings left a lasting impression on me, where the only sounds were of the ball off your tennis racket, the faint scrape of shoes against the baseline. Playing with my father was rewarding because it gave me time alone with him, something I always valued. I tried to mimic the motions I had seen, but even simple swings felt foreign, my timing off, my confidence flickering.

It was also during that time that I discovered something unexpected in myself, a "look at me" persona, which appeared whenever someone familiar stopped to watch us play. I ran harder, hit with more force, and exaggerated each movement. My father laughed it off, but I could feel the shift inside me. What needed to be seen was something I did not yet understand.

My physical limitations led to embarrassment, and struggling with instructions created a sense of judgment and inadequacy. I was still reeling from my experiences during the early years of grammar school, where I often felt lost and behind. My reaction toward authority was defensive, always reactive.

Lessons from a tennis professional, a family friend, felt more like report cards than guidance. I measured every correction as a sign of failure, which only pushed me to practice more aggressively. Once, my mistakes were visible to the entire neighborhood, and the embarrassment burned deeper than any physical exhaustion. In hindsight, those moments mirrored my struggles with basic learning skills like reading and math, each mistake feeling like proof I was not enough.

Subtly and quietly, I gave up tennis. The tennis racquets were put away, and the conversations surrounding tennis ended. Hoping its absence will simplify my life. Instead, I was straddling a line that I had not expected. My decision to stop playing tennis, in my eyes, real or not, strained my relationship with my parents. For years, the weight of responsibility pressed down on me, driving me to seek validation. I left tennis behind, but its reverberation stayed: how quickly joy can collapse under expectation.

What began as distraction became devotion. Sports were not just something I watched; they became the language that my father and friends spoke. Television schedules became sacred texts as I planned my viewing around every game.

In the fall of 1971, my father and I saw our first professional football game, a pivotal moment. The New England Patriots, in their inaugural season under that name, faced the Detroit Lions at Schaefer Stadium in Foxboro, Massachusetts. The game itself is a distant memory, but the stiff aluminum benches we sat on created an impression, as did the legendary players: Jim Plunkett, Randy Vataha, Greg Landry, and Hall of Fame player Lem Barney.

During the fall of 1973, new athletic doors opened when my sister and I took part in the National Punt, Pass, and Kick competition. This led to my joining Acushnet's pee-wee football team. Around the same time, my family moved into our newly built house, just up the street from where we had been living. My father's installation of a basketball hoop in our driveway seemed like a simple addition. Yet, this metal rim and backboard would reshape my life.

My father, noting my deepening interest in sports, particularly basketball, began taking me to professional games at Boston Garden. Watching the Boston Celtics revealed a level of athletic dedication that struck me. Even then, questions formed in my young mind about commitment and possibility; about what it meant to pursue excellence.

In November 1973, my family spent the day in Boston, culminating in a basketball game at the Boston Garden, where the Celtics faced the great New York Knicks. The Knicks featured players like guards Walt Frazier, Earl Monroe, and center Willis Reed.

The intensity and skill of each player captivated me; the raw competitiveness was unlike anything I had ever seen. Watching Dave Cowens sprint the court and battle inside against Willis Reed, seeing John Havlicek in a constant state of motion, admiring Walt Frazier's effortless cool with every play, and marveling at Earl

Monroe creating advantages with his mind and body, each moment burned into my imagination. After seeing this, how could anyone not want that in their life?

Over the next five years, we watched the greats in their sport: NBA icons Spencer Haywood, Connie Hawkins, Pete Maravich, Billy Cunningham, and Julius Erving showed basketball's artistic possibilities. Beyond basketball, my family experienced Carl Yastrzemski's mastery at Fenway Park and Bobby Orr's brilliance at the Boston Garden. We ventured to the Yale Bowl in Connecticut for a college football game and attended elite college basketball games at Boston College and Providence College.

One unforgettable afternoon, my father introduced me to Eddie "The King" Feigner in New Bedford. Watching this legendary softball player command his four-man team, *The King and His Court*, revealed how athletic excellence could transcend traditional boundaries.

Playing sports with my friends often left me unfulfilled. Their endurance faded while my drive held fast. In learning how to play basketball, I welcomed solitary practice, allowing me to embrace the repetition others avoided. While my friends sought easier paths, I discovered and pursued daily improvement with relentless focus. My friends left early. I stayed. When darkness plumes, an unrelenting pursuit begins.

During Thanksgiving week in 1973, our family traveled to New Orleans to visit my mother's sister. A basketball came with me everywhere: my cousin's driveway, street surfaces, even the chimney walls echoed with my dribbling. My aunt's patience wore thin. My uncle, a former Tulane University football and baseball player, took me to a nearby park. Two hours of shooting brought me perfect athletic satisfaction. Unfortunately, it would be the only visit to that park during our stay.

As if the stars had aligned, I was fortunate to grow up in a neighborhood with former athletes who had played in high school and college. They gave their time and support throughout my formative years. My neighbors and my father introduced me to Acushnet's men's league and its weekly games at Ford Junior High School gymnasium. The competition with experienced former high school and college athletes sharpened my skills and sped up my development.

My promotion to the sixth grade in 1973 would bring the conversation back to the basketball league my friends referenced. During one dinner, I casually mentioned to my mother I would be interested in playing in this league. Unbeknownst to me at this point in my development, I did not know this conversation would directly change my future. The next evening, I would learn that the Ford Junior High School gymnasium would host tryouts.

Through my father's connections, he secured practice locations across the New Bedford area, each carrying its own history. The most memorable was the old New Bedford High School gymnasium, a court once home to the area's most talented players and teams. Stepping onto that floor felt like walking into a legacy. Another unique venue was Hope Evangelical Community Church in North Dartmouth, where the auditorium doubled as a makeshift gym. We played only after every chair was stacked and moved aside from Sunday services, but the effort never mattered. The chance to play was always worth it.

On the night of the tryouts, I showed up at the gym in blue jeans, a white t-shirt, and sneakers. Kids packed the gym, and I noticed unfamiliar players. While I had not expected to know every kid in Acushnet, I would learn later the unfamiliar players attended St. Francis Middle School, a private school in Acushnet.

The tryouts involved basketball drills to evaluate players. During the draft, the coach of the Acushnet Citizens Club (ACC), Tom Viera, picked me as the first choice. Mr. Viera, though I am inexperienced, he liked my aggressiveness and overall athletic ability. During the brief period when I had taken tennis lessons, my father was the only person to have formally coached me. Mr. Viera was an excellent first coach. The display of patience and his ability to walk me through each phase of instruction were important to me.

Practices began, and what stood out at once was my pure athleticism. In my basketball skills, I excelled around the basket, especially in defensive rebounding. My quick reflexes set me apart from my teammates, and I pursued every rebound. However, the rest of my basketball skills were underdeveloped, and my understanding of the game was immature. For example, not reacting to a weak side play or standing in the lane creating consistent three-second violations. What I lacked in skill, I made up for in sheer competitiveness.

We had four practices scheduled before the season began. While I felt confident, I was also eager to see how I would perform in an actual game. During practice, I learned to play in a 2-1-2 zone defense. Our coach positioned me as the "one" in the middle. Also, learning the basic skills and concepts to play one-on-one defense.

We ran a 2-1-2 offense, with me again in the middle, playing a medium to high post position. I realized I could beat my defender down the lane for layups, which became my go-to move.

Besides learning the physical skills for playing basketball, someone introduced me to a new language. The terminology of basketball is unique unto itself. I would learn over time that each sport has its own language.

The basketball league games took place at Ford Junior High School, where the basketball court was small and confined. Each end line sat tight against the walls, and the sidelines ran close to the benches. Full-sized white wooden backboards stood at each end, with four half-backboards mounted on the walls.

While practicing with my team, someone introduced me to the give-and-go play: a "give-and-go" or "pass-and-cut" is an offensive move where a player passes to a teammate, then cuts toward the basket or gets open to receive the pass back and create a scoring opportunity. Its effectiveness surprised me. Passing the ball, cut to the basket, and my defender, focused on the ball, lost track of me. It was simple, yet immensely powerful.

At the end of our dead-end street, our house bordered dense woods. At night, the neighborhood was silent. The only sounds were the rhythm of my basketball ricocheting off the driveway, the thud of the ball, the scuff of my sneakers, and the swish of the net. My father had installed garage lights, not meant for practice, but they illuminated just enough: the white backboard glowing, the orange rim suspended in the dark, while the surrounding woods dissolved into shadow. From a distance, it must have looked unworldly, an island of light floating in the night.

For me, it was my world. Each dribble and shot cut through the silence, carrying across the neighborhood. Sometimes it carried too far, a neighbor complained, and the police were called. But I kept practicing, drawn to the ritual. The surrounding darkness only heightened my focus.

Those nights belonged to me, and they shaped the player I was becoming.

And when the nights faded into days, the driveway was waiting again, no shadows, no silence, just the repetition of practice that became my constant companion.

I prepared myself as well as possible for the upcoming basketball season. There were six teams, three per division. We played each team twice. My coach selected the starting five, and I earned the center spot. A mix of excitement and caution led to both anticipation and dread.

Joining the basketball league brought an unfamiliar experience: nervousness before a game. I had read stories about Bill Russell vomiting before every game, showing anxiety not just about playing, but playing *well*. I never thought of myself as an impressionable kid, but that story stuck with me and enhanced my unease.

Reading about other athletes with similar experiences gave me a sense of relief. I was not alone. This was not abnormal. And with my ambition bursting at the seams, I came to accept that pre-game anxiety would be part of the process. Unfortunately, I would learn that anxiety was not a guarantee of success, or playing well, or even winning. But it was a part of me.

During this period of adjusting to formal competition, I discovered a psychological syndrome where certain athletes may have instinctively pursued physical contact or engaged in high-energy activities to regulate their nervous systems and enhance performance.

Sports performance anxiety, sensory activation, and psychological arousal regulation relate to this phenomenon, where physical contact or an intense moment could awaken you, letting you play freely. Clinically, it may have been a form of sensory grounding, a psychological process where a physical stimulus refocuses the mind. It also reflected the inverted-U theory in sports psychology, which suggested that best performance occurred at a specific level of arousal, not too low (lethargic) and not too high (overanxious). I remember one game where a hard screen jolted me out of my nerves, my heart steadied, the court grew quiet, and everything slowed enough for me to play effectively.

Through the first five games of the season, my team remained undefeated. Our sixth game was against the American Legion team, coached by Mr. Koczera, which was also undefeated. That team included Bobby Langlois, who later played for Bishop Connolly High School in Fall River. Bobby and I would eventually become teammates on the New Bedford Buddies off-season tournament team.

The American Legion team was well-balanced and well-coached. We matched up well, except at the guard position, where they had two quick, skilled players.

In the winter of 1974, one afternoon after school, a friend and I walked across the junior high school soccer field to watch the junior high school basketball team play. It was my first time seeing them in action. What stood out most was the size of the players. My friend noticed it too. Watching one player take the ball out of bounds near us, he asked, "Do you plan on playing here next year?" I nodded affirmatively.

"Good luck with that," he added.

My team lost to the American Legion team twice during the regular season and again in the playoffs. We finished second in the league. Four teams made the playoffs, with two from each division advancing. We were the second seed and made it to the finals, but we still could not beat the American Legion team. Their guard play outmatched ours.

A key moment during the season came when Albert F. Ford Junior High School basketball coach, Ron Hall, served as the lead referee during our league championship game. For me, it showed the level of importance our league held in the eyes of those looking to the future.

By the end of the season, I had proven myself as the team's top scorer, averaging twelve points and eight rebounds per game. I made the All-Star team and won Most Valuable Player (MVP) in the All-Star game, scoring sixteen points and grabbing ten rebounds. I also earned Rookie of the Year and finished second in league MVP voting.

After the season ended in February 1974, my father mentioned he had spoken with the American Legion coach. The team had a tournament the following weekend at St. Francis Middle School. He asked whether I wanted to join them. Without any hesitation, I agreed.

The next evening, I practiced with the American Legion team at the junior high school gym. Initially, I was nervous about joining a new team, but I felt at ease thanks to my welcoming teammates. Practice began with a full-court three-man weave, a drill I had never done before. This team played faster and had more skilled players than my league team. Thanks to the drills my father had taught me, I kept up.

The guards were sharper, and I quickly developed chemistry with their center. We practiced a zone offense designed around an overload play. It allowed the center and me to work inside while the guards stretched the defense. I was familiar with the 2-1-2 zone defense, but now I play the wing and baseline instead of the middle. Practicing one-on-one defense was tougher because of my teammates' speed and skill.

At the end of practice, the coaches reviewed the tournament rules. This was a four-team tournament, double elimination. Teams could press for the entire game. This was new for me, but my teammates, experienced in tournament play, seemed unfazed. At the next practice, we would focus on press defense. The coaches then shared a scouting report of St. Francis, our opponent. The scouting report focused on one player: Mike Verronneau. An eighth grader in 1974, he was strong, agile, and capable of scoring inside and outside. He rebounded well and played with relentless effort. Our strategy was clear: stay active on offense, use pump fakes before shooting inside, and avoid fouling on defense. The challenge ahead proved why the team had recruited me.

They held the tournament across town at the St. Francis gym. Our first game was the second of the afternoon. My family and I arrived early, and the atmosphere overwhelmed me. Spectators packed the gym to watch the first game. Cheerleaders flanked both teams. Coaches paced the sidelines, giving instructions and encouragement. I had not expected the event to feel so serious.

The basketball court at St. Francis was part of the auditorium. Not a traditional basketball court. Tiled floors in the auditorium would create challenging footing. The court layout was larger than I had played on previously. The backboards had a half-moon shaped. There was ample space around the sidelines and end lines.

Soon after we arrived, my father tapped me on the shoulder to let me know my coach and teammates had shown up. On the way to the locker room, I noticed Mr. Viera and Mr. Hall sitting together. Their presence underscored the tournament's importance in our town.

I hurried down the corridor to catch up with my team. Our coach nodded as I entered the locker room, acknowledging my arrival. My teammates were getting ready, quietly focused on preparation. The mood was tense. Following their lead, I stayed silent and got myself ready.

Taking the court for warmups, the eerie quiet of the gym despite the packed bleachers. St. Francis cheerleaders watched curiously, almost dismissive as we ran through the three-man weave and two-line layup drills. But when the St. Francis team entered the court, they erupted.

Leading them was Mike Verronneau. He looked taller and more imposing than I expected. As he moved through warmups, I noticed he wore a knee support, something I had never seen before. He ignored our team completely. His cool, detached demeanor left an impression on me and became a persona I would later adopt.

The game began, and we lost the opening jump ball. We settled into our zone defense, but St. Francis easily fed Verronneau. He hit a quick turnaround jumper from ten feet, banking it in. The crowd and cheerleaders responded as you would think they would, with a loud roar. This was another new encounter for me. Playing before a crowd. A hostile crowd. Your mind gets in the way when you are trying to work through what your senses are seeing and hearing. It is overwhelming. Following my teammates' behavior and not letting all this distract me. I was not sure whether I could pull this off.

We struggled early, turning the ball over multiple times and giving up easy baskets. Within moments, we trailed 6–0.

Our coach called a timeout. Sensing our nerves, he reminded us to support each other and play smart. Regrouping, we executed better. Our center hit the high post, and I flashed to the middle, but Verronneau stayed with me. The ball went to Bobby Langlois on the wing. He hit a smooth twelve-foot jumper, putting us on the board.

St. Francis responded. Verronneau caught the ball at the high post and drove past our center for an easy layup. On our next possession, we adjusted, placing me at the high post. I received the ball, turned, and saw our center screening Verronneau, creating space. Taking one dribble, I hit a ten-foot jumper, a shot I had practiced countless times. But I was always reluctant to try the shot in a live game. Executing it in a game felt surreal, almost instinctual.

Throughout the first half, we kept the game close, but Verronneau made the difference. Whenever St. Francis needed a basket, he delivered. Tracking him proved to be challenging.

Trailing by six points entering the second half, something changed. St. Francis seemed indifferent, so we played more aggressively. Our offense exploited their zone defense, finding patterns that led to points or fouls. Lob and controlled bounce passes improved our inside game.

Our overload offense forced their defense to hesitate. If they collapsed inside, Bobby Langlois was open on the wing. If they focused on the perimeter, we attacked inside, where we had an advantage. These adjustments helped us close the gap.

As the game wore on, fatigue set in. We committed more fouls, and our offense became unsettled. What worked in the third quarter broke down in the fourth. Slowing down only seemed to backfire, and we trailed by four to six points.

Feeling a sense of urgency, I became more assertive, focusing on scoring. Our inside passing became predictable, so I adjusted by taking more shots, half-hooks, short jumpers, and layups.

Verronneau stayed involved in the game, but my actions led him to adjust, creating opportunities for passes. Sensing the advantage for the first time playing organized sports, I felt I could use my position, and I wanted the ball on every possession. With the score tied, St. Francis called a timeout. We felt like our third-quarter energy had returned, but it was an illusion.

Coming out of the timeout, St. Francis found Verronneau for an easy basket. On our next possession, we turned the ball over, leading to a breakaway layup. Just like that, we were down four points.

I received the ball at the high post. Feeling emboldened, I drove straight at Verronneau. He bodied me up, but I pump-faked him into the air. I released an awkward shot, and somehow it went into the basket, while Verronneau fouled me. He slammed the ball down in frustration, which startled me more than the shot going in.

In a daze, I went to the foul line and made the free throw. We were now down just one point. St. Francis called another timeout.

With ninety seconds left, we switched to man-to-man defense, hoping to force a turnover. St. Francis responded by stalling, executing the North Carolina four corners offense. I had seen this strategy only on television. They ran it well, forcing us to foul. St. Francis capitalized by making their free throws.

We never recovered and lost by three points. Disappointment hit me, but I did not know how to process the loss. We played hard, but we still lost. My teammates were upset, so I mirrored their demeanor as we walked to the locker room.

Despair clung to the quiet locker room walls. When I stepped out, I saw my father talking to our coach. They called me over and praised my performance against tough competition.

Reflecting on the game, I felt proud of how I played. I finished with sixteen points, six rebounds, four assists, and two steals. I played the entire game. One result of this tournament was the sudden realization that I could play at the next level.

The next day, in the loser's bracket, we won, fueled by frustration from the St. Francis loss. St. Francis won the tournament, with Mike Verronneau earning most valuable player honors.

The following week, talk began about competing in future tournaments and forming an all-star team from our league. The all-star team was created and registered to play in a tournament at Keith Junior High School in New Bedford. My father, Mr. Viera, and Mr. Koczera agreed to coach the team together. Practices began at Ford Junior High School twice a week. The coaches installed a simple offense and defense, nothing unfamiliar. Tournament rules allowed full-court pressure, just like the games at the St. Francis tournament.

Despite the excitement, I felt distracted, unfocused in practice and disconnected from my teammates. My frustration boiled over at home, where I could not shake the apathy that had set in. Even when I practiced alone in my driveway, I went through the motions, unable to explain the shift. For the first time, I noticeably sulked. Until then, I had imagined myself as someone who thrived on competition, drawn to the professionals' discipline and composure. But with expectations mounting, I bent under the weight and quietly realized I did not yet have the tools to become the player I hoped to be.

We won our first game of the tournament. My team played well, but I did not contribute. The second game was close, but we lost. Again, I had no meaningful impact. Frustration overshadowed my disappointment. I felt confused and demoralized, unsure why I had checked out.

The drive home after the game with my father was silent and tense. Once home, he sat me down, disappointment clear. If I did not want to play anymore, he said, he would respect that. However, he stressed the importance of honesty. Before investing more time and money, I needed to decide. He reminded me of my talent and the responsibility that came with it. If I wanted to succeed, I had to take ownership of my abilities. My father asked why I had been acting this way for two weeks. I answered, but my responses only frustrated him more. My father pressed for answers I could not give; my mother stayed silent.

Though it felt like hours, the discussion lasted about thirty minutes. The weight lingered long after. My parents sent me to my room, saying we would talk again in the morning. Before bed, frustration consumed me. Part of me was ready to walk away and deal with the fallout. Lying awake in the early morning, I suddenly saw what was right in front of me, opportunity. Emboldened, I decided to go all in.

I reflected on my father's frustration and realized it mirrored my own. His message was clear: I needed to own my talent. It was time to grow up. The shift in my behavior was out of character, and even now, I am not sure why I took that step. I had already convinced myself and my parents that I was the kind of person who gave up at the first sign of a challenge. The memory of my tennis lessons and how that experience played out in my mind still plagued me. Looking over my shoulder, second-guessing myself and my parents, was not healthy for any of us.

The next morning, I woke early and went straight to the driveway. My father soon joined me. We played twenty-one, H-O-R-S-E, and Around the World in silence. When we finished, he asked, "What are your plans?" Completely out of character, my response is, I am going to try out for the junior-high team. I want to start, lead the team in scoring, and break the school scoring records.

Setting ambitious goals was becoming a pattern. My father, ever measured, raised an eyebrow, and asked, 'How will you do it?'

I told him I had overheard the American Legion players talking about a basketball camp at Mass Maritime Academy and that I wanted to go, believing it could help me reach my goals.

My father nodded, said he would investigate the camp, and left it at that. In the same conversation as if he had predicted my decisions, my father also mentioned a summer league in New Bedford and the idea of forming a team. When he asked what I thought, I told him it was a great idea. The New Bedford Summer League would become one of the launching points of my athletic career and, more importantly, the foundation of my reputation years later.

As spring 1974 approached, my father began recruiting. His first call went to Phil Gelinas, Acushnet Junior High School's single-game scoring record holder. Phil suggested Kevin Pelletier from his junior high school team and Mike Verronneau from St. Francis. Both eagerly joined. Mr. Hall, the junior-high school basketball coach, recommended Jeff Pina from Old Rochester Middle School, a gifted, team-first athlete who excelled in multiple sports. His contribution gave us an enormous boost.

With the team coming together, my father secured sponsorship from St. Luke's Hospital. Their support legitimized our team and commitment. We began practicing, building chemistry and understanding each other's playing styles. Each session helped turn us into a cohesive unit.

One evening, my family watched Mikhail Baryshnikov perform. His athleticism and grace captivated me. Ballet seemed as demanding as any other sport.

The next afternoon, my father mentioned ballet's physical rigor. He wondered aloud whether strength, balance, and agility from ballet could help me. I dismissed the idea at once. My ego, tied to immature fears, rejected outright. The conversation ended, never revisited.

That night, while I was alone in my room, the idea lingered. Stripped of stigma, ballet looked different, a study in flight, strength, and balance that could have complemented my training.

The next morning, I wanted to bring it up with my father, but I hesitated. Doubt crept in. I stayed silent. Looking back, I see a missed opportunity.

The experience taught me the value of open-mindedness. At that age, I was not mature enough to see its worth. The real lesson was learning to push past the inner and outer voices where criticism and ridicule hide.

The New Bedford Recreation Department managed the summer league, which featured future high school teammates and rivals. My role was clear: I was there to watch and learn. I studied how these players prepared, how they managed in-game situations, and how they carried themselves. Watching opponents, I began recognizing patterns. Could they dribble with both hands? Were they catch-and-shoot players, drivers or pass-first guards? Did they defend? Even then, I was dissecting the game, building a basketball IQ that would serve me well.

Traveling from park to park, I understood the weight each matchup carried. Each neighborhood park carried its own reputation, creating a level of competitiveness you didn't find in high-school basketball. This was different. The anticipation felt more complex than I had been prepared for. The pressure was real, and every game carried elevated expectations. These games were about more than ability; they built your reputation. I learned that early. The league demanded focus and maturity.

Our regular-season success earned us a playoff spot, but Sonny Silva and Gary Dias formed a strong guard duo, a difficult matchup for us. We lost in the first round of the playoffs. Sonny's game was smooth and controlled; Gary was quick and explosive. We could not match their guard play. Later in my career, both would become familiar adversaries in high school.

Buttonwood Park hosted the finals for each division. While the junior and senior divisions interested me, the open division was more captivating. The best players from the New Bedford area competed there: Tom Baroa, Eddie Rodrigues, Brian Baptiste, Nunu Gonsalves, Paul, and Billy Walsh. Countless pickup games, as well as their high school performances, had built their reputation. Their chemistry and competitive edge left an impression. I saw what years of dedication could produce.

Meanwhile, my father enrolled me in the basketball camp at Mass Maritime. We discussed it briefly. True to form, when I showed interest in something, my father made it happen.

I was optimistic about attending, but my mother had concerns. She insisted I would not stay overnight, as the camp preferred. Instead, I would commute daily, with someone driving me back and forth from camp. This was a significant commitment from my parents and family.

Their dedication to supporting my development did not go unnoticed. Seeing their effort made me realize how pivotal this moment was. This was not just another activity; it was a step toward becoming the player I aspired to be.

In the summer of 1974, I watched the senior players in the New Bedford summer league and noticed the reverence they inspired. Kids craned their necks, grown men paused conversations just to watch. People spoke about them with respect, admiration, even awe.

The discussions I overheard drew me in. My eyes lit up whenever talk of that world surfaced. Even as a young athlete, without fully understanding why, my curiosity kept me close.

The level of evaluation was always present, circling, watching, listening, advising as you developed. To overhear those same words about yourself felt almost otherworldly. Whether or not anyone ever spoke of me that way, I carried the thought with me.

The idea of a virtual passport, one that allowed entry and acceptance into what felt like an exclusive club, captivated me.

I often searched for other interests, hoping to find the same challenge, the joy, and the torment that basketball offered. The thrill of practice, the rush of competition and the exhilaration of leaving everything on the court. Each game felt like a story unfolding, a new puzzle to solve. Where else could a kid find such intensity, with parents encouraging the adventure?

Even then, I did not fully understand the pull. But my parents gave me the freedom to explore sports in ways my friends could not. Older athletes had access to it, the opportunity to chase dreams, and I wanted to be part of that world.

Sports offered freedoms that felt exclusive. Once I stepped inside, I did not want to leave.

By the end of that summer, the distance between watching and belonging shrank. What had once felt like a world reserved for others, the older players, the familiar faces, the ones whose names carried weight, suddenly felt within reach. I could feel the pull, the invitation to evaluate myself against that measure. The curiosity that once kept me on the sidelines had turned into something else, something restless. I was not just dreaming of being part of the club anymore. I was ready to find out if I truly belonged there.

This is my first experience at a basketball camp. The unrecognizable dynamics that hits you right in the face are sounds and movement. From the beginning, it is disorienting. Basketballs bouncing, whistles blowing sounding like metronomes, players moving swiftly before my eyes in a color stream. Watching the coaches veiled attempts to quell the chaotic behavior whirling around the gym.

Gerry Alaimo, Brown University's head basketball coach, led the Mass Maritime Academy basketball camp. The coaching staff and guest speakers were impressive, Jack Leaman from the University of Massachusetts, who coached Julius Erving; George Blaney from Holy Cross; and Gary Walters from Dartmouth. As a young player, I did not yet grasp all their philosophies, but the seriousness of their delivery left an imprint. When Coach Walters spoke about ball handling, you could feel his belief that discipline and mastery were inseparable.

The coach who influenced me most was Vic Colucci, a Providence College standout who once scored thirty-six points against Lew Alcindor's UCLA team. Under his guidance, we drilled the fundamentals of shooting, hand placement, squared shoulders, hips and feet aligned, full follow-through. His lessons felt less like instruction and more like initiation. Each correction carried weight. These teachings became the foundation of my future as a player.

The camp-built structure into my game. Mornings and afternoons were divided into skill stations that challenged but never overwhelmed us. Each session reinforced the fundamentals from the last lecture, linking repetition with understanding. The afternoons ended with scrimmages, where instruction met competition. My biggest takeaway was simple but enduring success demands equal commitment to skill and conditioning.

Later that summer, encouraged by my father, I began playing pickup games at Pope Park in Acushnet. Competing against high school players from Fairhaven and New Bedford. Hearing the words, "Do you want to play?" meant everything; it was the invitation for which I had waited. Those moments under the fading light and the rhythm of the ball off the pavement made me feel like I belonged.

By summer's end, I had a shot I trusted, a handle that held up under pressure, and a hunger I could not shake. The question was no longer whether I would chase this; it was how far it would take me.

When summer ended, the rhythm of the game followed me home. Back on my driveway, the memory of the park and the summer leagues became part of my daily life. What I learned that summer was not just how to shoot or dribble; it was how to prepare. The lessons from Mass Maritime stayed in my muscles and my mind, quiet reminders that work done in solitude mattered most when the lights came on. By the time seventh grade arrived, I was not just hoping to make the team. I was ready to prove I belonged.

Chapter Two

Albert F. Ford Junior High School, Seventh Grade, 1974–1975

S eventh grade marked yet another new beginning, my fourth school in six years. Albert F. Ford Junior High, a long, low-slung building in Acushnet, held its seventh graders at one end and the older students at the other, a silent division that made the place feel bigger than it was. Each morning's announcements crackled over the loudspeaker, reporting soccer scores and school news. I listened intently, imagining the day those same speakers would announce basketball results. Even before I set foot on the court, I carried that anticipation with me, like a ball tucked under my arm, knowing this season could shape everything that came next.

One day, a classmate caught wind of my plan to try out for the basketball team. Someone had informed him of my earlier achievements, but he stayed skeptical. My classmate challenged me to a one-on-one game. He did not think I had what it would take to make the team.

Despite my father's advice to avoid those kinds of challenges, I accepted. My father was not thrilled, but he understood.

We set the game for Saturday at Pope Park, 10:00 AM. My father drove me, arriving early. I warmed up alone on a court that already felt familiar. The sun and heat rose over the park, enhancing the quiet stillness. I settled into my routine, waiting for my classmate, who showed up thirty minutes late, dragging his feet and looking half-asleep.

We laid out the rules: first to twelve and winner out. We would check the ball after every basket or change of possession and call our own fouls.

On my first two possessions, I drove by my classmate only to receive two hard fouls, with me ending up taking a face full of chain-linked fence. My classmate looked at me as if I were crazy for not calling the foul. On his first possession, he drove right. I cut him off and forced a rushed jump shot that clanged off the rim. I took the rebound and checked the ball to keep my possession.

As we continued, I started noticing patterns. He always went right. He had no countermove. I began beating him to his spots. Frustration crept into his body language, slower recoveries, lazy cuts. He built a 4–0 lead before fatigue wore him down. His feet got heavy. His form, sloppier. That is when I turned it on.

I stole the ball on the next possession and drained a set shot. On the next possession, I blew past him for a layup. 4–2. Then 4–4. He looked smaller somehow, like the confidence had drained out of him.

He did not score again.

I ran off eight straight points and closed out the game 12–4. We shook hands, his head down. We never made eye contact, and without a word, he walked off and disappeared into the park.

I stared at the empty court, the ball heavy in my hands, wondering why winning felt unfinished. I had proven myself but also had a hollow feeling. The game had not challenged me. What stayed with me most was how I had played: under control, strategic, disciplined.

Six months earlier, I would not have known how to analyze an opponent's weaknesses. Now, it felt like second nature. The hours I had spent alone in the driveway, running drills and playing out scenarios in my head, had paid off.

On the drive home, my father glanced at me from the driver's seat and asked, "So, what did you learn?"

I hesitated, then admitted, "You were right. I should not have accepted the challenge."

He just nodded, eyes forward.

"My motivation was mostly… ego," I added quietly.

That got another nod.

"In pickup games," he said, "if you take a hard foul, call it. Otherwise, you will get hurt."

I said nothing, but the words stuck. I hated calling fouls. Something about it felt like weakness, but I knew he was right. That mindset would matter as the competition got tougher.

Back at school on Monday morning, unknown to me, curiosity had already spread about the game. During lunch period, my friends circled around me, eager for details. This reminded of the "tell the stories or he goes" position, where I felt circled, a demand to know. I purposefully kept the details vague, careful not to humiliate anyone. I said it was a good game and gave my classmate credit for his effort. My classmates reacted disappointedly, wanting something more detailed and conspiracy filled than I would commit to.

"You should try out for the team," I told my classmate when we crossed paths later that day.

He just nodded, never looking at me directly. My friends noticed. They studied my words, trying to read between the lines.

As school and basketball found their own rhythm, life at home offered a vastly different kind of classroom. While the court drilled me in discipline and competition, my father's books, music, and family weekend outings showed me just how wide the world could be. *"Those two worlds, one of sweat and blacktop, the other of ideas and sound, ran in parallel, shaping me in ways I could not yet understand."*

Cultural advantages appeared in our home through literature and music. My father fed my curiosity with newspapers, magazines, and books, each one widening the lens I looked through. Looking back, I realize how deeply a parent's interests could shape an impressionable child.

I still remember the first time he brought home the *Boston Sunday Globe*. He sat fully absorbed in its pages, while I lingered nearby, subtly observing, eager to see what had captured his attention. I did not always understand the political or economic pieces, but I knew they mattered, *because they mattered to him*. Noticing my interest, he broadened our household's literary landscape.

Soon, *Sports Illustrated*, *Tennis*, and *Sport* magazine appeared on our coffee table. Through them, I came to know sportswriters like Bob Ryan, Peter Gammons, Frank Deford, and Curry Kirkpatrick. When I asked and displayed an interest in my father's music taste, Rolling *Stone* magazine appeared, and with it came prominent authors like Jann Wenner, Hunter S. Thompson, Tom Wolfe, and Cameron Crowe. I did not just read about music; I *experienced* it, one album at a time.

Music became another portal, another way into the world. Bruce Springsteen, Bob Dylan, Van Morrison, Elton John, Chicago, The Beatles, and Stevie Wonder, artists who filled our home like family friends, but it was not just background noise. Their voices are present on Saturday mornings and late evenings. Live concerts became our family tradition, something that set us apart from other families we knew. Where others went bowling or to the movies, we immersed ourselves in live performances that felt larger than life.

These stood out:

- David Cassidy, April 1, 1972, Boston Music Hall, Boston, MA.
- Jerry Lewis, August 6, 1973, Cape Cod Melody Tent, Hyannis, MA.
- Paul Revere and the Raiders, July 10, 1974, Brockton Fair, Brockton, MA.
- George Harrison, *The Dark Horse Tour*, December 11, 1974, Providence Civic Center, Providence, RI.
- The Beach Boys & Chicago, June 29, 1975, Schaefer Stadium, Foxboro, MA
- Bob Dylan, *Rolling Thunder Revue*, November 1, 1975, SMU, Dartmouth, MA
- Elton John, *Bicentennial Concert*, July 4, 1976, Schaefer Stadium, Foxboro, MA
- Newport Jazz Festival, George Benson, Maynard Ferguson, Buddy Rich Big Band, July 3, 1978, Fort Adams State Park, Newport, RI.
- Steve Martin, October 8, 1978, Hynes Civic Auditorium, Boston, MA.

One concert stands out: George Harrison's Dark Horse Tour at the Providence Civic Center. It was a benefit to Bangladesh, which made the night feel even more monumental. Seeing a Beatle live, it barely felt real.

Back at school, Monday morning, a girl I had been passing notes with asked how my weekend went. I told her about the concert, excited to share. Her reply stopped me cold. That must have been fun! I love his song "Cats in the Cradle." I stared at the note, stunned. George Harrison did not sing "Cats in the Cradle." That was Harry Chapin. We never passed another note after that. If she did not know Harrison was a Beatle... well. Cats in the Cradle, indeed.

Each event felt surreal. Sharing them with my parents and sister only deepened the magic. While other families followed predictable routines, mine leaned into culture and curiosity. These experiences did not just entertain me; they helped shape my worldview.

Weekends often meant heading into Boston. We wandered through Haymarket Square, tried new foods, and browsed record stores. These trips widened my cultural lens. My parents' adventurous spirit left a permanent mark.

I still remember spotting an interracial couple holding hands, and later, two men doing the same. I looked around, expecting a reaction, but no one even blinked. That silence taught me love should not be complicated.

Another memory lingers; the first time I smelled marijuana. My sister and I looked at each other, confused. The scent was unfamiliar, earthy, and sharp. My parents never shielded us from the world's complexities. They refrained from preaching or explaining. I craved those moments. They were strange and thrilling. They made me feel older and ready.

In the town of Acushnet, the sports scene revolved around baseball. The town's pride seemed to live in its Little League and Pony League teams. Summer revolved around diamonds and dugouts. But at Ford Junior High School, from my view, the athletic reputation went deeper. The school fielded strong teams in soccer, baseball, and basketball.

In the late 1960s, two names became legend: David Almeida and Joey Jason. David became a standout athlete at Fairhaven High School before playing football at Boston College. Joey set the junior high basketball scoring record and later made his mark at Fairhaven as well. Their younger brothers were my classmates, which made their legacy feel close, like something I could reach for.

Ron Hall, a science teacher at Ford Junior High School, coached both the basketball and baseball teams. He was a respected figure in Acushnet athletics, his name synonymous with discipline and quiet integrity. A former standout athlete himself graduated from Fairhaven High School in 1956 and later attended the New Bedford Textile Institute. He excelled in basketball, baseball, and track, eventually earning the school's first Coach's Award.

Mr. Hall's coaching style mirrored his personality: calm, patient, measured. For some players, this kind of coaching builds confidence. For me, it felt at odds with what I was about to experience.

The basketball tryouts began the Monday after Thanksgiving and lasted two days. On Wednesday morning, the final roster was posted. Having made the roster was one step towards my goals for the season, which were making the starting five, breaking the season scoring record and leading the team to win every game on our schedule. Ambitious for sure. My father had set my mind on achievement, not participation. From the start, I felt confident. I was the best player on the floor, the fastest on the team. My footwork, anticipation, and quick hands gave me an edge. The team had solid athletes, but most lacked refined basketball skills. One detail surprised me: none of my classmates were at tryouts. I was the only seventh grader. Twelve players made the roster, seven freshmen, four eighth graders, and me.

After each practice, Coach Hall often asked if I wanted to stay for extra shooting drills. I never turned him down. My teammates noticed the one-on-one sessions. At first, they watched quietly. Then came the murmurs. "Why him, not me?" I did not have an answer for them, nor did I owe them one.

My father and I began a quiet tradition: dinner at a local restaurant before and after each season. Those meals became small celebrations, moments to pause and reflect. They were not just about basketball. They were about us. His quiet encouragement shaped me, not just as a player, but as a son.

A week before my first junior high game, my mother picked me up from practice. She had errands to run and asked if I wanted to come along. We planned to grab dinner afterward. As we drove, my mother asked the usual questions about school, teachers, and friends. I told her everything was fine. Then she said something that caught me off guard.

"Things might change with your friends once basketball season starts."

I looked at my mother with curiosity. "What do you mean?"

Keeping her eyes on the road, she said, "You might start getting more attention. People might not like that. And people who are not your friends today may pretend to be your friends once you gain popularity. Those people are not your friends; they will try to use you for their gain."

I had never thought of that. People had always liked me. I figured basketball might earn respect from teammates and opponents. But outside the court? That had not occurred to me.

Sensing my confusion, my mother added, "If you ever feel overwhelmed, your father and I are always here."

Something shifted after that conversation. Basketball felt bigger, no longer just a game, and no longer about me. It was touching on other parts of my life: my friendships, my family. The weight lingered. That night, I did not sleep well.

My sister especially weighed on my mind. Our complicated relationship had always been a factor. She attended a Catholic school in New Bedford, and now I worried that any recognition I might receive would only widen the space between us.

As late as the day of our first game, I still did not know if I had made the starting five. I felt I had practiced well, but no one had confirmed anything.

Game days brought new challenges. Because junior high games were played after school, I had to manage my diet and stress carefully. I discovered that playing on an empty stomach worked best; it heightened my focus and sharpened my performance. But managing my nerves was another story. I had experienced a level of anxiety in the Acushnet League and at the St. Francis Tournament, but now the stakes felt even higher. The nervous energy was familiar, but I still had no way of controlling it.

Laced with uncertainty, my nerves carried me into uncharted territory. I was a young athlete, just one year into organized sports, my only point of reference. And now, I found myself in the strange position of trying to manage my mind so it would not collapse and make me walk away for good. I knew that was not a reality; I had already bought into the belief that I was going to succeed.

Our first game of the 1974–1975 season was against Tabor Academy, a prestigious prep school in Marion, Massachusetts. I had a personal connection to the school. One of my aunts owned a summer home nearby. As a kid, I spent hours playing on the academy fields until I was exhausted. Those visits left me with fond memories.

"Before I ever played a minute of organized basketball, something had already taken hold of me."

On game day, I was distracted in school, counting the minutes until the last bell. When it finally rang, I rushed to the gym, eager to get ready. I could not hide my excitement. First one to the locker room, my first mistake. I tried to slow myself down, searching through my gym bag for something, anything, just to delay the moment.

But then it happened. Tremors. As I laced up my sneakers, my right leg started shaking. I had experienced nothing like it. Panic set in. My mind was racing. I did not want anyone to notice, so I covered my leg with a towel. When the shaking did not stop, I stood up, hoping to walk it off. Surprisingly, walking around the locker room made it stop. But the moment I sat back down, it returned.

This was my first encounter with the physical manifestation of performance anxiety. The body releases hormones like adrenaline as part of the "fight or flight" response. The shaking or trembling I experienced was classic. Of course, I did not have the knowledge or the coping skills to process what was happening to my body. Over time, tragically, I would accept it as part of my pre-game ritual.

Finally, stepping onto the court for warmups, the energy in the gym hit me like a wave. The space buzzed with noise and excitement. I jogged around the court, trying to steady my nerves. Scanning the growing crowd, I saw my classmates, my eyes wide with anticipation. Their presence reminded me how significant this game was, not just for me, but for everyone watching.

This was my first junior high school game. I felt the moment intensely. In my mind, the crowd seemed enormous, as if the gym might burst. It was my imagination, my excitement distorting belief, but it felt real. In one year, I had gone from playing in my first organized league to this, playing for my school. I tried to stay calm, but my nerves refused to settle.

I glanced over at the Tabor Academy team as they entered the gym. They looked composed, their warmups crisp and confident. Meanwhile, our cheerleaders chanted, filling the gym with chaotic energy.

The referees entered with an air of authority, their striped shirts and whistles adding gravity to the moment. They exchanged greetings with Mr. Hall as the clock ticked toward tip-off.

Throughout junior high school and my high school career, I had the privilege of having the best referees in the area officiate my games. For example, in my first junior high school game, the officials were John McKenna and Paul "Lefty" Duval, both widely respected across football, baseball, and basketball. Even then, I sensed that their presence meant the game would be managed with fairness and control.

My relationship with Mr. McKenna grew more meaningful. My father respected Mr. McKenna and sought his advice at a critical point in my life. When deciding where I should play high school basketball, my father turned to him. Without hesitation, Mr. McKenna recommended Jack Nobrega and Wayne Wilson, both of whom I would later play for during my high school career.

Years later, at my nephew's wedding, I noticed Mr. McKenna sitting across the room. I walked over, reintroduced myself, and after a brief pause, he greeted me warmly. We talked about our connection to the bride and groom and reminisced about the past. My grandmother had often expressed her disapproval of the officiating during my games. She once told Mr. McKenna she did not like him because of his calls. With a chuckle, he replied, "So that was your grandmother?"

His humor made the memory even more enjoyable. I reminded him of our first interactions at Ford Junior High School, when Mr. Hall was my coach. He smiled, shaking his head. "All those years ago?" he said.

I recounted the story of my father seeking his advice about the best high school coaches. Mr. McKenna did not recall the conversation, but I explained how my father had valued his insights. Then I asked if he remembered where I had played high school basketball. He admitted he did not.

When I told him, he placed a hand on my arm and lowered his head. "I didn't know," he whispered.

We sat in silence as the weight of shared history settled between us. He reached into his sport coat, pulled out a handkerchief, and wiped his eyes. "Thank you for telling me, he whispered, I'll never forget it."

Before I left, I waved my wife over, eager for Mr. McKenna to meet her. He greeted her warmly, making pleasant conversation. As we said goodbye, he thanked me again and told me how happy he was to have met my wife. That encounter left an impression, reminding me how deeply those past connections had shaped my life.

The noise in my head was overwhelming. I tried to block it out, but it consumed my focus. My teammates and I huddled around Mr. Hall as he gave his pregame instructions. When he called my name as part of the starting lineup, my heart raced.

This is happening, I thought.

I tried to focus on his words, but my nerves drowned out everything except one detail, we were starting in a zone defense.

The game opened chaotically. Neither team could find a rhythm. Early on, I had two breakaway layup opportunities and missed both. The crowd groaned, amplifying the pressure already building inside me.

At halftime, we trailed by two points. As the second half began, I knew I needed to step up.

Grabbing a rebound off a missed Tabor shot, I dribbled up the right side and passed to a teammate in the corner. As I moved into position, the ball came back to me. I was wide open, fifteen feet from the basket. It was a shot I had practiced countless times. I set my feet, released.

Swish.

Relief surged through me. The tension that had held me back vanished, and I played with more confidence. Momentum built. On the next possession, I chased down a loose ball, sprinted ahead of the defenders, and finished with a controlled layup.

Moments later, we ran our overload offense against Tabor's 2-3 zone. I noticed their top defenders were slow to rotate. I moved the ball to the corner, got it back, and attacked the gap. Driving into the lane, I floated a shot over their big man.

The game remained tight. Neither team could pull away.

With thirty seconds left and the score tied, Tabor held the ball for the last possession. One of their guards mishandled a pass. It rolled right in front of me. I quickly grabbed the ball, and Tabor fouled me.

I stepped to the free-throw line for a one-and-one opportunity. The gym is silent now. I took a deep breath, steadied myself, and sank the first shot. The crowd erupted. I blocked out the noise, refocused, and released the second shot.

It dropped through the net.

With fifteen seconds left, we led by two. Tabor called timeout. Mr. Hall huddled us together, his voice calm and clear: "Stay in the zone. Keep your hands up. No fouls. Be ready to rebound."

Back on the court, the tension thickened. Tabor swung the ball to the right wing, away from my side in our zone defense. I slid down the lane, ready to cut off any drive. A Tabor player launched a jumper from the right wing. It hit the back of the rim.

I grabbed the rebound as the buzzer sounded.

The gym erupted. My teammates and the cheerleaders rushed to the court, grabbing me, celebrating the win. I tried to stay composed, acting like it was no big deal, but something strange happened. For a moment, everything went silent. The entire gym was muted. Then, suddenly, the sound came crashing back, loud and jarring. Catching my breath, I felt a sudden sensation of relief and sadness. What now? I thought. Back to being a normal kid?

As I stood there trying to process it all, one referee walked past. Without even looking at me, he said, "Nice game, Semiao."

Team Record: 1–0 Points: 8 Assists: 2 Rebounds: 2 Steals: 1

That night, I replayed the game in my mind repeatedly, dissecting every missed opportunity and rushed decision. I was unsatisfied. My anxiety had limited me, held me back. Waiting for the next game felt like an eternity.

I was determined to prove that I could play better.

The next evening, my father and I sat down to discuss the game. His feedback, as always, was direct and honest. "Do not overthink it. Become a more instinctive player. Get out of your head," he said. His words cut through my self-doubt. "Are you taking all the steps to excel as a player, not to be good, but great?"

The question hit me hard. It was not just a challenge; it was the standard. One he had set for me. One I would carry with me for the next six years.

Days later, my mother shared a story that stuck with me. During the first game, my mother had been sitting with a close friend whose daughter was a cheerleader. As excitement swelled after I grabbed the final rebound, my mother turned to her friend and asked, "Is this how it's going to be?" Her friend smiled, an unspoken acknowledgment of the journey ahead. My mother realized this season would be a ride, interesting, unpredictable, even transformative.

The next day in gym class, one of my classmates wanted to know how many points I'd scored. "Eight", I said.

Before I could say more, our gym teacher, Mr. Goulet, chimed in. "You should have had more." His blunt comment hit harder than I expected, not because it was unkind, but because I knew he was right. Another reminder is that I had not played to my full potential.

Leading up to our second game, practice was a mix of preparation and playful teasing from the older teammates. The freshman girls had asked about me, giving my teammates new material to tease me with.

"Do you have a girlfriend?" they asked.

Before I could have answered, someone shouted, "Do you want one?"

During practice, Mr. Hall emphasized smoother transitions into our offense. He urged us to exploit mismatches but to avoid rushed decisions. Over the next two days, we drilled with those concepts in mind.

After practice, I stayed behind for my usual shooting routine. Mr. Hall fed me passes, encouraging me to move into the spots where I would take shots in our offense. He stressed rhythm and decisiveness.

"When you are open, take the shot. Do not hesitate."

Simple advice, but invaluable. I took steps to incorporate it. As I practiced, I sometimes noticed my teammates lingering at the other end of the court, watching. Naively, I hoped they would notice my improvement, even as I ignored everything else.

The day before our second game, I got a crash course in team dynamics and faulty leadership. After practice in the locker room, the team captain called out players by name, raising issues he felt needed addressing. His tone was sharp and direct. This was not the leadership style I had envisioned. I assumed captains managed things privately. Instead, he aired grievances in front of everyone.

When my name came up, his focus was on my sneakers. "You shouldn't wear those Adidas with the black stripes," he said. "We stand for the school. Everyone should wear navy blue Converse Chuck Taylors."

I did not respond. The comment felt petty, more about asserting authority than addressing an actual issue. I made a mental note of it. Not because I felt targeted, but because it was the first time a teammate had publicly called me out. The topic never came up again, but the moment stuck with me. It reminded me that leadership, or the lack of it, could affect a team's chemistry.

Our second game of the 1974 season was against Friends Academy, at their gym. Founded in 1810, the school had a distinguished history in New Bedford and Dartmouth. Their gym reflected its age, small, worn, and dated. Bleachers lined one side of the court, packed with students, faculty, and parents. The atmosphere was intimate yet lively.

Unlike our first game, this contest lacked drama. We won.

Team Record: 2–0 Points: 10 Assists: 2 Rebounds: 1 Steals: 0

Winning both games exhilarated us. Camaraderie grew, and I felt optimistic about the season. With eighteen games ahead, we had the potential for a strong season.

The following Monday's practice prepared us for a tough week: back-to-back home games. First against Diman Vocational on Tuesday, and then Bristol-Plymouth Agricultural on Thursday. Unfortunately, our two wins made the team relaxed. We played sloppily, misplaced passes and missed defensive assignments. I felt restless, eager for practice to end so I could focus on shooting. While my teammates rode high after two wins, I stayed wary. Even then, I knew success could slip away without discipline or preparation.

After practice, Mr. Hall and I refined my shooting routine. That session emphasized stepping into my shot with rhythm, not just catching and firing. By the end, I had taken fifty shots, making thirty-eight. It was also the first time we tracked my stats during the shooting drills. As I wrapped up my drills, I noticed my teammates watching again from the other end of the basketball court. An annoying pattern was emerging.

Our first game of the week was against Diman Regional Vocational Technical High School, founded in 1912 to serve Fall River and the nearby towns of Somerset, Swansea, and Westport.

On game day, the energy in the locker room was electric. My teammates were loud and animated, but I stayed quiet. I changed into my uniform and headed to the court. The noise and chaos of the locker room felt distracting, so I left it behind.

When I stepped onto the court, it was empty. I was the first one out there.

I started with light sprints to loosen up, then grabbed a ball and began dribbling, alternating hands, through my legs, behind my back, crossovers, spin moves. Without thinking, I sprinted down the right sideline, banked the ball off the gym wall, caught it in stride, and pulled up for a twenty-foot jumper.

Swish.

Energized, I repeated the drill on the left side. Swish.

I paused and looked around the gym, noticing spectators, coaches, cheerleaders and players watching me with curiosity.

Where did that come from?

The sequence felt effortless, instinctive, as if my body had taken over. My father's advice came to mind: *Trust your instincts. Get out of your head.*

Two Diman players stood at the far end of the court, exchanging glances before hurrying back to their locker room. Picking up the basketball, I continued warming up but avoided repeating the sequence. The moment felt too perfect to try again.

When my teammates arrived on the basketball court, their behavior did not change. They laughed and joked during warmups. I looked at Mr. Hall for guidance, but he said nothing. That frustrated me.

The game began, and we quickly fell behind by six points, plagued by mistakes on both ends of the floor. Diman started with a 2-3 zone defense. Once I recognized it, I knew where my opportunities would come from.

I missed my first two shots, but after that, everything clicked. I hit ten straight baskets. The basket looked enormous, three times its normal size. I could feel every dimpling and seam on the basketball as it left my hands. Shots fell from everywhere, even from distances I had not dared to try before.

It was one of the first times I experienced what athletes call being "in the zone, the flow state."

I did not know it then, but I would spend the rest of my basketball career chasing that feeling. It became both my greatest strength and challenge; a benchmark I would chase every time I stepped on the court.

The phenomenon of a quiet mind during intense athletic activity is known as "the flow state" or being "in the zone." It is a state of deep focus and complete immersion where actions become effortless, decisions are automatic, and time seems to alter. This optimal performance state occurs when the brain's prefrontal cortex quiets negative and distracting thoughts, allowing for seamless coordination between movement and thought, leading to heightened awareness, confidence, and enjoyment of the activity.

Disappointingly, my teammates struggled. We trailed by eight to ten points throughout the game and never mounted a serious challenge. The deficit forced us out of our zone defense and into man-to-man coverage, a shift that exposed our weaknesses. Diman exploited us with solid pick-and-rolls on both sides of the lane. We had not practiced how to defend that. The result was a string of easy layups and fouls, widening the gap.

I thought back to the Boston Celtics games I had attended with my father at the Boston Garden. Sitting close to the court, I could hear the players talk through plays. One voice stood out, Dave Cowens, the Celtics' undersized but relentless center. His booming commands, "Screen on your right!" "Man coming through!" were like a masterclass in leadership. Cowens did not just play. He orchestrated. His athleticism, aggression, and constant communication made up for what he lacked in size.

From those games, I learned that success in basketball, or any sport, needed more than skill. It demanded trust, coordination, and a near-telepathic connection between teammates.

We lost by eight, dropping our record to 2–1. The reasons were obvious: poor practice habits, lack of preparation, and our inability to adapt during the game.

Sitting at my locker afterward, I felt the sting of the loss, and my inability to do more to help. As I changed out of my uniform, I noticed the Diman coach talking to Mr. Hall. I turned back to my locker when I felt a tap on my shoulder.

It was the Diman coach, extending his hand. "Nice game, son," he said.

Surprised, I shook his hand and thanked him. He smiled and walked out of the locker room.

The interaction did not go unnoticed. My teammates saw it but said nothing. I did not grasp the full weight of the moment. Looking back, I recognize it as a turning point, a subtle shift in how my teammates viewed me.

Team Record: 2–1 Points: 20 Assists: 2 Rebounds: 1 Steals: 0

The next morning during announcements, they shared the game's score and listed each player's contributions. I sat in my classroom, trying to focus on the day ahead. At lunch, a friend teased me: "Semiao twenty points? Do not forget us when you are playing for the Celtics!"

We laughed, but the attention made me uneasy. I was not sure how to balance recognition with staying grounded.

After school, I headed to practice. The locker room's energy had shifted. Gone was the usual banter. In its place, there was tense silence. The weight of our recent loss lingered.

Mr. Hall took us back to fundamentals: dribbling with our heads up, catching passes with two hands, meeting the ball, pivoting, boxing out. He also emphasized on-court communication. The practice felt grueling, but it was necessary.

For the first time, I did not stay after practice for extra shooting. Instead, I called my father to pick me up. I showered, changed, and began packing my gear.

That is when I overheard a teammate say, "What, Semiao scores twenty points and thinks he's too good to stay and practice shooting?"

The words stung. When they realized I was still in the locker room, the conversation went quiet. I said nothing, but I carried the comment with me.

I met my father in the school lobby. The drive home was silent. He sensed something was wrong.

"Are you okay?" he asked.

I did not mention what I had overheard. Instead, I sat in frustrated silence, wondering if the rest of the team felt the same way. Following my father's words of advice, deep down, I knew I could not control their opinions. I just had to keep working, believing that effort and winning might earn their respect.

That evening, while I was doing homework, my father came into my room. I shared my frustration, admitting that no matter how hard I worked, it did not always feel like enough.

He listened, then said, "Sometimes, even your best will not be enough to win every game. But that does not mean you stop trying. Keep playing hard, and good things will come." His reassurance helped, though I still did not mention the locker room comment.

Noting after every game, I struggled to sleep. Replaying each possession, every decision, repeatedly in my head. Before the games, I could not eat. Afterward, I was always starving. These routines revealed the rawest parts of who I was. Over time, they created distance between me and my friends and even girlfriends. They could not understand the intensity I carried.

The next day at school, I was in a fog, hungover from what I had overheard in the locker room. I grappled with feelings of mistrust and emotional distance from my teammates. The sense of unity I had hoped for felt out of reach. Leadership, which I had expected from the older players, seemed to focus on trivial things, like the color of my sneakers.

As the day wore on, my mood lifted, thanks to the lighthearted chatter of my classmates. Endless talk about girls filled the lunchroom. None of us had experience with girls, but that did not stop the fantasizing or daydreaming. Boys being boys. By the time the last bell rang, my focus shifted to the afternoon game.

Our next opponent was Bristol-Plymouth Regional Technical School, a vocational high school in Taunton, Massachusetts, founded in 1972. Despite being new, their basketball team had already developed a formidable reputation. The school catered to over 1,200 students and had competitive teams in various sports.

In the locker room before the game, the tension was palpable. No one made eye contact or spoke to me. The silence and isolation were unsettling, but I brushed it off and stuck to my routine. I was the first player on the court, just as I had been in earlier games. Warming up alone, I moved well and shot with confidence. This pregame solitude was becoming my way of centering myself before the chaos of competition.

Unfortunately, we started the game by falling behind again. A disappointing pattern was forming. Bristol-Plymouth had two sharp guards and dominant forwards. They dismantled our zone defense with an overload offense, a concept we should have been able to defend since it mirrored our own zone strategy. We had assumed familiarity would give us an edge. It did not. We looked unprepared and played like it.

Bristol-Plymouth ran a 1-3-1 zone defense that shut down our offense. It was clear they had scouted us. They knew our tendencies and exposed our weaknesses with discipline and poise. We could not adapt. Watching the game unfold, I felt the weight of not just our lack of execution, but a deeper lack of preparation. They had outplayed us in both skill and strategy.

During the timeout, Mr. Hall called for a shift to a 3-2 offense. The idea was simple: attack the zone, draw defenders in, and find the open man. But it was not something we had practiced. Still, we had little choice.

One possession stood out. My backcourt partner tried to drive into the defense but lost the ball, which led to an uncontested layup for Bristol. On the next play, he passed to me just before half-court, a silent gesture that said: *your turn.*

I dribbled into their zone, looking for an opening. I spotted a seam and threw a bounce pass to a teammate under the basket. He hesitated, surprised, then passed it out to the wing. The defender deflected it out of bounds.

It was emblematic of our basketball IQ; we fumbled a playable opportunity. At halftime, we were down six points, but it felt like more.

The second half brought a slight improvement. We hovered within six to eight points but could not close the gap. I had been deferring to my teammates, hoping it would build unity, but the effort went unnoticed.

Early in the fourth quarter, with our deficit at fifteen points and my frustration mounting, I shifted gears. A deflection led to a quick score. Then another steal. Then a fast-break layup. I threaded a jump pass to our captain for a layup that cut the deficit to nine with three minutes left.

On our next timeout, Mr. Hall called for a full-court zone trap. The strategy was to increase the pace of the game and force turnovers. The trap worked. We caught Bristol off guard and created steals. But we could not convert. My teammates looked rattled; their decisions were erratic; our execution was poor. We were working harder, not smarter.

Sensing the momentum slipping again, Mr. Hall switched to a full-court man-to-man press. He assigned matchups and reminded us there was still time. I appreciated his persistence, even as I sensed my teammates' confidence was unraveling.

Back on the court, Bristol slowed the game. As their guard crossed the half-court, I saw a chance to double-team. I made my move. My teammate mirrored me. We trapped the ball handler, who panicked and lobbed a pass toward my original assignment. I leaped, deflecting it. The ball bounced toward the top of the key.

Three of us sprinted for the basketball, two Bristol players and me. I reacted first, splitting them and racing toward the basket. One defender closed in from the left, another from the right. I ignored them, locked in. As I entered the lane, I heard their coach yell, "Don't foul!"

I drove hard, absorbed the contact, and released the shot. It kissed the backboard, bounced twice on the rim, and dropped in.

Whistle. Foul.

I stepped onto the free-throw line. No one on my team approached me. No handshakes. No pats on the back. Just silence. I brushed it off, sank the free throw, and cut the lead to six.

Rattled, Bristol inbounded the ball and passed to the high post. It slipped through the player's hands. I reached for it, sidestepped a diving defender, and took off down the left sideline. Three defenders converged as I neared the lane. I split them again, drove hard, and heard the familiar shout, "Don't foul!" just as the whistle blew. The shot went in.

Whistle. Foul.

I hit the free throw. The lead was down to three.

Bristol called a timeout, their composure cracking. The gym roared. For the first time, we had momentum.

Mr. Hall, usually soft-spoken, raised his voice, matching the crowd's intensity. He laid out our next moves with urgency.

When play resumed, we pressed. A panicked pass, too high and too fast, went down the sideline. Our captain intercepted it near our bench.

From the far side of the court, I moved five feet to his right, just below the foul-line circle. I was wide open. A simple outlet pass would have given our team possession and the opportunity to close the deficit to one point.

Instead, he raised his arm and launched a one-handed, football-style pass down the court, aiming at our teammate, who was up the floor. The pass sailed over everyone's head and out of bounds.

I stood frozen, disbelief washing over me. He had chosen the low-percentage, flashy play over the smart one. That moment confirmed what I had suspected: my teammates did not want to rely on me. They would rather lose the ball than pass it to me at a critical moment.

Our opponents forced our team to foul in the last minutes of the game. Bristol hit their free throws and extended the lead. The buzzer sounded. We lost by six.

The sting was not just in the loss; it was in what it revealed.

My teammates, whether out of jealousy or immaturity, had no interest in lifting each other up. They did not want me to succeed. Even if it meant the team would fail. An unfortunate diatribe of events and sentiment that would follow me throughout my career.

With sixteen games left, I did not know how I would make it through the season.

After the game, I sat by my locker, motionless. Replaying the last minutes in my mind. Then I heard my name.

I looked up. The two Bristol guards were standing in the doorway of our locker room, searching for me. Finding me at my locker, I heard, nice game, another compliment. I was not sure of anything at this point. I heard a question; they wanted to know if it was true. Am I just a seventh grader? Surprisingly, I understood the question, and I smiled and confirmed it. They seemed genuinely impressed.

They mentioned they had not played on a court with white backboards in a long time and talked about how excited they were about their new field house. I told them I was looking forward to playing at their gym in a couple of weeks.

Their respect was refreshing, a contrast to the tension I felt within my team.

As they left, my father entered the locker room with the Bristol-Plymouth coach. The coach introduced himself and praised my performance. The abbreviated time I had been playing also surprised him. I thanked him, grateful for the acknowledgment. As he left, I noticed my teammates exiting the locker room, casting suspicious looks my way.

As the Bristol-Plymouth coach left the locker room, he said, "We'll be ready for you in two weeks."

My father, following the Bristol-Plymouth coach, turned to me. "I'll be right outside if you need me."

Team Record: 2–2 Points: 25 Assists: 2 Rebounds: 2 Steals: 2

That night, I could not speak. I felt a volatile mix of emotions, mostly anger. I had hoped my teammates would recognize my abilities, and that we would grow together. Instead, those hopes felt as if they had evaporated.

I never expected us to become close friends. The age and grade differences made that unlikely. But I had not expected backbiting or resentment. I often wondered if Mr. Hall was aware. From what I could tell, he was not the type to confront issues head-on.

In games, I saw him experimenting with strategies, trying to give us a chance to win. But the truth was unavoidable; we did not have a team full of skilled players. Meanwhile, I was still learning the game from scratch. Scoring was the one thing I did well. I had my flaws, but I knew my contributions were solid. That should have been something to build on. My teammates did not see any value in me.

That night, my family gave me space. I sat in the dark, staring at the ceiling. As usual, I did not sleep, replaying every possession in my head, wondering what else I could have done.

Early the next morning, I had a quiet conversation with my father. He pointed out the positives and reminded me to stay focused on the coach, not the noise. His words grounded me. I left for the bus stop feeling more optimistic.

My friends were already there. Two stood apart.

"How'd the game go?" one asked.

"We lost," I said, giving them the score.

Then came the inevitable: "How many points did you score?"

"Twenty-five."

They stared at me.

"You've scored forty-five points in the last two games?"

I nodded. Their reaction caught me off guard. I had not realized my friends were keeping track of my stats. It became clear my games mattered to them. That realization added a layer of pressure: I did not want to let them down.

They asked about the season scoring record. I told them it was 342 points, and the single-game record was 40 points.

"Who set the scoring record?" one of them asked.

"The season scoring record belongs to Joey Jason", I said. Joey is Jimmy and Patti's older brother, our classmates. I then added that Phil Gelinas, the older brother to Danny and Kevin (also our classmates), held the single-game record.

Another friend asked, "Are you planning to break those records?"

I smiled, letting my silence answer for me.

Practice on Monday was uneventful. Mr. Hall reviewed our offense and defense, focusing on the finer details. While the concepts were new to me, I was eager to learn and paid close attention.

After practice, I wanted to stay for extra shooting, but Mr. Hall had to leave early. I asked the team manager if he could rebound and pass me the ball during my shooting practice. He agreed with a smile, but as we started, my teammates began teasing him. Sensing his unease, I said, it's fine, you can go. See you tomorrow. He hurried out of the gym.

I stood there for a moment, holding the ball under my arm, staring into space. As I turned toward the equipment room to return it, I heard a familiar voice. "Are you done shooting?" It was my father. Surprised, I tried to act unfazed. Without missing a beat, he said, "Let's shoot."

We worked on catch-and-shoot drills, focusing on five spots on the court, around the key, both wings and the corners. After two rotations, he introduced a new drill: after each shot, he would toss the ball high, leading into a no-dribble, left-handed layup. Exhausted at the end, I realized he had always known what I needed, and in this case, it was to stay in the gym just a little longer.

Our game against the West Bridgewater freshman team did not go well. Founded in 1968, the school served grades 7–12, with about six hundred students. We lost again, our third straight defeat. The ride home was quiet, the weight of another loss pressing down on me. I was getting fewer touches. Word of my recent scoring had spread around school, and the attention only fueled my teammates' resentment.

Team Record: 2–3 Points: 16 Assists: 2 Rebounds: 3 Steals: 1

Wareham Middle School, founded in 1950, had a strong basketball program. Three standout players: Marty Cardoza, a dominant forward/center who could score from anywhere; Randy Andrews, a two-way threat who thrived when defenses focused on Cardoza; and Willie Santiago, a poised point guard, who controlled the tempo with ease.

All three would later become my teammates on my father's second summer league team, but that is a story for another time.

Wareham dominated us. Their offense ran through Marty Cardoza, with Willie Santiago orchestrating from the top. "Marty high" as Wareham executed their high-post offense to perfection. Their pick-and-roll plays were sharp, calculated, and deadly. Each time we cheated on defense, they made us pay with quick passes and making open shots. By the final whistle, they had dismantled us. We had little left to offer in response.

Team Record: 2–4 Points: 15 Assists: 2 Rebounds: 1 Steals: 0

After the game, I showered and joined my parents for dinner. They did their best to lift my spirits with stories and neighborhood gossip, but my mind stayed fixed on what was not working. We were not a team. In theory, we should have come together, defined roles, played to each other's strengths. But we were not even close.

That night, it hit me: the freshmen were not interested in winning. For them, basketball was a social activity, a rite of passage. I was a seventh grader who disrupted their plan, the one who wanted to win. Their indifference baffled me then. It still does now.

At dinner, my father shifted the conversation to the upcoming Christmas basketball tournament at Southeastern Massachusetts University (SMU), a local college. He said area high schools would compete, including Holy Family High School, a team I had been eager to watch.

Later that evening, my father told me more. According to scouting reports, Holy Family High School was one of the top teams in the state. He mentioned their star players: Mickey Gonsalves, Peter Ribeiro, and Joey Gaudreau from Acushnet, players I had seen dominate in the New Bedford Recreation Summer League finals. Hathaway Oil sponsored the Holy Family High School summer league team, which crushed the competition.

Their coach, Jack Nobrega, had a long, respected career. My father listed the standout players who had come through the school: Steven Lawless, Dennis Kennedy, Billy and Paul Walsh and Steve Gomes.

Just hearing those names sparked something in me. A flicker of excitement in an otherwise dim moment.

As if I needed nothing else to happen in my life, the following morning I noticed my school clothes were hanging loosely on me. I was losing weight. No one said anything, but I saw the concern in my mother's eyes.

The next morning, she told me I would be late for school. She had scheduled an appointment with a doctor at her hospital. My mother had noticed the weight loss and knew I had not been sleeping. Her intuition always outran my sense of what might be wrong.

At the doctor's office, the physical went smoothly, but the "what ifs" sat heavily in my mind. What if I were sick? What if I had to stop playing? I could not help but spiral. The fear of missing games replaced my usual pre-game anxiety.

With games every Tuesday and Thursday, there was little time to reflect, no time for practice. I was not sure if more practice would help the team, but I knew I could always use more time in the gym.

Our next game was against Somerset North. Surprisingly, we played well. We stayed competitive. Then something strange happened.

During the timeout, my mind began racing. I could not focus on what Mr. Hall was saying. Out of character, I mumbled a response. The words got jumbled. I saw the concern on my teammates' faces. I bent over, humiliated, trying to steady myself.

The rest of the game felt off. I could not shake the unease. With five seconds left, Somerset North committed a time violation on an inbound play. It was our chance to win.

Our out-of-bounds play was simple: a four-man stack in front of the inbounder. I was the third man breaking to the corner. The play worked. I was open. The pass came. Eighteen feet. A shot I had practiced thousands of times. I missed it short. We lost. I stood there stunned. I had failed.

As Somerset celebrated, their head coach approached me. "Hey, Semiao, nice game," he said, extending his hand. I shook it, too embarrassed to speak. "You'll make more of those than you will miss in your career," he said, then walked away.

I moved slowly to the locker room. After showering, I waited until everyone else had cleared out.

From a distance, near the coach's office, Mr. Hall called out: "Nice game. Let the missed shot go. You will make the next one. And the one after that." Then he added, "See you tomorrow."

Team Record: 2–5 Points: 16 Assists: 1 Rebounds: 1 Steals: 0

Outside, my family waited in silence. My father approached first. "Nice game," he said, extending his hand. I avoided his gaze, staring at the ground.

"Look at me," he said. I met his eyes. My father spoke again. "When the out-of-bounds play was called, did you know the shot was yours?" I nodded.

"And when you knew it was yours, did you shy away from the responsibility?"

"No, I whispered. I wanted the shot." His expression shifted, serious but proud. "Outstanding players are not afraid to fail, he said. Tonight, you failed, and you will fail again. But skilled players move forward. They prepare to eliminate failure." He paused, letting it sink in. "You need to decide what comes next, how you'll prepare for the next time you're in that situation."

His words landed like a storm, harsh but clarifying. I understood what he was saying: I had to rise above the distractions, above the resentment, and focus on the work. That was his way, logic over emotion. And now, he was asking me to do the same.

My mother, her voice soft with concern, asked, "Are you okay?" That moment captured my family: my father pushing me to grow, my mother offering comfort.

Later that week, my father told me Channel 2 in Boston would broadcast the Catholic League Basketball Tournament Finals. He urged me to watch Ron Perry from Catholic Memorial High School. "He's one of the top high school players in the state."

The game lived up to hype. Perry played with confidence and precision. When he missed, it felt like a glitch. He made the game look easy. Watching him, I felt both inspired and humbled.

I also realized something deeper: my basketball journey was shaping my whole family. They felt my wins and losses with me. Though we tried to act like everything was normal, this was uncharted territory for all of us.

I wanted to protect them from my emotional highs and lows. But I did not have the tools yet.

One memory lingered: the moment during that timeout when I could not form a sentence. It haunted me. I never shared it, not even with my family.

Days later, the results of my physical results came in. I was in good health, but underweight. The doctor recommended more protein in my diet and noted my limited eating habits, just one meal a day. That, combined with poor sleep, had affected my health and performance.

That weekend, my father and I went to the Christmas Tournament at the SMU gym. Holy Family High School defeated New Bedford Vocational.

On the ride home, my father asked, "Would you be interested in attending Holy Family for your freshman year?" Without hesitation, I excitedly said yes.

Excitement surged through me. I had not even finished seventh grade, and already, we were talking about high school.

As we drove home, my father shared more about Holy Family's basketball history, stories of their Tech Tournament wins. My father spoke about other standout athletes from southeastern Massachusetts: Tom Barao, Frank Nightingale, Eddie Rodrigues, Brian Baptiste, and the Gomes brothers. He even recounted legendary games at Boston Garden featuring King Gaskins of Catholic Memorial and Reggie Bird of Boston English.

Listening to these stories, I felt connected to something larger than myself. The reverence my father and the community held for these players was unmistakable. It was more than just a game; it was part of our region's cultural fabric. I saw that athletic success was not only a personal journey. It was a shared tradition, steeped in history and pride. I knew I would dedicate myself to this pursuit, even while recognizing how much of it was beyond my control.

Weeks later, my father and I attended a game between Holy Family High School and Fairhaven High School at the Kennedy Youth Center in New Bedford, Holy Family's home court. The smaller, more intimate gym buzzed with excitement, even more so than at the Christmas Tournament. People packed the gym before the junior varsity game even started. I sat wide-eyed, absorbing every detail: the sound of the ball, the rhythm of the game, the players' calm intensity despite the crowd.

Holy Family's junior varsity team featured Gary Dias, a flashy point guard and one of the best young players in southeastern Massachusetts. I had seen Gary play against my father's St. Luke's Hospital team in the summer league. Also on the team were Phil Gelinas and Mike Verronneau, both from Acushnet and familiar faces from the St. Luke's Hospital team. Watching them play together created a level of anticipation for me.

I could not help doing the math. If I kept improving and made it to Holy Family, these players would be juniors when I arrived. Together, we could continue the great Holy Family tradition and even win a state championship. The future felt wide open.

The varsity game was a blowout; Holy Family dominated from the opening tip. They looked like a team destined for the state tournament. The idea of playing under Coach Jack Nobrega, and being part of something so respected, only strengthened my desire to attend Holy Family.

After watching the Holy Family games and the Catholic Tournament, something struck me: those games seemed to matter in ways mine did not, I was walking around with this collared sense of responsibility, where, unfortunately, my teammates opposed me, a situation I was not prepared for.

It started subtly. Fewer passes. Cold shoulders. Then it became deliberate. I would be open, and the ball would swing the other way. It was not about winning. It became about making a point. We would rather lose without him than win with him.

That season was my first lesson in team politics and how quickly the concept of "team" can fall apart when ego and status get in the way. I did not know what to do with the feelings. So, I buried them.

I started internalizing everything. My appetite got worse despite my doctor's advice.

My sleep stayed inconsistent; Sleeping only when exhausted. I stopped being honest with myself, family, and my friends, especially about how I felt. This was a troubling time for me to live in at this moment.

In completing our season, the cracks deepened. We finished with 5 wins and 15 losses. We never came together as a team, and my relationships with most teammates deteriorated further. By season's end, I stopped taking the team bus back to Acushnet after away games, choosing instead to ride home with my parents. I was not sad to see the season end. I was ready to move on.

Two games of note versus Fairhaven closed out our schedule. Fairhaven Junior High School's 1974–1975 freshman team stood out as one of the finest in Massachusetts and maybe even the country. Their players had grown up playing with and against each other, forming a cohesive, talented unit. From a distance, I admired them. They embodied the foundation I longed for.

Fairhaven's success was not just about talent. It was about tradition. The town had a long history of developing athletes through excellent coaching, solid fundamentals, and well-organized league play. Despite its small size, Fairhaven regularly competed with and beat larger schools across the state. The teams displayed discipline, skill, and toughness.

Upon reviewing our season schedule, I promptly focused on our upcoming matches against Fairhaven. There was weight in those games, a chance to measure myself against a legacy.

Our first meeting was at our gym in Acushnet. During warmups, I noticed how smooth Fairhaven looked and how fluid their movements were. Their preparation was clear.

The game began with Fairhaven in a 2-3 zone. Early on, I found a seam and hit a 15-foot jumper. Then another from the same spot. Then a third, slightly deeper. We jumped out to a 6–0 lead and forced a timeout.

After the break, Fairhaven shifted to a man-to-man defense and effectively neutralized my efforts. Their adjustments were surgical.

In the second quarter, after a turnover, I sprinted back on defense. Fairhaven launched a long pass over my head. I jumped to intercept it, colliding in mid-air with one of their players. I hit the court hard, landing on my back with my right elbow slamming the floor. The ball rolled out of bounds.

As I stood up, I knew something was not right.

Mr. Hall, for the first time all season, took me out of the game. At halftime, we were down by twelve points.

The second half did not go any better. Fairhaven kept its lead. At one point, trapped in a corner. I split the defenders and took a 12-foot jumper. My attempt failed. Fairhaven grabbed the rebound and scored in transition. As I brought the ball back up, I heard it: "Semiao, pass the ball!"

The words rang through the gym. Time froze. It was the first time someone had publicly criticized me like that. Feeling exposed, I was useless for the rest of the game. We lost.

After the game, I learned who had made the comment: one of my teammate's parents. Officials removed him from the gym. That moment lingered, another bruise in a season full of them.

Team Record: 5-14 Points: 10 Assists: 2 Rebounds: 2 Steals: 0

The following week we played the rematch against Fairhaven in our last game of the season. We fell behind early and never recovered.

During the game, I grabbed a long rebound and sprinted down the court. Near the top of the key, I switched the basketball to my left hand and looked around. None of my teammates were running with me. Three Fairhaven players waited in the lane. I slowed, hesitated, and pulled up from eighteen feet. They closed in as I released the shot.

The ball swished through.

As I turned to get back on defense, one of the Fairhaven players muttered, "Nice shot."

That simple compliment, spoken in the middle of competition, meant more than anything I had heard from my own teammates all year. It stayed with me.

Fairhaven won by twenty-two points.

Mr. Hall left me in until the final buzzer, letting me play alongside the eighth-grade players who would return for the next season. They brought energy and effort. I made it a point to involve them, setting them up for scoring opportunities, sharing the ball. It was a small but hopeful way for me to close out a difficult season.

After the game, my father introduced me to Mr. George Graves, whose son, Phil, played for Fairhaven. Mr. Graves had been a standout on the Fairhaven championship team and was now a respected business executive. He complimented me on my performance, and we had a pleasant conversation.

Before we left, he invited us to attend the Fairhaven vs. Holy Family game the next night. We accepted.

Team Record: 5-15 Points: 17 Assists: 3 Rebounds: 2 Steals: 1

I finished the season with 277 points, an average of 14 points per game, falling 65 points short of the school's single season scoring record.

The next evening, we went to Fairhaven vs. Holy Family game at Fairhaven's gym. Holy Family had dominated the earlier matchup, and I was curious to see if Fairhaven would respond.

We arrived during the junior varsity game. As we entered the lobby, Mr. Graves greeted us warmly. After a brief conversation, he waved over Mr. Walter Silveira, a Fairhaven town selectman, and introduced him to my father. They talked about basketball, community, and other things, while I stood nearby, trying to listen.

Eventually, Mr. Graves led us to seats behind the Fairhaven bench. It felt like an odd place to sit, but I said nothing, curious about the view. Then he disappeared into the crowd, and we did not see him again that night.

The varsity rematch was much closer. Fairhaven, led by their star Luke Janusz, found gaps in Holy Family's defense that had not been visible in the game before. From our seats, we could hear every word of the coaches' strategy during timeouts. Wayne Wilson, Fairhaven's head coach, commanded the sideline. Fairhaven pushed hard, but Holy Family's talent held. Another victory for the Holy Family team.

As we stood to leave, someone called my father's name. It was Fairhaven's assistant coach, David Fernandes. They clearly knew each other. My father made the introduction. Coach Fernandes shook my hand. "I have heard good things. Enjoyed watching you play yesterday."

The comment stayed with me. I was not sure what he meant, but I did not forget it. He said Holy Family was a good team and would go far in the state tournament. As we parted, he added, "I hope to see you again soon."

On the ride home, my father mentioned scheduling our end-of-season dinner.

"How about this Friday night?" I suggested. My father nodded, pleased. "I'll make a reservation."

At dinner, we did not dwell on the season's struggles. We looked ahead. My father talked about the upcoming tournament at Keith Junior High School in New Bedford. It would feature junior and senior divisions. He wanted to assemble a team for the junior bracket like the St. Luke's Hospital team from the summer.

Knowing the caliber of players he planned to recruit, I doubted I would get any playing time. I was excited to be part of something strong again.

We also talked about returning to the Mass Maritime basketball camp that summer. Then he shifted the conversation to rebuilding the St. Luke's summer league team.

He asked who I would recruit. Without hesitation, I said, "Marty Cardoza, Randy Andrews, Willie Santiago." He smiled, pleased with my response. "They're already on my list." We also talked about reaching out to Mike Verronneau. He could help bring in more talent.

The season had ended, but something new had already begun. With the season over and no access to indoor courts, I returned to my sanctuary for self-improvement, my driveway. It was a space where I could experiment, free from the judgment of teammates or opponents. My cold-weather routine was meticulous. I kept one basketball inside by the baseboard heater, rotating it with the one I used outside when the cold sapped its bounce. A glove protected my non-shooting hand from the frigid air, but the spinning ball still cut my fingertips. I treated them by soaking my hands and applying salve until they toughened up.

◇ ◆ ◇

One of the dribbling drills I included was to dribble the basketball with winter gloves on. The lack of feeling with the winter gloves created the necessity to concentrate on your technique, your feel for the ball and dexterity with both hands. Essentially, making dribbling, passing and shooting more difficult. Creating those challenges encouraged creativity and entertainment for those tough days in the cold, rain, ice and snow. Also, I backed up onto the lawn near my mother's potted plants to try one-handed push shots from thirty feet. As I grew stronger, I worked on jump shots from that distance. I also stood on the two-step porch by our back door, jumping from the porch into the air to take shots, trying to land on the walkway.

After gym class, I asked my gym teacher how I could strengthen my legs. He paused, gave me a curious look, and replied with a single word: "Run."

That afternoon after school, I told my mother my plan to run to the junior high school. She looked surprised. "Today? Now? It is cold and drizzling." "Yes, today," I said without hesitation. Concerned, she offered to follow me in the car in case I got tired. I reassured her I would be fine. I changed into wool sweatpants and a wool sweatshirt. Without proper running shoes, I laced up my Converse Chuck Taylors, not ideal for running.

The route to the junior high school was a 1.7-mile stretch down Middle Road, the farthest I had ever run. The road was narrow and lined with construction zones. As I ran, I became hyper-aware of everything, the rhythm of my breath and footsteps, the rustle of my clothes and the wind in my ears. I could hear birds calling in the distance and recognize cars by the hum of their engines. Those sensations stayed with me and became part of every run from that day forward.

When I got home, tired but exhilarated, I told my mother all about it. It felt like the beginning of something new, a routine that would help me grow as an athlete.

My family realized I was serious about this conditioning routine. Days later, my father surprised me with a pair of Nike LDV running shoes, blue nylon, and suede with a bright yellow swoosh. The shoes looked odd with their waffle bottoms but were perfect for running.

Unbeknownst to me, my gym teacher, who is also our summer mail carrier, shared a story with my parents. He told them about our brief conversation and his one-word advice. When other teachers mentioned seeing me run down

Middle Road in the drizzle, he just shook his head. He said, "That kid's got dedication." He also talked about watching me in the driveway all summer, practicing in the heat. To him, my determination was undeniable.

From that point forward, I ran to the junior high school each day, except on game days. I began sprinting up and down my street, building explosiveness. My father and I pieced together a cross-training routine from books and articles, a full regimen that pushed my limits.

At an early age, I embraced a disciplined approach to fitness. Stories of how athletes trained and lived left a mark on me. Their habits became my blueprint. My father supported me with every step, timing my sprints, buying me free weights, urging me to grow.

Those challenges reflected who I was. I wanted to push myself further. One day, I created my own "Fitness Day." No basketball. Just intense workouts: jumping rope, distance running, cycling, sprints, full-body exercises. I set goals for running and biking, two full circuits without stopping. It took time and stubbornness, but once I hit that mark, I shifted to speed and efficiency.

Each time I finished the routine, I felt a deep sense of accomplishment. This discipline, this commitment, was how I would set myself apart.

One spring afternoon in the driveway, my father introduced me to a new concept, the mental side of sports. He had bought a book called *The Inner Game* by Timothy Gallwey. It was not about technical skills but about the "inner game," the mental battle: overcoming self-doubt and anxiety through visualization and Zen thinking. I devoured it, convinced it gave me an edge.

That day, we also discussed visualization. My father explained how athletes mentally rehearsed success to find calm and focus. These tools became emotional anchors. Though I was young, I embraced those advanced ideas.

Before spring sports began, the junior high school scheduled three events: a father-and-son basketball game, an alumni basketball game, and a basketball-cheerleader outing. I was reluctant to face any of them.

The father-and-son basketball game was only for the ninth graders and their fathers. The alumni basketball game felt like a letdown. Three minutes in, the coach subbed me out for a ninth grader who had not played all season. It was a game meant for fun, and I spent a significant amount of time on the bench. Mr. Hall sat beside me. I felt humiliated. I expected more. Afterward, I changed quickly and slipped out the side door to meet my family.

Spring arrived, and so did the awards assembly. I expected to receive the top scorer award and quietly hoped for the most valuable player (MVP) award. Sitting near the back with my friends, I watched the soccer awards, then basketball. When Mr. Hall announced the top scorer, I walked up to receive my trophy. The upperclassmen's response was tepid. Only my classmates and a handful of eighth graders clapped. The silence of the older players and students was not surprising, but it stung. Then came the MVP award. Mr. Hall awarded it to a player who had scored 100 fewer points than I had. Someone from the same group that had dismissed me all season. I sat frozen. I had led the team in points, minutes, and assists. None of it mattered. When the assembly ended, I left my trophies behind, eager to forget the day. That moment introduced me to the emotional conflict of splitting, viewing situations or people as all good or all bad. I felt abandoned, unsupported. These feelings shaped how I managed relationships and rejection. During this phase, I built a defense: turn the page. Feel the sting, then move on. It became a skill I relied on more than I understood.

The rest of the school day felt especially disappointing. When I got home, I changed clothes quickly and left for my run before my mother could see me. Instead of running to the junior high school, I headed toward Pope Park. Halfway there, I realized I had not planned the route. I adjusted, veering toward White's Dairy Farm and looping home through Nye's Lane.

When I got back, I took off my sneakers on the porch and headed to the driveway with my basketball shoes. Before I could leave, my mother stopped me. She stood in the doorway, holding my two trophies.

"Mr. Hall dropped these off," she said evenly. "He thought you forgot them."

"No," I said. "I left them on purpose."

My mother's stance shifted. "Why?"

"Am I supposed to just accept this without reacting?" Silence hung uncomfortably in the air between us. My mother's expression softened. The look of disappointment lingered, not on me, but on the situation. As I look at my mother, a surge of regret washes over me. I can see it in her eyes. This was more than anyone should have to carry, and unfairly, I just left it at her feet. "You have workouts to complete," she whispered. "Your father will be home soon." My mother turned and walked into the house, carrying my two trophies.

My mind raged, because I do not have the tools to express myself or the experience to process what was happening. I picked up my basketball and slapped it into action. Right hand, left hand, crossover, behind the back. My dribbling intensity climbed with each sequence. I lost myself in the rhythm. Sweat blurred my vision. When I finally stopped, I noticed three neighborhood kids watching from the end of my driveway. They smiled, giggling, and waved before running off.

Then I heard the hum of a car engine. My father pulled into the driveway, careful not to disrupt my practice space.

I passed him the ball and made a sharp cut. He delivered a perfect bounce pass. I laid it in.

"Nice pass," I called out.

My father smiled. "Give me a minute to change, and we will work out." We did not talk about what had happened at school. We did not need to.

When he came back out, we worked on an updated shooting drill. Five spots, twenty to twenty-two feet out. Slide right, receive the pass, shoot. Slide left, repeat. Ten shots per spot, fifty in total.

Then the variation: slide right, dribbling left before shooting. Slide left, dribble right. Another fifty shots. One hundred in total.

Breathless, I bent over. My father walked toward me; the ball tucked under his arm.

"Feel better?" he asked.

I nodded. "Yeah"

My father understood the frustration and betrayal I carried. But as always, he focused on the bigger picture. "You're doing everything right," he said. "Sometimes, the things that hurt now will shape your future."

It was hard to hear, but I knew he was right.

Next, the conversation shifted to the upcoming tournament at Keith Junior High School. We went over the roster, age limits, and deadlines. Despite everything, I felt a flicker of excitement again.

Over the weekend, he began recruiting. Through sheer persistence, my father could recruit half of the original St. Luke's Hospital team. He especially wanted Gary Dias, convinced Gary could anchor the team.

But the team never fully came together. Conflicting schedules and commitments got in the way. Only half of the team showed up for the first practice. The second was no better. A weak performance felt inevitable before the game even started.

We drew Fairhaven Junior High freshman team in the first round, the same team that had beaten my junior high school team twice in the last few weeks. Fairhaven played exactly as expected and won by eight points.

One play stuck with me. During a lengthy possession, they adjusted mid-flow: a screen, a handoff, a perfectly timed lob. It was so smooth, so intuitive, it looked instinctive.

The next day, I felt better, ready to finish the school year and move on. When the sign-up sheet for the cheerleader outing made its way around school, I ignored it.

When my classmates asked why I was not going, I said I had a medical appointment. They tried to talk me into it, mostly out of hormonal curiosity, not camaraderie.

I never told my parents about the basketball cheerleaders' outing. But it did not go unnoticed. My mother's best friend mentioned it.

That night, the phone rang.

"I didn't know… I don't know why he didn't go."

Afterward, my mother turned to me. "If anything is bothering you, you can tell us. We will always try to help."

I nodded. "I'm fine."

The subject never came up again, but I sensed they understood.

That evening, my father came home with two boxes: ankle weights. "They'll help strengthen your legs," he said. "But never wear them while playing, running, or walking. Only for exercises." My dad showed me how to use them. I started that night. Leg extensions and leg raises became my nighttime routine, lying on my living room floor. I had no strategy. Reps until my legs burned. I learned quickly to create more resistance by attaching both sets of leg weights to my legs while I did my exercises.

One afternoon during study period, Mr. Hall asked if I wanted to work out after school. For two weeks, we drilled and played one-on-one. We talked little, but his invitation made me feel seen.

Looking back, it was his way of helping me move on. But I had not yet learned to forgive. I poured my frustration into the workouts.

One day, Mr. Hall asked if I still practiced in my driveway after our workouts. I told him yes. My mother limited my time outside, but I stayed outside until someone called me in for the night. Practice after practice had become part of my routine.

Mr. Hall also mentioned a job opening at the Acushnet Recreation Department. I said I was interested. He planned to call my father about the opportunity. The job included teaching basketball to young kids. My "bosses" would be Joey Gaudreau, Phil Gelinas, and Kevin Pelletier. I hoped that when we were not coaching, we would play two-on-two.

The freshman graduation ceremony took place on the last Friday of the school year. Organizers asked my friends and me to be ushers. My history with the freshman class did not make the idea appealing. I hesitated, but my friends pressured me to go.

After the ceremony, a friend, an eighth grader, invited me to his sister's graduation party. I asked whether my friends could come. To my surprise, he said yes.

We all got permission from our families to go to the party. The house where the party would be held was close enough to the junior high school to walk there. I knew the house; we all knew the house; it belonged to one of the wealthiest families in town. The backyard was stunning, with a glowing pool and manicured landscaping.

While I admired the patio and pool, the girl whose graduation party we were attending grabbed my hand. "Come with me," she said. She led me through her house. Through a doorway. A stairway ahead of us. Down the stairs we went. *If I am to be honest, my fourteen-year-old hormonally active mind thought…well, I think you can understand.* At the bottom of the stairs to our left was a hallway and then another hallway. I am dizzy with anticipation, and now I am extremely disappointed because I am now standing in front of her parents. The next sound is the girl saying smugly, "I told you he would come to my party." This conversation was taking place right in front of me as if I were not there. Her parents greeted me warmly. I was asked about my season and about my summer. When I told them I was going to Holy Family my freshman year to play for Jack Nobrega, her father smiled. "He's the best coach in the state," he said. "I will look forward to following your progress. Best of luck to you." With that, I hurried back outside to my friends by the pool.

Later, I found their tennis court, which doubled as a basketball court. My friends teased me. "Semiao, you look like you're ready to move in." They were not far off.

The next day, I told my parents about the party. I pitched buying the vacant lot next to our house and building a pool and tennis and basketball courts. My persistence did not change their answer. I asked for a month, but their answer stayed the same: no.

When the school year finally ended, I was tired and angry but also strangely relieved. Summer 1975 would be my chance to start over, to rebuild my game and my confidence.

Even as that first season ended in disappointment, a different rhythm took over, runs down Middle Road, home workouts with ankle weights, jump shots in the fading light. What I lost in camaraderie I tried to rebuild in solitude. These rituals became the quiet scaffolding of my next chapter, preparing me for the leap from survival to self-mastery.

The second generation of the St. Luke's Hospital basketball team came together in the New Bedford Recreation Summer League, thanks to my father's recruiting efforts. He recruited three talented players from the Wareham High School freshman team Marty Cardoza, Randy Andrews, and Willie Santiago and added Steve Pires, a rising star from Holy Family High School. Together, we formed a strong nucleus that promised a competitive season. Marty, a natural leader, led our team. While he could be vocal, it was his quiet focus and relentless work ethic that struck me most. I watched how he moved through practices deliberately, calm, composed, and tried to mirror that same presence.

Even as the team thrived, I wrestled with growing pains. My performance swung between flashes of confidence and stretches of frustration. The weight of the junior high season clung to me, making it hard to fully settle into this new rhythm. I leaned on the older players, watching how they carried themselves, asking questions when I could. There were more days than I will admit when I felt like a visitor in someone else's game.

Recognizing the talent on the roster, my father used the summer league to experiment with lineups and strategies. At home, we would sit in our living room, flipping through coaching books and sketching defensive schemes on scrap paper. He tried different zone defenses, evaluating their impact in live games. That process sharpened our team's readiness and deepened my grasp of the game's nuances.

The summer league became a turning point, not just for my skills, but for how I saw the game. Watching my father blend strategy with instinct taught me how adaptability and preparation could shape outcomes. I realized then that basketball was not just something you played; it was something you studied, felt, lived. That lesson stayed with me.

One of the more aggressive systems was the 1-3-1 zone defense. It relied on anticipation, quick hands, and smart rotations to disrupt passing lanes and spark fast breaks. It was high-risk, high reward, leaving soft spots in the corners and on the low block.

He also introduced full-court presses, both zone and man-to-man. The 1-2-1-1 zone press created traps and chaos in the backcourt. Our ability to adapt from game to game showed just how sharp our collective basketball IQ had become.

Our toughest regular-season matchup came against Pepin's Electric, a gritty, well-coached squad from the North End of New Bedford. The game was at Brooklawn Park, their home turf, one of four venues the Recreation Department used. The park's bright lights made shooting tricky, but I had logged hours under similar lights in my driveway. That night, it felt like all those solo sessions had been leading to this moment.

As we warmed up, the crowd grew. The sidelines swelled three to four people deep, creating an intense, almost claustrophobic atmosphere. From the opening tip, the competition was fierce, and by the fourth quarter, the score was still deadlocked.

Early in the game, Pepin tracked me closely, limiting my offense, so I focused on defense. As a team, we shifted between a full-court man-to-man press and a 2-3 zone, hoping to keep them off balance. Then came a turnover on the far side of the court.

My game always chased drama, a satisfying conclusion, the hero arriving to save the day.

Seeing my teammate scoop up the turnover, I sprinted down the left sideline, signaling that I was open. He threw a perfect pass. Catching it in stride, I pushed the ball forward with my left hand, attacking the basket. A defender closed in from the opposite side. I adjusted, cutting under the hoop and laying it in with my right hand on a reverse. The ball spun off the backboard and dropped through just as my momentum carried me into the crowd.

From somewhere behind me, I heard, "Nice shot, Semiao. About time you did something." I smiled to myself, knowing they were not wrong. In the last minutes, I strung together key plays: an 18-foot bank shot, a 22-foot jumper, and finally a three-point play after drawing contact in the lane. That last basket sealed the win. Beating Pepin's in that kind of environment electrified us, especially knowing we might see them again in the playoffs.

After the game, Joey Gaudreau mentioned that Holy Family's summer league team had a game later that night. Curious to see how they were shaping up, I stayed to watch. As expected, their strong guard play carried them to another win.

Late in the game, one of their top guards went down with a knee injury, a reminder that summer success did not always carry into the regular season.

We entered the playoffs as the number one seed. The format was best-of-three, with each team selecting a home court. We chose Buttonwood Park as our home court for its neutral feel and well-kept courts. In the first round, we swept the series two games to none, heading to the finals with momentum and confidence.

In the same week that the summer league playoffs began, I attended the Mass Maritime Basketball Camp in Buzzards Bay. Like the earlier summer, I attended only the day sessions. My family was still not comfortable with my staying overnight. It was my second summer at the camp, and I was eager to show how much I had improved. I felt more confident, more aware, and ready to dive into every drill from day one.

Returning to camp at this stage in my development was pivotal. The first time had humbled me. I had watched polished, confident players who were clearly ahead of me. I hesitated, afraid of making mistakes. My fundamentals were not strong, and fear of embarrassment kept me from fully joining in. But I watched, absorbed, and brought those lessons home.

This summer, I came back to camp a different player. Hungry to learn and eager to compete, I threw myself into every challenge. Each day, we rotated through skill-specific stations, rebounding, shooting, ball handling, and more. Expectations were clear: focus, execute, be ready.

By the third day, my team earned the privilege of playing two games on the main indoor court, a coveted opportunity. That morning's stations focused on rebounding and shooting.

At the rebounding station, we drilled positioning, leverage, and securing the ball. The coach emphasized holding the box out until the ball hit the floor, using balance and footwork to gain an edge. Each rep demanded precision, legs shoulder-width apart, eyes tracking the ball, securing it with both hands. It was one of the best rebounding sessions I had ever experienced.

Next came the station I had been waiting for: shooting. I wanted to hear what the coach thought of my jump shot.

As I have noted previously: Vic Colucci, a former standout at Providence College, led the session. His reputation spoke for itself: he once scored 36 points against UCLA at Madison Square Garden during the 1969 Holiday Festival, with Lew Alcindor (later Kareem Abdul-Jabbar) anchoring their defense.

That session would change my game forever.

Coach Colucci demonstrated a shooting form you could build a game around, repeatable, balanced, clean. He called each camper to the foul line to take five shots, offering feedback after each one. I stepped up fifth.

I expected minor adjustments. Maybe even praise. What I really wanted, though I didn't know it then, was validation, an attitude I now recognize as arrogance for someone still so raw.

After my first shot, Coach Colucci stopped me.

"Keep your shooting elbow tucked in at your hip," he said. "Eliminate any extra motion."

I froze for a second, stunned and a little embarrassed. Then I nodded and adjusted.

Then came the detail that would flip everything.

"You're a right-eye-dominant shooter," he said. "Close your right eye and shoot."

I hesitated, confused, then I shot.

Swish.

"Again," he said, tossing me another ball. Swish.

"One more."

Swish.

He gave me a quick smile and moved on. I just stood there, holding that feeling.

No one else got that kind of correction, or that kind of result. The adjustment seemed small, but it shifted everything. I walked away, knowing something had changed.

The biggest takeaway was not just the improved shot; it was how the ball felt leaving my hand when it was right. That feeling was unmistakable. More importantly, I had learned how to correct myself, to feel when something was off and visualize the fix. That session taught me to ask better questions: Why was my shot flat? Why didn't the ball have the right backspin? Why was my release hard? And more importantly, what could I do about it?

Through trial, error, and endless repetition, I found answers. I did not just improve my form; I understood it. And from that understanding, I grew. I transformed my jump shot from a playground fling to a polished, mature shot. It was a momentous change. For a young athlete, developing self-correction and awareness felt advanced. But once I grasped it, my game changed forever. I felt energized. Every spare moment that day, I practiced my new jump shot, elbow tucked just as Coach Colucci taught. I even skipped lunch, grabbed a ball and a rim, and drilled through the break. It felt like I had unlocked a new level in my game.

That evening, when my father came home from work, I could not wait to show him what I had learned. Out on the driveway, I let the shots fly. My release was consistent; the ball's rotation was tight. I could shoot from deeper without changing my form. My dad watched silently, gave nothing away, then turned and went inside, leaving me to practice. I kept shooting well past 10 p.m., until he finally came out, took the ball from my hands, and told me it was time to call it a night. Even then, I could not stop.

Lying on my bedroom floor, I rehearsed the technique repeatedly, balancing the ball on my fingertips, tucking my elbow, following through. Thinking back, finding another reason not to sleep, "Sugar plums dancing in your head."

For the rest of the week, camp focused on agility and endurance. One drill locked us in a defensive stance, feet wide, knees bent, hands up, sliding side to side within the foul line circle for thirty seconds at a time. It burned, but we pushed through.

That summer, I learned more than mechanics. I understood defensive posture, the value of endurance, and the discipline it would take to rise higher. It was transformative, proof of how far I had come in a single year.

New Bedford Recreation Summer League Junior Division Finals - Game One

Meanwhile, the St. Luke's Hospital team was preparing for the finals against Pepin's Electric, the same team we had beaten earlier in the season. We had expected to see them again. We knew they would be ready.

When the first game of the finals tipped off, something was off. For the first time all summer, we played scared. We were flat-footed on defense, committing avoidable fouls and giving up easy points. My father cycled through lineups, searching for a spark. I played timidly, reflecting on the team's hesitancy like a mirror.

We had not faced a challenge like this all season. Pepin's Electric pounced on our mistakes, and we crumbled. The scoreboard recorded our first loss of the summer, but it did not show the part that mattered most: for the first time all season, there was no fight in us.

After the game, my father gathered us for a short meeting. He broke down our performance, but his focus was not on what we had done wrong. It was about how we would respond.

My father's words, "Learn from this loss and come ready to win tomorrow."

The drive home was just as quiet. Once we got home, I went inside, changed, and headed straight to the driveway. I launched into drills, fifty to seventy shots in rapid succession. Midway through, I saw someone at the bottom of the driveway. I turned. I already knew who it was.

Our neighbor pointed out something as he approached our driveway, yelling about the noise and saying I was violating the town ordinance. He had already called the Acushnet police. Moments later, my father stepped out of the house and stood beside me, calm but firm. He told the neighbor to leave.

Then headlights swept across the driveway; a police car pulled in. The officer stepped out, spoke briefly with the neighbor, then approached us. Polite and professional, he reminded us of the noise ordinance, then shifted gears. He asked where I went to school and whether I played basketball. When my father mentioned I played for the junior high school team under Ron Hall, the officer nodded. He knew Mr. Hall.

"Ron's an excellent coach," he said.

My father added I had been the leading scorer as a seventh grader. The officer raised his eyebrows. We laughed, thanked him, and promised to stop for the night. Before leaving, he encouraged me to keep practicing.

After the officer drove off, my father and I went inside. Still, I could not sleep. My mind looped through the game, the loss, and now the bizarre confrontation in the driveway. During the summer and fall, the Acushnet police continued to stop by. The officers were consistently professional and courteous. One even gave me advice on a training run, telling me to run against traffic for safety. I followed his advice from then on.

The next day was the last session of camp. Thoughts of the game, the police visiting our home and my still-imperfect jump shot swirled. Determined to stay focused, I pushed through the drills and performed well. Getting out of my head made all the difference.

Before leaving camp that day, I sought coaches Alaimo and Colucci to thank them. They wished me luck and said they hoped to see me next summer. I promised I would be back.

On the drive home, my focus shifted to the game ahead and my teammates. We pulled into the driveway with two hours to spare. I did not waste a minute, grabbed a ball, hit the driveway, and started warming up. Following my pre-game ritual, I showered, dressed, and was ready to go by the time my father got home.

Game Two

The evening air was thick with tension at Buttonwood Park. My teammates were somber, still weighed down by the loss. Warmups passed in near silence.

When the game tipped off, it felt like déjà vu. We fell behind by six points. The deficit did not grow, but we could not close it. For three quarters, we trailed by four to six points, stuck in neutral.

At the start of the fourth quarter, my father made a critical change. He moved Steve Pires and me into the backcourt together, with me running point. His plan: increase the tempo and press full court after every score. We scored, set up the press, and forced a deflection that led to another basket. The gap shrank to two.

Pepin's Electric called a timeout. My father switched us to a 1-3-1 half-court trap, using sidelines and corners to create turnovers. It worked. We forced another stop and scored to tie the game. The teams traded baskets. With under a minute left, Pepin surged ahead by four. My father called a timeout and laid out our plan at both ends.

Out of the huddle, Pepin went man-to-man in the backcourt, then dropped into a 2-3 zone defense once we crossed half court. We executed our zone offense. I found Marty flashing to the high post. Marty caught the pass, pump-faked, and drove past his defender for the bucket and the foul.

Down one, we set up a full-court press. Steve deflected the inbound; I caught the deflection and passed it right back to Steve, and he converted a layup. For the first time in the series, we were ahead. With ten seconds left, we led by one.

Pepin called their final timeout. My father told us to press hard but not to foul. I picked up their point guard full court, forcing him to his weaker right hand. He crossed half court with me on his hip, boxed in by the sideline. As he spun, with a slight bump, I held my ground; their bench screamed for a foul. He pulled up for a desperate shot that grazed the backboard and bounced away. We won.

The sudden relief we each felt was not surprising. The toll of the regular season, the punch in the face we received from the first game of the finals and then getting this win, like a giant exhale. This was the first time in our athletic lives we had been in a fight. You could not blink because the competition was so heavy. We felt genuine relief, but knowing we still had work to do made everyone cautious about celebrating this win. The unspoken truth is this would be our last opportunity to play together.

That night, I lay in bed replaying the game, every moment I hesitated, every time I could have done more. I promised myself no more hesitation. And for the first time in days, I slept.

The next morning, my parents told me my sister would not be going to summer camp today, and I would need to take her with me to work. We set off on our bikes towards the junior high school. My sister struggled to keep pace. I realized during this trip that my sister was not in shape enough to make the ride to the junior high school without enduring significant difficulty. My training runs made Middle Road familiar to me. I knew every inch of this road, and my sister did not. I spent the entire ride slowing down, encouraging her, pulling for her, trying to create a pace which moved us forward. By the time we arrived at the junior high school, we were both worn out.

At work, I listened to the older guys tell stories, laughing alone but staying mostly quiet. Then someone teased me about girls. "What social life?" My sister blurted out. "Michael always has a basketball in his hands!" "Don't worry," they said. "That'll change when you get to high school."

Later that afternoon, with the gym pulsing with heat, I slipped in to get shots up. An hour in, drenched in sweat, I drilled my new jump shot, pushing myself harder with each attempt. Noticing my focus, my coworkers reminded me about the game that night. I nodded and kept going.

Afterward, they offered my sister a ride home, leaving me to ride back alone. I arrived home exhausted. I tried to follow my pre-game ritual, shower, reset, but something was off. In the shower, there was a wave of fatigue. My body felt heavy. I realized I might have pushed too hard.

Back in my room, I sipped water, suspecting dehydration, then noticed a slight tremor in my hands and arms. I sat on the floor, staring at my hands, trying to make sense of it. For the first time, I wondered: Am I sick? Can I play tonight?

I felt a level of embarrassment I did not expect. The expectation was that you should have known better than to push that hard with a big game ahead. I went to my mother and explained. She listened calmly. When I finished, she held my hands, asked me to squeeze, and checked my arms, temperature, pulse, and stomach. Her approach was steady, clinical, but reassuring.

"Your temperature and pulse are high," she said, guiding me to the kitchen. "You're dehydrated and need nourishment."

She told me to sip water and then to make a peanut-butter and banana sandwich. It was not surprising; she knew I would eat it and that it would address the immediate issues.

"You need quick hydration and carbohydrates," she said. "Small, steady nutrition and fluids."

I followed her instructions and retreated to my air-conditioned room to rest. Sitting quietly, I reflected on how I had let myself reach this point. I vowed to be smarter from now on. As I calmed my mind, visualizing to clear the panic and refocus, my body recovered. The tremors eased. My breath slowed. I felt grounded again.

My mother checked on me and suggested I stretch and use the breathing exercises she had taught me.

"Stretching helps calm your body and psyche," she said. "It prepares you for what's next."

I moved through the stretches she had shown me. Over time, I had developed a rhythm, each stretch flowing into the next. The repetition soothed me. For the next thirty minutes, I alternated between stretching and visualization, slowly returning to myself.

As I recovered, a strange realization came into focus. Thinking back to seventh grade, the tremors, the mumbled sideline talk, the weight loss, the sleepless nights, was I edging toward self-sabotage? Where had today's recklessness come from? This was not like me. How had I put myself in a position to fail?

Dwelling was not something I had time for. I had to steady myself and get ready for the biggest game of my life. I changed into my game clothes and waited for my father to get home.

Game Three

The drive to the game was silent. Between father and son, coach, and player, no one spoke. When we arrived, the scene was electric. The packed parking lot hummed with energy. My father and I walked toward the courts, surrounded by voices and movement.

On the sidelines, my teammates had already gathered, whispering among themselves. We nodded subtle acknowledgments of what the night meant. All season; we had been the favorites. We had not underestimated our opponent. We just had not played to our potential. Last night's win gave us a chance. Now we had to finish the job.

My father's pre-game instructions were simple:

"Man-to-man at half court. Move the ball. Be aggressive."

The game opened with tension hanging thick. Both teams played tight. Shots clanged off the rim. Possessions dragged. Pepin opened in their usual 2-3 zone. We traded missed baskets, neither side breaking through.

I missed my first two but kept hunting for my shot. I had to shake off my nerves. Then it happened. I found a rhythm. I hit four straight: top-of-the-key, corner, foul-line pull-up, and a leaning bank from the left lane. We jumped out to an 8–0 lead. Pepin's called an early timeout. Our bench erupted.

For the first time in the series, it felt like we were playing our game. We held the lead through the first half. When Pepin switched to man-to-man, we responded, moved the ball, ran our sets, and closed the half up twelve. But no one thought it was over.

Pepin clawed back, cutting it to four by the end of the third. Midway through the fourth, it was down to two. It turned into a battle of nerves; every possession carried pressure. With under a minute left, Pepin took a two-point lead.

Then I found myself open for the first time since the opening quarter. I rose for a 20-foot jump shot from the right sideline, clean form, clean release.

Swish.

The score of the game was now tied. The crowd grew uneasy; they wanted our game to end so the senior finals could start. They would have to wait. Our work was not done. But neither team scored again. The buzzer sounded. Overtime.

In the huddle, my father was direct: "Stay aggressive. Force mistakes."

On their first possession, Pepin turned the ball over. We converted. During their next possession, the referees called a charging foul on Pepsin's. We scored again. Their coach called timeout.

Out of the break, my father shifted us into a 2-2-1 three-quarter press to burn the clock. Once they crossed the half court, we dropped into a 2-1-2 zone. It worked. Our defensive pressure rushed them, throwing them off rhythm, and forcing a quick shot. We rebounded. Less than a minute to go.

My father called one final timeout. "They'll foul now," he said.

As predicted, Pepin's fouled one of my teammates right after the timeout. Unfortunately, he missed the front end of the one-and-one, and Pepin's raced down the court, scoring quickly. Our lead shrank to two with thirty seconds left.

Pepin's called timeout.

In the huddle, my father laid out the plan: spread the offense, keep the ball between Marty and me, and either score or get to the free throw line.

Pepin's stayed in man-to-man defense as we set up. I started on the right wing and cut along the baseline to the left side. Marty occupied the high post. He read the defense, set a screen, and posted himself up on the left block.

I caught the ball on the left sideline and settled into a triple-threat position. My defender stayed tight, but I saw Marty seal his man inside. I fired a bounce pass to him. As soon as he touched it, two defenders collapsed. We both saw the same thing, an opening.

I sprinted to the corner. Marty kicked it back to me. With no hesitation. I caught it, squared up, and released it. Swish.

We were up by four. The game was ours to lose. Pepin answered with a quick basket, cutting the lead again. We inbounded the ball to Marty. They fouled. Calm and composed, Marty stepped to the line and sank both shots. The game ended quietly as Pepin's tried a rushed shot, which missed wildly. We are champions.

The excitement was not just about the win; it was about the journey. For me, the moment carried a deeper charge because of my father. He had been there the whole way, coaching on the court, father at home. It was a difficult role to play, but this championship was his too.

After the game, the New Bedford Recreation Department handed out the awards. The New Bedford Recreation Department named Marty Cardoza MVP of both the regular season and the playoffs, honors he fully earned. They selected both of us for the playoff all-star team.

This was the team experience I had always hoped for when I first started playing. A group united, locked in, chasing something bigger than ourselves. As the celebration swirled around me, I stood at that moment, taking it in. I made a silent vow right then: I would carry this focus, this energy, into my eighth-grade season at the junior high school.

By the time the school year ended, there were dynamics surrounding me I did not yet understand. Ford Junior High School had given me a taste of organized basketball and, just as powerfully, a taste of isolation and politics. But the summer league title and the lessons at camp changed everything. In the same driveway where I had once played alone, I now rehearsed Coach Colucci's shooting form and my father's drills, rebuilding myself piece by piece. The season had bruised me, but the summer rebuilt me. Standing on the edge of eighth grade, I felt a flicker of new resolve. With a stronger shot, a stronger body, and a clearer sense of who I was becoming, I was ready to step into the next chapter carrying everything I had learned.

Chapter Three

Eighth grade began with proof that the work I had put in over the summer was paying off. My skills had sharpened, and my confidence had grown. The previous year had been full of milestones: leading the junior high school team in scoring as a seventh grader, attending Mass Maritime basketball camp, and helping my father's summer league team win a championship. Now the game felt different, less like a dream I was chasing and more like a life I was living.

As my experience deepened, I had learned to push through pain, to treat it not as a warning but as part of the process. That mindset gave me strength, but it also fed something else. Beneath the surface, anxiety and insecurity whispered in quiet moments. I had to work harder than everyone else just to prove I belonged. That pressure sometimes pushed me into darker, more introspective places.

The scars from the seventh-grade basketball season at Ford stayed. My family quietly questioned whether this was still the right school for me, exploring other options. But competitive leagues in our area were scarce, so I returned to the junior high school for eighth grade. To supplement my time on the basketball court, my father found another league at the Fairhaven Boys' Club.

A large part of my development and maturity came from my inclusion on the junior high school soccer team during the fall. Never having played competitive soccer before, not counting my time at Camp Massasoit. The nuances and the rules of the game created a unique opportunity for me as an athlete. Each day at practice, I learned another technique. For example, trapping the ball where you use your body, not your hands, to stop and control the ball. Learning to corner kick and the offside rule. I was open to all of it. I was the best-conditioned player on the team from my days running Middle Road and running sprints on my street at home. What was most unexpected about the experience was how my teammates appreciated my eagerness to learn. They saw how hard I worked each day and how supportive I was of their efforts. These traits were like what I experienced playing for my father's summer league team, where we supported each other, and that positioned our team to play and win the summer league championship.

Tryouts showed how belief could shape outcomes. During a scrimmage, I sprinted ahead on a fast break, calling for the ball. I caught the pass, fumbled, and missed the layup. One teammate laughed, mocking me loudly enough for the coach to hear. My jaw tightened, and I stared at the gym floor, heat rising to my face. Mr. Hall waved it off as if to say, forget it, I followed his cue, letting it go.

I entered the season with clear goals: win every game and break the scoring record. In theory, it felt simple. The greatest challenge was the unknown, my teammates. Would they be ready for the pressure?

Game days carried their familiar rush. In our first game, everything clicked. For the first time, I played at my pace, confident and in control. My teammates matched my energy, feeding off every possession. One play stood out: a two-on-one fast break. As I neared the foul line, I stopped, planted, rose, and released. Clean. Running back on defense, I realized I was executing what I had drilled countless times before.

As the clock wound down, Tabor Academy tried to close the gap. Their last shot missed and dropped into my hands. Just seconds left. I dribbled past the scorer's table, stopped at half court, squared up, and let it fly.

Swish.

My teammates exploded. I stood in disbelief. I had never taken a half-court shot in a game before. Sure, it was unnecessary, but it felt incredible.

We won, 66–58.

Team Record: 1-0 Points: 29 Assists: 8 Rebounds: 6 Steals: 3

Later that evening, after a quick change at home, I played my first game at the Fairhaven Boys' Club. The atmosphere there was looser, more like pickup basketball, and I scored forty points in a win.

In Acushnet, athletes rarely found the spotlight. Attention went to players from neighboring towns. That bothered me. Yet small gestures, like a classmate, who was a hockey player, giving me a pair of blue-and-white skate laces "that would never come untied," reminded me of the shared commitment that transcended sports.

Our second game was against Westport. The game was tight, but I took over in the final two minutes. I hit a 20-foot jumper, followed it with a reverse layup, and capped it off with a fast-break score that sealed the win. Final score: 59–51. Two wins in a row.

Team Record: 2-0 Points: 29 Assists: 6 Rebounds: 5 Steals: 2

This season, my connection with my teammates grew stronger. Familiarity with the soccer season carried over. They had seen my work ethic and respected my commitment. That mutual respect-built trust on and off the court.

In our third game, we faced West Bridgewater, the team that beat us twice last season. This time, we controlled the game from start to finish and earned our third straight win.

Team Record: 3-0 Points: 26 Assists: 5 Rebounds: 4 Steals: 0

Our fourth game was against the freshman team from St. Anthony's High School. A friend of my father's, a fraternity brother, coached the team. He also taught at Holy Family High School, the school where I hoped to play the following year.

My team struggled throughout the game, and with less than two minutes left, we trailed by twelve points. Our only chance was to foul and hope St. Anthony missed their free throws.

They missed the first. I sprinted down the court and pulled up for a 20-foot jumper, cutting the lead to ten. Another miss. I caught the ball in the left corner and drained a 22-footer. Eight points down, with thirty-five seconds to play. When they missed again, I hit a jumper from the foul line. Now within six, with thirty seconds left.

We fouled again. Another miss. I took the ball at the top of the key, surrounded by defenders, and nailed the shot. Our bench erupted. The lead was down to four with eighteen seconds left.

St. Anthony's missed once more. I raced from baseline to baseline, caught a pass in the corner, and felt their defense collapse around me. In that split second, I had a choice: trust myself or pass to a teammate slipping under the basket. I chose to shoot.

Swish. The lead was now two. Eight seconds remained in the game. We pressed hard on the inbound. Their guard panicked and threw the ball away. We had a chance.

My teammate prepared to inbound the ball on the sideline in front of our bench. I faked right, then left, darting and spinning, trying to shake free. I cut left again, but my teammate passed to where I had been a second earlier. Our opponent intercepted the ball. St. Anthony's regained possession and ran out the clock. We lost by two.

The outcome haunted me. I blamed myself and silently vowed to do better the next time. After the game, I avoided the St. Anthony's coach, though he and my father talked for a while. It felt strange watching two old friends catching up after such a gutting loss.

Team Record: 3-1 Points: 31 Assists: 4 Rebounds: 6 Steals: 2

Weeks later, I learned that the coach, my father's fraternity brother, had bragged about how he had guaranteed I would not score over 30 points. He had made that promise before the game. Hearing that unsettled me. It was a reminder of how people you trust can surprise you with their words and how easily pride can twist into something personal. This turns out to be a foreshadowing moment for me and for the person who had tried to limit my points.

Human nature at its best is an awkward dance. Sometimes, adults look to make a name for themselves or chase attention, hoping their behavior will advance their careers. Strapping themselves to the back of a junior high school student was beyond anything I could understand.

That moment stayed with me. It was an early lesson in trust, loyalty, and how easily someone could exploit you for their own gain. My mother's words were now in front of me, "Those people are not your friends; they will try to use you for their gain." You make this vow to yourself never to be exploited, regardless of the temptations that are presented to you.

At fourteen, I saw how quickly life could shift. Just two years earlier, I had been learning how to dribble a basketball. Now, I am the best player in every game I played. The path had been difficult, and it was not always clear why things unfolded the way they did.

Balancing basketball, school, and daily life wore me down. Anxiety had crept back into my life; more than likely, it had never really left. Persistent patterns showed up: little sleep and poor recovery from the physical toll of my junior high school season and the grind at the Fairhaven Boys' Club. My appetite fluctuated, so my nutrition suffered. Each day, I barely managed a single meal. My ambition and focus on the goals I set for my team and myself were the overriding issues in front of me. I knew nutrition and rest mattered, but I ignored that guidance and kept pushing.

That night, alone in my room, my thoughts stretched beyond the game. I reflected on the countless hours I had spent practicing alone in the driveway and shooting in the gym. I knew there was still work to do, but the stress was building. In my mind, I kept coming back to the question: could I keep up with the physical and mental demands? Obsessing and calculating everything, analyzing the weight of my schedule: twenty games with the junior high school team, two games a week, with practices on non-game days. Add to those two more games a week with the Fairhaven Boys' Club team. A minimum of three games a week, every week.

Over the weekend, my father and I attended a game at the Kennedy Youth Center, where Holy Family High School hosted the team from Martha's Vineyard High School. At halftime, I drifted into the lobby and overheard my father speaking with someone. As I got closer, I realized he was talking to Jack Nobrega, the head basketball coach at Holy Family.

My father introduced me, sharing highlights from my season, including the half-court shot from an earlier game. Coach Nobrega smiled, saying he had heard about our game against St. Anthony's. His acknowledgment surprised me, but I quickly realized the details were unimportant. What mattered was the connection he was building with me.

As the conversation wrapped up, my father stepped back and let me stand on my own. Coach Nobrega shook my hand and encouraged me before going back to his team. My father gave me a small grin and patted me gently on the lower back, a silent acknowledgment that he understood how uncomfortable those moments could be for me.

Meeting Coach Nobrega left an immediate impression on me. I realized that stepping outside my comfort zone, no matter how awkward, was necessary to create opportunities for my future. That day's events helped me move on from our first loss and refocus on what mattered most: continuing to grow and preparing for what lay ahead.

The following week, unfortunately, my calculations proved to be true. I played four games and attended practices on non-game days with the junior high school team, leaving barely any time to rest. At school, the atmosphere was shifting as I inched closer to the scoring record. Classmates suddenly paid closer attention to the morning announcements, especially the basketball scores and individual stats. Crowds at our games were growing. The excitement was genuine.

For our first game of the week, we traveled to Somerset South. We dominated from start to finish.

Team Record: 4-1 Points: 32 Assists: 4 Rebounds:8 Steals: 2

The second game of the week was against Somerset North, at their new gym. From the opening tip, they were ready for me. They double-teamed me the entire game, giving my teammates a four-on-three advantage, but we could not solve their triangle defense. We lost.

Team Record: 4-2 Points: 21 Assists: 2 Rebounds: 2 Steals: 0

My performance disappointed me. I had not expected the pressure defense and struggled to adapt. Frustrated, I took it out on our opponent later that evening at the Fairhaven Boys' Club, scoring 46 points in a 15-point win.

As the season progressed, the pressure mounted. I was more than just physically exhausted; somehow; it felt like my game was shrinking. My versatility had vanished. We won four of our next five games, but I felt disconnected.

My poor shooting frustrated me even after I hit a game-winning shot against Friends Academy. I almost cost us the game.

Team Record: 5-2 Points: 31 Assists: 2 Rebounds: 3 Steals: 1

We faced Diman Vocational next, a team that had beaten us twice the previous season. I came in hoping to redeem myself, but I played cautiously. Fortunately, we controlled the game early and cruised to a win.

Team Record: 6-2 Points: 29 Assists: 3 Rebounds: 4 Steals: 0

Then came a home game against Apponequet Regional High School freshman team. By this point, the weight of the season was undeniable. I struggled to stay locked in for an entire game. My focus drifted in and out. We won, but it was because my teammates stepped up, not me.

Team Record: 7-2 Points: 29 Assists: 2 Rebounds: 3 Steals: 0

Our rematch against Tabor Academy exposed my growing vulnerability. Their aggressive play and constant taunting completely threw me off. I was not engaged. I did not fight back. We lost, and it stung.

Team Record: 7-3 Points: 18 Assists: 1 Rebounds: 2 Steals: 0

Determined to respond, I shifted my focus to our rematch with Westport, a team that had become something of a rival. We played with intensity and won. Still, my struggles lingered. After the game, my father summed it up perfectly: "Twenty-nine points, and you didn't play well."

Team Record: 8-3 Points: 29 Assists: 2 Rebounds: 4 Steals: 0

That night, I could not stop thinking about how far I had slipped. I felt disconnected from my game, from myself. I could have presumed that the pressure I felt was self-imposed, but I quietly would not admit that to anyone. It was like revisiting a barrier where self-sabotage reappeared in my life. Is the pressure real or imagined? The struggle I had with my psyche was not something I trained for or even knew there was coaching for. I was aware of the expectations, considering the investment in my success.

But I also knew one thing for certain: I could not keep going like this.

Our next game against Bristol Plymouth began with hesitation. But a single play in the second quarter changed everything. Breaking their full-court press on my own, I drove through two defenders and floated in a shot from the lane. That moment shattered the mental barriers I had been wrestling with. From then on, I played with confidence, rediscovering the joy and rhythm that had been missing.

Team Record: 9-3 Points: 33 Assists: 4 Rebounds: 6 Steals: 3

The rematch against Somerset North gave me a chance to confront my earlier struggles head-on. I had been circling this game in my mind since our first matchup at their gym. Their relentless double teams had frustrated me. Now I was ready, and I knew the school scoring record was within reach.

I came out strong, hitting my first six shots and setting the tone. In doing so, I broke the single season scoring record. We won handily, and my coach, always understated, simply praised my shooting percentage. But this time, there was no hesitation, no letdown. I played with the freedom I had been searching for.

Breaking the school record, previously held by Joe Jason with 342 points, brought a deep sense of satisfaction. I was proud of the effort; of the demanding work it took to reach that moment. Still, I knew I could not dwell on it. It was a milestone, yes, but just another step forward. The future demanded focus, and I was determined to keep building.

I had reached my two-year goal. More importantly, our team had made history. Our team's record of ten wins and three losses was the best record in southeastern Massachusetts at any level. That consistency was a testament to our collective effort and filled me with immense pride.

Team Record: 10-3 Points: 26 Assists: 3 Rebounds: 4 Steals: 2

The next day at school, I was still buzzing. The school principal read my name and the accomplishment aloud during homeroom morning announcements, and applause streamed through the hallways throughout the entire school. Even in the first period, my classmates clapped when I came into the room, and, unexpectedly, my first period teacher walked over and shook my hand, and he leaned in to say, "Congratulations." Heady stuff for a fourteen-year-old. That moment of recognition felt new, and it signaled that more "firsts" were on the way.

That weekend, my friends, teammates, and the cheerleaders organized a surprise party to celebrate breaking the scoring record. The attention was both flattering and overwhelming. Though unfamiliar, this recognition reminded me of my growth as both a player and a person.

During halftime of the game with Somerset North, a photographer took pictures of me. Feeling embarrassed by the attention, I moved awkwardly, as if being dragged along. The pictures taken that afternoon were part of an article that will appear in the Sunday sports section of our local paper.

Seeing my name and photo in a full-page article was surreal. My eyes glazed over when I first saw it, struggling to take it all in. My family and I functioned as if it were just another day, but we all knew it was not. The increase in phone calls, visits, and letters of congratulations was flattering, and on the other side of this was the precedent being set. None of us had been prepared for this level of attention. Oddly, we never acknowledged that our lives would never be the same from this point forward.

Hearing people talking about me, people I did not know, was unsettling. Reading about my accomplishments in the paper felt oddly impersonal, like I was seeing someone else's story. I realized I had changed by noticing how others treated me. Their belief had shifted, and I was now adjusting to a reality

I had not expected: one where ego, humility, and identity had to coexist in a strange new balance.

On Monday morning at school, the Sunday newspaper's full-page profile drew even more attention. Students stared as I walked through the halls. I had become a point of interest, and the weight of that visibility felt inescapable. At basketball practice, my teammates' energy lifted my mood and provided a welcome distraction. My mind, though, was already drifting toward the Fairhaven Boys' Club game later that night. Staying focused was becoming its own challenge.

At home, my parents tried to keep things normal, though I could tell they were not sure how to manage the sudden attention. I had not considered how their proximity to me would draw the spotlight onto them too. They laughed about it in good humor, but my sister struggled. She had become "Michael Semiao's sister," and despite our efforts to shield her, the spotlight on me had cast her in shadow. From that point on, my parents became determined to ensure she had her own path, her own space to thrive, even as the surrounding attention grew.

A Teammate's Point of View

Going into the rematch with Somerset North, we all knew what this game meant to him. He never said it outright, but we could feel it. The first matchup had left him frustrated because of the double teams and physical defense. Nothing was easy. This time, though, he looked different. Focused. Locked in. He had been replaying that first game repeatedly in his mind, just waiting for the chance to rewrite it.

From the opening tip, he was in complete control. Every shot looked effortless. Six straight baskets to start the game. It was one of those performances where you just knew something special was happening. We were not just playing to win; we were making a statement. A response.

Coach Hall, true to form, kept it simple. He complimented his shooting percentage like it was just another day. However, we were better informed. We had seen the weight he carried. We had seen the pressure, the expectations, the long hours he poured in. This was not about scoring points; it was about proving something. To himself. To all of us, too.

By the final buzzer, our record stood at 10–3, the best in southeastern Massachusetts. And that was the part he seemed most proud of. For all his individual success, he never made it about him. He wanted us to be great. That made him different.

That afternoon, walking out of the gym, I remember thinking: This is just the beginning.

The following week, on Monday, I had a game scheduled at the Fairhaven Boys' Club. I felt off. My body ached in unfamiliar ways, and I went to bed early. The next morning, I woke up with a fever. I missed school for the entire week, including our game against Wareham. By the time I recovered, I had dropped five pounds and returned to school feeling weak and drained.

The illness resulted from overplaying, pushing myself to the brink. I had not been honest with myself or my family about the mounting pressure I was under. Falling ill forced me to confront my limits. I scolded myself for not having had the courage to speak up earlier. The obedient son, trusting his parents to guide him through everything, had reached a breaking point. As a family, we were learning together how to navigate this new reality, and it was becoming clear there would be no smooth path forward.

In the days after breaking the scoring record, I felt unexpected emptiness. I had reached the goal I had poured so much of myself into. Now what? That question lingered. The constant pressure to meet impossible expectations, with the fear of failing, was becoming too much to carry.

Returning to school and basketball felt strangely complicated. My teachers had sent homework through friends, helping me stay on track academically. But something was missing. The misguided expectation I fell into, along with everyone else, was that I would pick up where I left off athletically. The fire that once drove me was gone. On the court, I hesitated. I replaced my defined confidence with anxiety and caution. I could not immerse myself in the game the way I once had.

We won only one more game that season, finishing with 11 wins and 9 losses.

Of note: Our last game of the season was against the freshman team from Fairhaven. Arriving at Hastings Junior High School, I found the lobby buzzing with activity. Students, staff, administrators, and spectators filled the space, creating a noisy, chaotic atmosphere. As I walked through the crowd in the school's lobby toward the court and into the locker room, I could feel the weight of their attention. All eyes were on me.

Inside the locker room, the mood was unsettling. My teammates were unusually quiet, unfocused, and tense. We were not an animated group to begin with, but the silence only deepened the nerves.

Our pre-game warmups brought everything into focus. Walking to the court from the locker rooms, which were behind the stands, you could feel the buzz, the intensity from the gym. I noticed the school's administration only opened one side of the stands, and they were full. I would have ventured that if they had opened both sides, those seats would have been filled too. The carnival act, the kid from the newspaper, was playing this afternoon, and everyone wanted to see me play. Wanting to know if I was real. As I led the team out, I stuck to my usual routine, guiding us around the entire court. It was my silent way of telling my teammates: *We belong here.* But settling into our rhythm was hard. Fairhaven's reputation for dominance loomed large, and it felt like we were already behind before the first whistle.

The pregame atmosphere brimmed with anticipation. I could feel the focus tightening on me. People had come to see if I was really that good. I could almost hear the skepticism: *He cannot be that good, can he?*

As a team, we did not play well, and we lost. But for the first time in weeks, I played hard and without fear. I tried to lead by example, but it was not enough. The same fear I had known before, that quiet paralysis of doubt with no effortless way out gripped my teammates.

Throughout the game, Fairhaven chased me relentlessly. Wherever I went, they followed. Every time I drove to the basket, they met me with hard fouls. One of them left me with a shoulder injury that limited my ability to shoot from the outside and at the foul line. But I did not back down. I kept going. Exhaustion crept in by the final buzzer, but I left the court with a new understanding: I had become a marked player. Opponents were going to step up against me, using my performance as the benchmark for their own.

Team Record: 11-9 Points: 22 Assists: 2 Rebounds: 4 Steals: 4

A Teammate's Point of View

I remember the Fairhaven game, but not for the reasons most people would expect. It was not just about the loss. It was about the way it unfolded, the way we walked into that gym already carrying the weight of the game before it even started.

You had this one circled on your calendar. We all knew it. You had something to prove, not just to yourself, but to all of us. Acushnet did not have a reputation like Fairhaven. A win against them meant something. It meant we belonged.

I could see it in you, even before we got there. On the bus, you were quiet, not just your usual pre-game focus, but something sharper. Heavier.

And then we walked into Hastings Junior High, and the energy shifted. The gym lobby was full of people. They were not just there to watch a game; they were there to watch you. You had become the story. The way they glanced at you, whispered, sized you up, they were not sure whether to believe the hype.

I was not the one they were watching. No one cared how I played that afternoon. But standing beside you, I felt their expectations pressing down, a weight for which I had not prepared. And judging by the look on our teammates' faces in the locker room, I was not the only one.

We were not the most animated team; it was nerves. Doubt had crept in before the tip-off. And when we stepped onto the court for warmups, I felt it spreading.

You tried to lead, circling the court, owning the space, showing that we belonged there. It was your way of saying; We are not backing down. But it was hard to settle in. Fairhaven's reputation, the noise, the crowd, it got in our heads.

I learned something that day: before a big game, some players disconnect completely. That is how my team felt before the game even began.

You played hard, without hesitation, without fear, for the first time since you had come back from being sick. I saw that. Even as the rest of us hesitated, you pushed forward. But Fairhaven came prepared. They were not just playing our team; they were playing against you.

Wherever you went, they followed. Each step brought pressure, close contact, and no room to breathe. When you drove to the basket, they made sure you felt it. Every foul was hard. Every hit meant something.

Then came the shoulder injury. I did not see it happen. I just noticed you were not shooting the same. Something on your form had changed. But you did not back down. Even tired and facing defeat, you played to prove something beyond the score.

By the end of the game, we knew.

We lost on the scoreboard, but something shifted. I saw it in the faces of the Fairhaven players. They came to shut you down. Instead, they left knowing who and what you were.

From that day forward, you were not just another player.

You were the target.

You have become the one they will measure themselves against. The benchmark. That is what I remember most about that game. Not the crowd. Not the score. The moment you became the one everyone was chasing.

Weeks later, I would come to understand, regretfully, that I had not fully seen the world I brought to the team. We were all still kids, playing a game. But I carried those games with the weight of something heavier. I made them bigger than they were. My seriousness and my ambition had unintentionally put my teammates in the firing line alongside me.

I wanted to win every game, to break every scoring record. But those were my goals, not theirs. I expected and maybe demanded they follow me. I dismissed them when they did not pretend to understand or blindly adjust to my drive. That pressure was not fair.

The regular season had ended, and I knew my next chapter would begin at Holy Family High School in the fall. I planned to use the spring and summer to sharpen my skills and gain experience, though I was not yet sure how that journey would begin. One last event remained: the annual alumni game.

I felt conflicted about playing. I remembered the previous year's game with frustration. It was not competitive; it was more of a reunion, a casual gathering of current and former players. Maybe I did not fully understand the underlying meaning of the alumni game or its true intention. This was my way of justifying my ambivalence towards this game. My family, especially my father, was not buying into my manipulation.

My father reminded me that leadership often requires showing up, even when the moment feels insignificant. Meeting expectations, he said, is part of your growth. In the end, I agreed to play.

On the Friday night before the alumni game, a snowstorm dumped over eight inches of snow. Determined to prepare overnight and through the early hours of the morning, I shoveled the driveway in shifts, hoping to clear enough space for a workout.

By late Saturday morning, the sun was shining brightly; the temperature had climbed to sixty degrees, and the driveway was dry. I set up my pitch back under the hoop to protect the ball from the melting snow dripping off the garage roof.

That afternoon, I shot for six hours. My father urged me to rest, but I ignored him. Focused. Driven. Somewhere along the way, my ambivalence about the alumni game disappeared.

That evening, my family traveled with me to the gym. My father and I headed straight to the locker room, where my teammates greeted him like one of their own. I appreciated the moment.

I had developed a pregame routine to block out the noise and distractions, especially for a game like this. The gym buzzed with energy. Staying grounded was going to be a complicated task.

From the opening whistle, I dominated. I scored 16 points in the first quarter, jump shots, bank shots, drives to the basket. I did not miss a shot during the entire first quarter. As a team, we scored 18 points total in the first quarter; the last two came from an assist while in the right corner triple teamed. I spotted a teammate open at the foul line and fired a chest-high pass. He hesitated. I shouted for him to shoot. The noise in the gym drowned me out, but he let it go and scored.

Here are the notes: a junior high school basketball game is played in four eight-minute quarters. The clock stops for fouls, foul shots and balls out of bounds. Our team scored 18 points in eight minutes. All field goals, no foul shots.

As the quarter ended, I caught the way my teammates looked at me. The crowd surrounding the court had the same stunned expression as my teammates did. They were not just watching; they were processing what they had just seen. I knew none of them had seen a performance like this in that gym; none of them.

Then it happened.

Our coach called out the second-quarter lineup, replacing the starters with the reserves.

"No," I said.

It came out sharper than I intended, but it was instinctive. I was not ready to sit. Not after last year's alumni game, where I had felt humiliated and dismissed. This was my chance to rewrite that memory. I was not stepping off the court.

But it did not matter.

I walked to the end of the bench and bent at the waist, head down, breathing quick and shallow. A familiar ache returned. It was not just disappointment; it was that feeling creeping in, the feeling of abandonment, resurfacing once again.

I lifted my head and looked at my parents. My father pointed toward the locker room.

I nodded and walked to the locker room in a daze.

Inside, the locker room was silent and empty. The gym noise faded as the door slammed behind me, feeling the silence as it pressed in. Alone, I stood in front of my locker, adrenaline still coursing through my body. My hands and arms trembled as I tried to open the locker. I had to steady one hand with the other just to turn the handle.

Eventually, I pulled myself together, and my family and I left the gym in silence. The drive home was tense. I never understood the phrase, "the silence was deafening," until now.

When we got home, someone asked, "Are you okay?"

My mother moved towards me, then stopped and turned away from me. Her shoulders rose and fell. She was crying.

My father panicked, scrambled to change the subject. He suggested I change so we could go to the Holy Family game, hoping to create a distraction.

While at the Holy Family game, I consumed myself with replaying the alumni game, my performance, the substitution, the emotional spiral. Although I had delivered on the court, something deeper had cracked. I longed for reverence, for acknowledgment, but what I really wanted was unconditional support. And when that did not appear the way I expected, I reacted.

That night, I realized the connection between my athletic performance and my mental health. I was not blind to the fact that my physical progress had always been more advanced than my emotional state. But suddenly, tonight, I understood how deeply intertwined they were.

On the drive home, the silence lingered until my father finally spoke. "I've never seen you so focused as I did tonight," he said. "I had points to prove", I replied.

Satisfied, he then shared that he had spoken with the assistant basketball coach at Holy Family, Dennis Kennedy. They wanted me to practice with the varsity team the following Sunday morning.

The next day, my father suggested we play tennis at a local club. For ninety minutes, I lost myself in the game's rhythm, grateful for the distraction. On the drive home, he mentioned things that piqued my interest.

First, he mentioned the Fairhaven School Department still hoped to enroll me as a freshman. I had not given it any thought before, but now I reflected on playing against their freshman team, their attitude, the hard fouls, the personal targeting. When you are learning how to adjust to being a marked player and welcome the competition, you are not interested in games clouded by resentment or aggression. The Fairhaven game had left a mark.

Sensing my hesitation, my father shifted the conversation to the upcoming practice with Holy Family's varsity team. The opportunity excited me. I had worked toward this. After setting the scoring record, I knew what came next.

Returning to school on Monday, I braced for the fallout from my decision to leave the alumni game. Late in the day, during study hall, my basketball coach, Mr. Hall, came into the library. He spoke briefly with the librarian before gesturing for me to meet him in the hallway.

Mr. Hall was not a confrontational man. He was thoughtful, measured. As I listened to him speak, I heard a balance of leadership, disappointment, and a challenge to grow. He was not wrong. Everything he said about my behavior and how it had affected the team, my teammates, and the school, was valid. I respected his approach, and I appreciated how he took the time to help me understand what growth looked like.

Before we parted, he told me about an upcoming middle school basketball tournament at the Kennedy Youth Center, where Holy Family practiced and played their home games. Mr. Hall asked whether I would be interested in playing in the tournament. I had reservations, but given my impending transition to Holy Family, I felt obligated to say yes.

The two weeks leading up to the tournament gave me time to focus on conditioning and rebuilding my strength. The invitation to practice with Holy Family was now just a week away, and I was optimistic, until everything shifted again.

That Friday, during practice, I came down from a rebound and landed awkwardly on a teammate's foot. My ankle rolled. The pain was immediate and sharp. I collapsed, grabbing my foot. Any thoughts of Sunday's varsity practice vanished in an instant.

My family quickly shifted into recovery mode. I cycled through ice treatments for the first forty-eight hours and wrapped the ankle tightly with an ace bandage. I could not walk properly, and despite my injury, my father insisted I still attend the Holy Family varsity practice. He believed it was important to build a relationship based on commitment to the team and the coaching staff.

That Sunday morning, I sat in the bleachers, watching closely. I visualized myself on the court, imagining my role. The varsity squad lacked a consistent outside shooter. I knew I could fill that role.

As I watched, I realized just how choreographed basketball could be. Offensive movement, spacing, and defensive rotations were like a dance. The most experienced players did not just react; they expected it. The great ones saw the play one or two steps ahead. Sitting there, I was more certain than ever: Holy Family was the right next step.

When practice ended, I stepped onto the court and introduced myself to the assistant coach, Dennis Kennedy, and the JV coach. The assistant coach invited me to take shots with him. Despite my injury, I accepted. Balancing on one leg, I began shooting from 18 to 20 feet.

Ten shots in a row, then fifteen in a row, I could not miss.

Just then, my father and Coach Jack Nobrega walked into the gym. The assistant coach shouted across the court with a grin, "Now that Michael's leaving, we can finally get some shots up ourselves!" Before we left the Kennedy Youth Center, Mr. Nobrega invited me to return for next Sunday's practice.

The two varsity practices I attended were eye-opening. For two hours each session, I did not touch a basketball. Coach Nobrega focused solely on defense, calling out my name from the first possession, correcting, instructing, challenging me in ways I had not experienced before. His approach was unfamiliar, but purposeful.

While exhausting, those practices redefined my understanding of expectations and responsibility. Being part of this team would demand more of me, but I welcomed the challenge.

What I did not realize at the time was that the varsity players were not exactly supportive of my presence. I stayed unaware of their feelings during practice, trusting the coaching staff to manage any issues. For now, my focus was on proving myself and preparing to compete for a starting position in the fall.

The Middle School Tournament was a double-elimination event held over two weeks. I was still recovering from my sprained ankle, and my play was inconsistent. Our team finished with two wins and two losses, falling short in the semifinals. I earned a spot on the all-tournament team, but the honor felt hollow. I had not played well enough to lead us to the finals and a championship.

This tournament marked the end of my junior high school basketball career, a journey defined by turbulence but also growth. These experiences became the steppingstones I needed, each challenge preparing me for what came next. Without them, I would not be ready to embrace the opportunities ahead, despite the uncertainty they brought.

Three moments from the final weeks of the season stood out. In the first round of the tournament, I met Marlon Burns, who would become both a rival and a teammate over the next four years. During that same tournament, the coach of the New Bedford Buddies scouted me and invited me to join their player development program, a clear path forward that expanded my vision of what was possible.

Each spring, the junior high school hosted an athletic awards assembly. The previous year, I had sat in the auditorium overwhelmed and stripped raw by internal struggles. This year, I felt more settled, more certain of my direction.

As expected, I received multiple awards. But the one that meant the most was the soccer team's Most Valuable Player. Before presenting the award, our coach explained that the entire team had voted for me. I had been the only dissenting vote, choosing our leading scorer instead.

While I knew I was the best athlete on the team, I had worked hard to *learn* the game, to master its techniques and improve every day. My teammates saw that. Their vote meant more to me than I could express. It confirmed the supportive, respectful environment we had built, and made the season's challenges feel worthwhile.

At the end of the assembly, the school principal approached with a smile and a handshake. In his other hand was an empty box. "You might need this," he said, offering it for my awards.

Team Record: 13–10 Points: 580

Spring brought the possibility of joining a new team. Through the Holy Family network, my father connected with Pepin's Electric, a team we had faced in the summer league. The coach, whose son had been Holy Family's starting point guard this past season, was assembling a roster for a tournament sponsored by the New Bedford Recreation Department. They offered me a spot on the roster.

We practiced for a week before the tournament, but I felt sluggish and mentally off. It was frustrating to revisit this familiar struggle, especially when I had hoped to be further along. Determined to improve, I went back to the basics, focusing on energy and purpose during games. My shooting was off, but my overall play was dominant. I was not dwelling on our first-round loss; my form was my concern.

Familiar faces from the junior league I had played in two years earlier appeared at the tournament, including players I had once competed against. Seeing them again and sensing their surprise at my growth was affirming.

Leaving junior high school in the spring of 1976 felt like a quiet but monumental departure. It marked the last time I saw my classmates. Life's realities, its complexities and demands, had already shaped my path. My success over the past two years, including breaking the school scoring record, had been hard-earned. It came from drive and commitment, with little support beyond my family.

Setting the scoring record at the junior high school was a goal I made when I was in the sixth grade. I achieved that goal. It was not just about numbers. It was about proving I could be a serious athlete. Yet, in achieving it, I placed a target on my back, which loomed large and grew every day.

Preparing for high school basketball meant setting new, clear goals: making the Holy Family varsity team, earning a starting spot, winning a state championship, leading the team in scoring, and earning a place on the All-Scholastic Team

Each goal required focus, discipline, and preparation. The Middle School Tournament and New Bedford Recreation leagues had exposed the areas I needed to grow. The feedback from the New Bedford Buddies coach, while humbling, was a reminder that growth never ends. I had come far, but the actual work was just beginning.

The next step in my basketball journey came with an invitation to join the New Bedford Buddies for a tournament in Waltham. Traveling for games during school nights was a serious commitment for me and my family, but it felt worth it. The intensity of the tournament hit at once; I felt the pressure like a vise.

Off-season basketball tournaments had a long tradition in Massachusetts, dating back to the 1950s. The atmosphere was electric. Top players from across the state competed with pride, and the level of play was like nothing I had seen before. Two of my teammates, Jimmy Hennessy from Fairhaven High School and Mike Borden from Somerset High School, stood out. Watching them was eye-opening.

The Waltham Boys Club gym was small and intimate, making every moment feel louder, faster, and more intense. Sitting on the bench for the first time in my career felt uncomfortable, but I used it as a chance to study. To learn.

After we lost in the finals, I headed to the locker room to change. The locker room was quiet as senior players arrived, preparing for their game. Then I realized the best high school players in the state surrounded me. All-American Ronnie Perry, Dwan Chandler, Craig Watts, and Joe Beaulieu. Stunned, I rushed upstairs to tell my father. He laughed, saying he had heard they might play, but I had not expected to run into them in the locker room.

Watching Ronnie Perry dominate the first half, he controlled the tempo with a calm authority, dictating every moment. It was inspiring. It made me hungry to improve.

After my eighth-grade season ended, new challenges surfaced. Practicing with Holy Family's varsity team gave me a glimpse of what awaited in the fall, but doubt crept in. Can I compete at Division I level?

To prepare, I joined Holy Family's summer league team. I was grateful to be involved, though it felt incomplete. I was not ready. The confidence I needed simply was not there. I did not believe in myself.

Translating my skills from junior high school to the high school varsity level felt daunting, if not impossible. My lack of conviction created a growing disconnect between my father and me. He had always believed in me. I felt as if I were failing a test; he was sure I would pass.

The coaching staff hesitantly introduced me to the team. My unfamiliar teammates did not trust me on the court, and I was not giving them a reason to. In one game, I collaborated with Jimmy Colbert, our point guard, to trap a defender and steal the ball. I then heard, "Nice play." But inside, I felt like an imposter. Just months earlier, I had led my junior high school team with confidence. Now, I was searching for that version of myself and failing.

In July, I received an invitation to join a workout in Stoughton, Massachusetts. It was a chance to train alongside other players in my age group. Billy McMillan, a former Bishop Stang High School star and current Stonehill College player, led the session.

The gym was hot and humid. Opening the doors offered little relief. The air felt heavy, and a quiet tension hung between the players as we adjusted to the grueling environment.

Billy exuded confidence. He greeted me with a playful jab about choosing Holy Family over Bishop Stang, adding a moment of levity to an otherwise intense setting. I laughed, appreciating the break in the silence.

What I did not realize was that this workout would challenge me in unexpected ways and reshape how I viewed competition, leadership, and my place in the game.

The workout began with shooting drills. The intense heat increased the difficulty of each movement, challenging our focus and essential skills. Sweat poured down my face, blurring my focus and soaking through my clothes. The dim lighting added to the challenge, yet I pushed forward, leaning in on my conditioning and mental toughness. I had learned how to find rhythm when struggling, and I refused to let fatigue dictate my performance.

Next came the passing drills. We moved with synchronized precision, each of us carried forward by shared determination. The heat became both adversary and motivator, demanding focus with every pass.

Then came conditioning. Sprints, slides, and agility drills. There was no time for rest or hesitation. The stifling air challenged everyone's endurance.

When the ninety-minute session ended, exhaustion and pride hung in the air. We endured it together. I left with renewed confidence, proud that I had performed well under such pressure. That day reinforced a truth I had grown into over the past year: I could thrive in discomfort. I had earned that belief.

Later that summer, I returned to the Mass Maritime basketball camp for the third year, eager to keep improving. On the second day, the instructors began questioning my offensive game. Though my jump shot was solid, I relied too often on runners and floaters. They pointed out that building my offense around the jump shot was essential. My current habits would not hold up. And they were right.

Hearing criticism from someone *other than* my father was difficult, but necessary. I was committed to change. I arrived early, skipped lunch, and stayed up late after evening sessions. Sacrificing social time for practice felt natural to me, a habit shaped by my father's lessons and my drive.

Midway through the week, I saw myself on video for the first time. Though I hit every open shot, I was not competing in other areas. It was a wake-up call. But by the end of the week, my progress was visible. Coaches and teammates noticed my progress, and they selected me for the camp's all-star game. That recognition confirmed I was on the right path.

After Mass Maritime, I attended the Sam Jones Basketball Camp at Stonehill College, still in search of a competitive edge. There, I met the depth of Massachusetts high school rivalries, especially between Holy Family and Cardinal Spellman. Edward Amaral, an assistant coach from Spellman, took an interest in me, already knowing I would be at Holy Family High School this coming fall.

One afternoon, I played three-on-three with Dana Skinner, an All-American player at Merrimack College, and Steve Kuberski, a Boston Celtic. Let me repeat that...a Boston Celtic. At 6'8" and 215 pounds, Kuberski was the biggest, most skilled player I had ever faced. His strength startled me.

After the game, Dana Skinner introduced me to Celtics legends Red Auerbach, Tommy Heinsohn, and John Killilea. Meeting them felt surreal. When Auerbach asked about my goals at Holy Family, I told him I wanted to help win a state championship. He smiled, shook my hand, and wished me well. That night, I called my father. His excitement was obvious, even as he tried to stay composed.

The camp lectures left their mark too. Doug Collins, a former top NBA draft pick, spoke about moving without the ball, a concept I realized I needed to learn. Sam Jones, famous for his bank shot, showed precision and poise that left me in awe.

Late in the week, I took an elbow to the face and needed six stitches above my left eye. But I returned and finished the week at camp. Dana Skinner and Coach Amaral's encouragement carried me through. At the awards ceremony, I received the "Best Guard" award. The honor was affirming, but it also reminded me of a recurring theme: my ambition often created distance between me and my peers. That tension, fueled by success, would follow me for years.

The themes were becoming constant: a target on my back and the steady progression of success. You think this is the normal course of action because this is what you are experiencing. The thought that everyone is there to support you is, at best, a naïve thought. This situation, however, is the stuff of conspiracy theories.

The New Bedford Buddies reserved the New Bedford Recreation gym for Sunday morning games, invitation-only sessions designed to evaluate both skill and commitment. The format was quick: the first team to seven points won the game, and no team played more than two consecutive games. These sessions were high-stakes evaluations, subtle tests of reliability, presence, and resilience. I looked forward to them every week. Each was an opportunity to measure myself against my peers.

These games happened in private, vacant gyms. The only sounds were the squeak of sneakers, the rhythmic thump of basketballs, and the occasional burst of instruction. On rare occasions, tempers flared into physical altercations. Sometimes, it felt like the competition teetered on the edge of something bigger than the game itself, like each possession carried unspoken consequences.

But those sounds, the effort, the hush between plays, meant something to me. They reminded me of my driveway in Acushnet, Massachusetts, where I had trained in solitude. I had learned to treasure those isolated moments, convinced they gave me an edge no one else could see or understand. I shaped my future in those quiet, unseen hours.

Following my persistent requests, I received an invitation to join the senior group for Sunday afternoon games. This was unfamiliar territory, reserved for established players. After completing a 90-minute junior session, I laced my sneakers up again for the senior group. The stakes felt high. Could I hold my own? That question was unrelenting in my mind.

The senior players included Kevin Whiting and Ken Fiola from Durfee High School, Jimmy Hennessy and Phil Graves from Fairhaven High School, and Mike Borden from Somerset High School. The adrenaline and nerves were intoxicating. For the first time, I was sharing the court with players who were better than me, and I welcomed the challenge.

On one play, I came off a low-post stack and caught a pass from Jimmy Hennessy on the wing. I saw Jimmy cut back through the defense, wide open for a layup. But I froze. The pass never left my hand. The moment slipped away, and I felt the sting of hesitation. A better player would not have blinked. It was a hard lesson: the game demanded more than skill; it demanded composure, instinct, and trust.

Later, overwhelmed by the speed of the game, I tracked a long pass on defense and leaped to intercept it. In that split second, nothing. My mind went blank. When I came to, Ken Fiola was standing over me, concern filled his eyes. My body would not respond. They told me to stay down. I wanted to fight it, but I could not. Disappointment crashed over me. This was not how I had imagined my debut. My time on the court had been brief. My presence, forgettable.

The next day, I sat in the emergency room at St. Luke's Hospital, nursing a throbbing headache. X-rays revealed no severe damage, but the pain was a constant reminder. The questions crept in. Can I really compete with these players? Was I out of my depth? The uncertainty unnerved me and shook me more than I expected.

Later that fall, on a quiet, nondescript evening at a local high school: Old Rochester Regional High School held a gathering of Massachusetts' top high school players. They split us into two groups: a junior group and senior group. The senior group included standout names like Joe Streater and Tim Chase (Lincoln-Sudbury), Ken Fiola and Kevin Whiting (Durfee), Tim Sullivan (Don Bosco), and Jeff Dickerson (Old Rochester).

The placement in the junior group frustrated me. I felt I had earned more. Determined, I proved I was the best player on the court. I wanted people to *see* the progress I had made in the past six months.

During our breaks, I watched the senior group play. Tim Chase commanded the floor, pull-up jumpers, drives to the rim, gliding through defenders. I watched with a mix of envy and admiration. That is where I wanted to be. But not yet. My time would have to wait.

Looking back, eighth grade was not just about wins or points; it was about stepping into a new identity. The record, the recognition, the camps, and the collisions, each piece was shaping me for what came next.

Chapter Four

The Sisters of Mercy founded Holy Family High School in 1891 as part of St. Lawrence Martyr Parish in New Bedford, Massachusetts. The school remained under their guidance until the 1970s.

Omnia per Mariam (Through Mary)

Catherine McAuley founded the Sisters of Mercy, a religious institute of Catholic women, in 1831 in Dublin, Ireland. They set up educational and healthcare institutions across the world, including Holy Family.

In the 1966–1967 season, Holy Family went undefeated, winning the Narragansett League, the Catholic Class B Tournament, and the Class C Tech Tournament. With a 27–0 record heading into the state semifinals against Melrose, the Class B champions. Holy Family had become a powerhouse. In that tournament, Steve Lawless set a state tournament scoring record with 52 points at Boston Garden.

In 1969, Holy Family earned a share of the Narragansett League title with Case and finished as runner-up in the Catholic Class B Tournament. They edged Andover 66–62 and bested Case 58–48 in the first two rounds of the Class C Tech Tournament. In the title game, before a roaring Boston Garden crowd of 11,000, they faced top-seeded and undefeated North Andover. Beat them 35-34. Billy Walsh led the Blue Wave.

The 1972 team brought home one of the most celebrated seasons in school history. Holy Family won the Narragansett League in its final year of existence, the New England Catholic Tournament, the Tech Tournament at Boston Garden, and the State Championship. That team featured All-State forward Stevie Gomes and All–Bristol County point guard Paul Walsh. Under Coach Jack Nobrega's leadership, Holy Family basketball reached legendary status. The team captured eight league championships, made fourteen appearances in the Eastern Massachusetts Tournament (including thirteen straight), received twelve invitations to the New England Catholic Tournament, winning three titles, and held a streak of 53 consecutive league wins from 1965 to 1968. Nobrega's teams won four state championships and amassed a career record of 285–97.

Holy Family High School, Freshman Year, 1976-1977

By the time freshman year arrived, everything I accomplished in seventh and eighth grade felt like a rehearsal for a harder stage. The work had sharpened me, but it had not quieted the questions: Am I ready? Will I belong? My father stayed steady through that uncertainty. He called the New Bedford Buddies coach. "I need an impartial evaluation," he said, setting in motion a relationship that would change my path. After months of weighing which high school to attend, we chose Holy Family.

Looking back, that summer marked more than a transfer. It marked the end of my childhood sense of inevitability. I was no longer just the kid from Acushnet breaking records. I was stepping into a bigger world, where every next step had to be earned twice.

Holy Family's strong basketball tradition had been the main reason for my decision, but in time, I grew to appreciate the school beyond the game. Still, the rigid school schedule disrupted my rhythm, creating frustration and unease. Basketball stayed my priority, my focus, and in those early days at Holy Family, it was my only purpose.

Holy Family felt different from my earlier schools. While my classmates moved through the halls supported by familiar friends and families, I often felt like an outsider. I projected confidence, but inside, I was still adapting. The school challenged me more than I expected, pulling me more into a constant tug-of-war between comfort and growth.

In the courtyard between St. Lawrence Church and the school, a single basketball hoop stood. During lunch breaks, we played H-O-R-S-E, Around the World, or three-on-three. I searched for signs of recognition from older students, hoping they shared my competitive drive. But my unremarkable performance in the summer league lingered in my mind. I wondered whether I was truly ready to compete at this level.

One day, the upperclassmen joined our lunchtime basketball game. Teams formed as we raced against the lunch-period clock. The game began at a casual pace, but I felt it differently. My classmates and I jumped out to an early lead. I was landing shots from both the right and left sides of the court. The upperclassmen, indifferent at first, soon pushed back, unwilling to lose to underclassmen. Drawing on hours of practice, I drove hard to the basket for a layup from the weak side, then followed with a clean jump shot from the wing. The game turned fierce, exactly the test I had been craving.

More students gathered to watch, knowing my classmates were seeing me play for the first time. We won, though the game ended early when the bell rang. Inside, I was beaming. It felt like a breakthrough, a quiet but undeniable display of my talent.

But as I walked back inside the school, still riding that high, reality hit; algebra class awaited. I arrived late, soaked with sweat, my dress shirt clinging to my back. The nun teaching the class stared at me with unmistakable disappointment. She did not need to say a word. Her silence cut deeper than anything she could have said. The thrill of the game quickly replaced my embarrassment. After class, I apologized to my teacher. She said little, but her stern look stayed with me. That day, I learned something about responsibility, and how pride sometimes comes at a cost.

As the school term wore on, the weight of exams and basketball preparation pressed down on me. One afternoon, the school principal, Mr. Finni, pulled me out of study hall. He needed help retrieving a missing certificate from the school's basement.

We descended into a dim and musty room stacked with dusty boxes and display cases. Trophies and plaques lined the shelves; decades of Holy Family's basketball history etched in bronze and gold. Names, dates, team photos, and game scores stared back at me. The silence in that room felt almost sacred.

"Do you think you could achieve something like this someday?" Mr. Finni asked, catching the awe on my face.

His voice was calm, but his question landed squarely in front of me. I nodded, forcing a smile, but inside, the pressure swelled.

That moment stayed with me. It lit a fire, but it also haunted me. In that quiet space beneath the school, the weight of legacy collided with my ambition. As a young player, you dream of the opportunity where, with every shot, every drill, every game, others will count on you. I pushed to carve out a place that would make our team's name echo through time.

Those trophies were not just symbols of past glory. They were standards, and I knew exactly what they demanded from me.

Following the encouragement from the New Bedford Buddies head coach, I committed to playing basketball at Buttonwood Park in New Bedford to assess myself and my game. My father often joked, "You're the best basketball player ever to play in a driveway."

One afternoon, I arrived at Buttonwood Park alone and waited. Players I recognized appeared, Eddie Rodrigues, Brian Baptiste, and Greg Parker, all local standouts. In the team selection process, chose me second to last. It stung.

The game was close, separated by just two points. I spotted a gap in their slow zone defense and stepped into an eighteen-foot jumper from the left elbow. Swish. As the game wore on, I kept attacking, finding holes, making them pay. With the game on the line, I drained a twenty-two-foot shot from the left wing to seal the win.

As I walked off the court, I noticed the New Bedford Buddies' head coach watching from the sidelines. He gave me a subtle nod. That acknowledgment meant everything.

That evening, he called my father to praise my performance. Word spread quickly. The other players realized I was the kid from the newspaper, the one who had broken the scoring record. Their recognition was not loud, but I felt it. It confirmed what I had been working toward. I was excited about what lay ahead.

Not long after that day at Buttonwood Park, I sat alone in the radiology department at St. Luke's Hospital, waiting to have my knees X-rayed. The goal was to assess my growth plates, to predict my future height, and by extension, my basketball potential. My father, always searching for an edge, wanted clarity about my development.

I experienced growth spurts during high school, but none that put me in the range for big-time college basketball. Still, we stayed focused on maximizing my abilities wherever they might take me.

An Evening with Doctor J, at New Bedford High School
Gymnasium, Friday, September 17, 1976

Amid everything happening to me, something big was unfolding at home.

In the summer of 1976, my father pursued an ambitious dream: launching a sports marketing business called *Sports in Action*. His first major project? Securing Julius Erving, "*Dr. J*" to host a basketball clinic in New Bedford, Massachusetts.

Every moment felt as if it revolved around something larger. While I trained for the upcoming Holy Family season, my family kept the event secret until they signed the contract. After confirmation, we put posters up all over the city. When I told my friends, their disbelief made me laugh. I could not blame them.

Then, one day, Julius Erving walked into our kitchen.

He wore comfortable clothes and carried himself effortlessly. I stood there, wide-eyed, watching people around him act like it was no big deal. No one showed the awe I was feeling. I wanted to run outside, grab the neighbors, and shout, *do you know who is in my house?*

Julius was gracious, smiling for photos before heading to New Bedford High School for the clinic.

The event opened with a semi-professional game before his appearance. The gym slowly filled with a mix of former and current players, coaches, and families. From my seat, though, I could tell the turnout was thinner than expected.

When Julius finally stepped onto the court, a wave of disbelief swept through the room. *Is that really him?* But as the clinic got underway, the crowd settled. He focused on fundamentals such as stretching, strengthening, and coordination. Seeing a legend emphasize the basics was surreal. It was a rare gift for anyone willing to pay attention.

But despite the excitement, the event did not meet expectations. The turnout fell short. The community's hesitation to embrace something new was obvious. Julius, gracious as ever, told my father he would consider collaborating with him again. But the second project never materialized.

The next morning, Julius, his agent, and one investor had breakfast at the Bridge Diner in Fairhaven. Surrounded by local fishermen and dockworkers, no one recognized him. A quiet end to what had started as a bold dream.

That moment lingered. It foreshadowed the uphill climb my father's business would face, and the limits of ambition when timing, support, and vision do not align.

The signs of fall were everywhere. Leaves blanketed the ground. A chill in the air told you winter was fast approaching, and so was basketball season. I was hungry to start. Inside the Kennedy Youth Center buzzed with energy. Aspiring athletes crowded the courts, all hoping to make the junior varsity or varsity basketball rosters.

During one pickup game, a varsity player suddenly called my name. Curious, I walked over, not expecting what followed. His tone turned sharp, his body language tense. He accused me of trying to take someone's spot on the team, complained about playing time, and even made physical threats. I didn't even know him. But the aggression was real. He had twisted a casual conversation I had had about earning varsity minutes into something entirely different. His anger felt like crows on a fence, waiting to pick apart my confidence and character.

"Hey, Semiao, come here for a second. I heard you talking about taking someone's spot in the starting five. Certain individuals find that kind of talk disrespectful. And that kind of talk will get you hurt. Personally, I don't want to hear you speak about this topic again, and if I do, I will kick your fucking ass."

Despite the bitterness of that moment, I refused to let it derail me. I had always known challenges like these would come. I was not about to let someone else's insecurity shake my purpose.

That night, a mix of frustration, determination, and even humor swirled inside me. I realized that my drive, my constant push to succeed, might sometimes lead to conflict or isolation. It reminded me of my earlier years: fleeting friendships, and the way my intensity could unsettle teammates. A simple first-year student's comment had stirred up an upperclassman's anger. His reaction, exaggerated and misinformed, showed me something. That I unknowingly got under his skin oddly satisfied me. I was seeing who and what I was up against.

Two adults steadied me during that fall: Father John Driscoll and Principal John Finni. They did not deliver speeches. They delivered presence, eye contact in the hallway, the right word at the right time, an invitation to a Holy Cross game where discipline sounded less like rules and more like a way through.

Early on, I struggled with doubt. I was not sure where I fit in, and my insecurities held me back. But these two men remained present. They checked in on me and made time for brief but meaningful exchanges. Their support became something I could lean on. It grounded me and gave me hope that I was not navigating this alone.

My hours of driveway practice mirrored a deeper fear: the fear of disappointing others and myself. Even now, reflecting on that period is difficult. Those solitary efforts came to define me in the eyes of my family, my friends, and my opponents. Once I committed to basketball, there was no turning back. It became an obsession, blurring the line between passion and compulsion.

As I wrestled with my insecurities, I wondered if I was sabotaging my success. I craved acknowledgment as a serious athlete, even as I struggled to reconcile that pursuit with the pressure it carried.

In high school, basketball became my world. I drew inspiration from players like Ronnie Perry Jr., the star from Catholic Memorial High School. The Perry family's athletic legacy became a blueprint for excellence. I wanted to follow that path, set records, and leave my mark. My admiration for the College of the Holy Cross and its connection to the Perry family only deepened when I discovered its link to Holy Family High School. It felt like a bridge between who I was and who I wanted to become.

One unforgettable moment was attending a Holy Cross game with Father Driscoll and Principal Finni. During the ride to Worcester and the Holy Cross campus, we talked about life, dreams, and the meaning of discipline. For the first time, I felt truly seen, not just as a player, but as a young man with potential. That evening became a turning point. It fueled my excitement about what might lie ahead.

Preseason practice was challenging. It exposed my weaknesses and forced me to rebuild from the ground up. Every pass, every movement had meaning. The coaches' constant refrain, *"Pass and move!"* became a rhythm that drilled itself into my body. I saw how those fundamentals could dismantle defenses, and I felt my confidence rising with each session.

Fatigue became my fiercest opponent, sharpening my focus through every grueling drill. But the pain had purpose. These sessions forged something in me, a deeper resolve, a hunger to become the player I dreamed of being.

As the season approached, a buzz filled the air. One day, I heard about a luncheon at Thad's restaurant, where teams from the Southeastern Massachusetts Conference would gather. When I entered the banquet room, I spotted Red Auerbach, the general manager of the Boston Celtics, seated at the head table. His presence instantly pulled me back to our brief encounter at the Sam Jones Basketball Camp.

When the luncheon ended, I worked up the courage to approach him. To my surprise, he said he remembered me. I was under no illusion that I had left an impression, but the recognition meant everything. As we talked, Coach Nobrega walked over and greeted him with ease. Their familiarity hinted at a shared history.

Mr. Auerbach asked about my role on the team. Coach Nobrega answered with quiet confidence, and hearing his response filled me with pride. As we parted, Red Auerbach left me with a simple but powerful message:

"Listen to your coaches and be a good teammate."

Walking back to the car with Coach Nobrega, he looked at me and said, "You're standing there talking to Red Auerbach and you're only a freshman." That moment stayed with me forever.

Back at school, the excitement surrounding the season became palpable. The basketball cheerleaders sold tickets to our first home game, fueling the buzz. On December 20, 1976, I stepped onto the court for my first high school basketball game at Taunton High School. Despite all my hard work, I was not in the starting lineup, and the continued theme of doubt was ever present.

As the game progressed, our early lead slipped away. With two minutes left in the second quarter, the coach called my name. I stepped onto the floor, sank two free throws, and secured a key possession, rising to the moment. My parents and former Holy Family team captain Joey Gaudreau were in the stands. I could feel a shift in the air.

When the second half began, I was in the starting lineup. Taunton's 2-3 zone defense had difficulty holding us, reminding me of my practice hours. My first shot of the second half, a twenty-foot jumper from the left wing, dropped cleanly through the net. Not a bad way to start. I followed it with three more shots, each one from farther out.

But fatigue set in. I thought I was choking under pressure, but in truth, I was getting sick right there on the court. My body failed me. I faded in the second half, and my team lost in double overtime. Still, despite the defeat, I saw promise in myself and in the team.

The next day, the coach sent me home from practice. I spent the next three days in bed, unsure if I would be healthy in time for our December 23 matchup against New Bedford High School. Strangely, the schedule had us playing New Bedford three times that season, twice in one week.

Our first home game against them was huge. The gym overflowed; bleachers extended onto the stage, and the roar of the crowd filled every corner. The energy throughout the Kennedy Center was something I had never felt before. Distracted, I retreated to the locker room earlier than usual. It was quiet. My teammates sat in silence, the pressure hanging in the air. They knew every player on New Bedford's roster.

Warming up, my heart raced. I ran harder than usual, hoping to burn off the nerves. I could feel eyes on me. Everyone knew who I was and had made me a target. A voice called out from the crowd: "Young fella! Hey, young fella, number twelve, Semiao! You are not in Acushnet anymore!" I did not acknowledge it, but the sentiment was not wrong.

The announcer introduced me last during the starting lineups: "From Acushnet, a freshman, starting at guard, number twelve, Mike Semiao." The moment felt surreal. Raw. Overwhelming. The noise crashed over me like a wave. I stayed there until my coach's voice brought me back to the present.

The game opened with both teams searching for rhythm. The court pulsed with chatter, trash talk, intimidation, and tension. Even over the crowd, I could hear the taunts directed at me:

"Hey, white boy! You have nothing, *fucking nothing!*"

Their words rattled me, but I refused to let them break my focus.

Three days later, we played New Bedford again in the Christmas Tournament. We stayed competitive but faltered late, losing a game we should have won. By the third matchup, they dominated us. Our coach pulled the starters, leaving me to guard Michael Fields, one of the best guards in the state. He was quick, explosive, and confident. He beat me to his spot and looked at me like I did not belong. But I stayed with him. I did not back down. I was determined to learn.

◇ ◆ ◇

Fast forward to spring 1978: I was playing for the New Bedford Buddies senior team in the city's recreation tournament. Once again, I guarded Michael Fields. But this time, things were different.

I had grown; my experience level expanded. I had been part of a National Youth Games gold medal team, attended Five-Star Basketball Camp, and competed daily against the best all-around guard in the state this past season, Jimmy Hennessy.

When Fields hit me with his stop-and-go move, I did not bite. I shadowed his right hand, forced him left, and gave him just enough space to deny the drive and neutralize his jumper. For the first time, I felt in control, trusting my instincts, my preparation, my earned confidence.

The satisfaction was immense. This was what I had worked for: self-management, problem-solving, and a real contribution to my team.

Holy Family's practices were unlike anything I had known. The coaches structured entire sessions around half-court drills, offense one day and defense the next day. Every practice ended with foul shooting and wind sprints. The format never varied, except on one unforgettable day.

Mickey Gonsalves, a 1975 graduate and the school's last standout player, walked into the gym. Back when Mickey was playing for Holy Family, he had just missed making the Boston Shootout Team, which featured stars like Ronnie Perry and Dwan Chandler. The day Mickey arrived at practice; the starters were playing offense, and suddenly Coach Nobrega flipped it, putting the starters on defense and assigning me to guard Mickey.

Covering Mickey was a masterclass in deception. His fakes and footwork left me spinning. I could not keep up. After practice, he pulled me aside and offered advice on spacing, timing, and how to vary my speed. His words stuck with me. That evening, I reflected on his presence. I hoped that one day I would pass that same wisdom on patiently and with purpose.

Durfee High School will go undefeated during the 1975-1976 season and win the Division I state championship. Led by All-Americans Ken Fiola and Kevin Whiting.

On January 11, 1977, we stepped onto Durfee's historic home court at the Fall River Armory. From the outset, their superior talent overwhelmed us. A month later, we faced them again, this time on our home court. I was determined to make an impact. Despite the challenge, I felt ready.

That season brought its own complications, including recent rule changes that affected both players and coaches. Referees could now issue technical fouls to coaches for sideline infractions and for arguing with them. A new penalty also prohibited dunking during pregame and halftime warmups. Durfee slipped up, and a player dunked, costing them a two-shot technical foul and possession.

The coach chose me to take the free throws. As the packed gym fell silent, I steadied my breathing, locked into my routine, and sank both shots. We opened with a two-point lead.

Durfee's relentless man-to-man defense pushed me to the edge. Positioned in the left corner, I executed plays I had practiced countless times with my father, each movement a product of muscle memory. But Durfee's defense was suffocating, and no matter how prepared I felt, it disrupted everything.

During a stop in play, I glanced over to the bench for guidance, only to see my coach laughing and chatting with Durfee's coach, Skip Karam. Confused, I stared. Coach Karam made a gesture to my coach, something like, *"You should see what I'm seeing." Coach Nobrega, catching my eye, turned and said, "Don't worry about what is going on over here. You have more than enough to worry about with what is happening on the court."*

I stayed silent, frustrated but wise enough not to speak. Coaches coach. Players play. That was the rule. We played harder than in our first matchup, but Durfee's talent still prevailed.

Still, something shifted. Competing against a dominant rival like that revealed more than gaps in skill; it revealed what I still needed to learn.

The last game of the season arrived on February 23, 1977, like an uninvited guest. It felt as if the season had slipped away, a series of moments clouded by uncertainty. For three years, this shadow had lingered, always arriving when least expected.

Our opponent for this game was Case High School. They were celebrating their last home game and senior night. Their gym pulsed with energy. For a young athlete, it drew you in. Outwardly, I stayed calm. Aside from my motivation to help my team that night, I wanted the home crowd at Case High School to see me as a player and someone they will have to track for the next three basketball seasons.

That night, I was the last to leave the locker room, which was not a normal circumstance for me. That moment felt almost symbolic, as if fate had predestined it. Leaving the locker room alone, I walked through the darkness of the school campus, where the parking lot lights guided me toward the team bus. I heard a voice; someone called my name. I stopped and turned toward where the voice came from. I saw a man standing in the shadows. I can make out another shape, a young boy. Stepping into the light, the man gestured toward me. I heard, "Excuse me, could you sign your autograph?" A piece of paper and pen appeared almost magically. In the next instant, others gathered, asking questions, and requesting signatures. I answered every question and signed every autograph. Their genuine appreciation left an impression.

The bus ride home was a swirl of emotion, frustration about our performance, reminding me of past seasons. My mother's words sat in my mind: *"Be kind to yourself."* I clung to them as I wrestled with doubt and the weight of my aspirations.

That autograph moment stuck with me. It reminded me that being an athlete came with responsibility, not just to perform, but maybe to inspire. In that moment, I felt what it meant to *matter* to others, to the game, and, finally, to myself.

But the season was not without cost. My success brought scrutiny. Whispers turned to questions. Pressure mounted. Teammates, classmates, even administrators said things I could not control. No matter how hard I tried, mistrust lingered. I understood that victories and losses were not only measuring points, but relationships, trust, and support were the fabric, the pillars of consistency I was looking for. Yes, wanting unconditional support may not have been realistic, but I thought I had earned a level of respect as a person and an athlete where those things went hand in hand. Over time, I will face disappointment in this belief.

The winter of 1977 marked my freshman year at Holy Family High School. I was the varsity team's top scorer and assist leader, and I played the most minutes. Before away games, I often detoured through the principal's office to read the Boston Globe. I was curious to see where I stood among the state's top players.

One name stood out: Tim O'Shea from Don Bosco. I saw his stats and thought, okay. Now I know about the competition. I did not know then that our paths would soon cross.

By season's end, I had scored 240 points, setting the freshman varsity scoring record. I became the first freshman in school history to earn an All-Scholastic Honorable Mention.

At sixteen, navigating and managing people's beliefs was both challenging and familiar. I questioned whether staying at Holy Family was the right decision. My father's words helped anchor me:

"Keep a broader perspective."

So, I did. I pushed through the noise. Focused on growth. On becoming the player and person I wanted to be.

As spring approached, Mr. Nobrega announced his retirement. The news shook me. The foundation I had built at Holy Family suddenly felt unstable, and for the first time, I seriously considered transferring.

His retirement marked the end of an era. But his lessons and his spirit stayed. Reflecting on the season, I realized this journey had always been about more than basketball. It was about resilience, growth, and finding purpose amid uncertainty.

The first spring offseason tournament with the New Bedford Buddies was the 42nd Annual Waltham Boys & Girls Club Basketball Tournament, a storied event dating back to the 1930s. The small second-floor gym had tight sidelines and end lines.

In the opening round, we blew past Framingham South, 84–33. The lopsided game gave me time to adjust to the strange, claustrophobic setting.

The second round was different. We faced the Talisman, a legendary team packed with talent, which included Jimmy Sullivan from Dom Savio, soon to be Massachusetts Player of the Year, Tim Sullivan, a versatile all-around threat and Tim O'Shea, a strong two-way guard, both from Don Bosco.

I rose to the challenge, scoring 36 points. With their defense focused on my teammate Mike Borden, I found space all over the court. Their zone left gaps, and I kept hitting shots from the corners, the wings, and the top of the key. Despite the gym's tight quarters and their coach yelling in my ear every time I touched the ball, I stayed locked in.

We won, 71–67.

In the semifinals, we rolled past the Waltham Hawks 86–64, setting up a showdown against Lee School in the final. Their star player, Karl Hobbs, brought a whole new level of competition.

Late in the fourth, down by two, I missed a pair of technical free throws, but I redeemed myself with a foul-line jumper to tie the game. Moments later, I drew a charge, and chaos erupted as the player I drew the charge on was rolling down the court fighting with the referee who made the call.

We won, 58–56. Mike Borden earned the Most Valuable Player award; I made the all-tournament team. That championship was unforgettable, a testament to collective effort, pressure, and grit.

Following the Waltham tournament, I received an invitation to take part in the selection process for the United States National Youth Games Boston team. They held the tryouts at the Roxbury Boys Club, a place I had never seen before.

My father and I drove up to Roxbury one Saturday morning. I had never been to that part of Boston before. We arrived early. As I stepped out of the car, an elevated train rumbled overhead, clattering across the street from where I stood. My eyes and brain could not process what I was seeing. Watching trains pass so close to homes where people lived was not something I expected to see. The tracks were so close you could reach out and touch them as they rattled past the windows. Unknowingly, this scene would stay with me for the rest of my life.

My father leaned in and whispered, "You don't know how lucky you are," before guiding me toward the gym.

Inside, 400 to 500 kids vied for a spot. The format was challenging; the organizers selected teams of five players each. The rules were simple; first team to seven points, win by one. My team did not lose for three hours. I played solid basketball, managing possessions, making smart passes, and scoring when needed. Afterward, my father spoke with the head coach, who praised my composure and decision-making. They invited me back the following week.

When I returned to school and told my friends, they were excited for me. I realized new opportunities were appearing, and accepting those challenges would become the foundation of my growth as a basketball player. I saw then that my ambition and basketball in southeastern Massachusetts did not align. My father's big-picture perspective changed how I viewed the landscape in front of us.

In May 1977, I learned I had made the team. We practiced every Saturday morning at the Roxbury Boys Club. My father and I made the drive each weekend. Playing alongside athletes who were better than I forced me to be ready each Saturday morning. There was no time to relax or take the day off. This was the next big step in my development. I thought I knew what it meant to play hard, but seeing others go beyond what I believed possible was eye-opening. It taught me that sometimes, the greatest challenge is to stop being a spectator and push yourself to new heights.

Following my success with the New Bedford Buddies and the National Youth Games team, our local newspaper authored an article about those achievements. The school administration was proud of my success and placed the article outside their office for the entire school to see and read. Later that day, someone scrawled crude graffiti across it.

The sting of betrayal cut deep. It felt like more than vandalism; it was a direct hit on my dreams and identity. Still, I poured myself into basketball, refusing to let it break me.

But the anger did not stay buried for long. I struggled with how to express it without compromising the image of the "good kid." The incident forced me to confront the double edge of admiration: the spotlight came with scrutiny. It marked a turning point. Basketball was no longer just a refuge. It came with its own shadow.

Next tournament with the New Bedford Buddies is the Lexington Tournament at the J.W. Hayden Recreation Center. The venue was quieter, more structured than the Waltham Boys and Girls Club. What remained consistent between the two tournaments was the strength of the competition. We had to adjust quickly. Despite the progress we had made, we lost in the semifinals to the Titans, a skilled, tough team. My performance fell short of what I had done in Waltham. I left frustrated, but focused.

The last tournament of the spring with the New Bedford Buddies was on our home turf, the New Bedford Recreation tournament. Because of age restrictions and scheduling conflicts, we had a depleted roster, yet we fought our way to the finals and faced the Titans again.

They were talented. Their internal dynamic felt like it might explode at any moment, but on the court, they performed. The Buddies lost in a close game. I struggled. I felt like I had let my team down.

That summer, I attended the legendary *Five-Star* Basketball Camp in Honesdale, Pennsylvania, about thirty miles northeast of Scranton. Five-Star had an almost mythical status. It was not about comfort; it was about fearlessness, sweat, and transformation.

Founded by Howard Garfinkel ("Garf") and Will Klein in 1966, the camp became a proving ground for elite players. Garf, who also ran *High School Basketball Illustrated*, turned Five-Star into a pipeline for future stars. Over 600 NBA players and 10,000 Division I athletes came through *Five Star* basketball camp.

Indiana basketball coach Bobby Knight introduced the camp's signature format, station instruction, in 1968. Every twenty minutes, players rotated through skill-building stations designed to expose weaknesses and sharpen fundamentals. No shortcuts. No soft landings.

Our bunkhouse resembled a military barrack: six beds lined each side, with two RA bunks in the center. Bathroom facilities sat at the back. Rustic. Challenging. Perfect for testing resolve.

The gym, with its aluminum siding, trapped heat like an oven. Even the outdoor courts punished us, blistering with sun, wind, and bugs. Nothing came easy.

My father believed *Five-Star* was the next natural step, and he was right. It challenged me in ways I had never experienced.

Among my bunk mates were talented players: Jimmy Hennessy (Fairhaven High School), Mike Borden and Chris Correia (Somerset High School), Champ Godbolt (Springfield) who would one day be drafted by the Boston Celtics and one of the bunk RA's Jack Barry, a forward / center at Hofstra.

That week, the camp drew future stars: Tony "Red" Bruin and Ed Gooding (Syracuse) Sidney Green (UNLV), Rodney McCray (Louisville), and Percy White (DeMatha High School / Western Kentucky) who was coached by the legendary Morgan Wootten.

At *Five-Star*, you quickly learned that success required more than talent. The camp demanded mental toughness, adaptability, and an unwavering commitment to growth. Each player had to confront his vulnerabilities, stripped of the accolades and confidence brought from home. Reputation meant little. The only currency that mattered was performance.

One of my earliest games took place in the sweltering, tin-can-like indoor gym, where the heat turned the air into a suffocating blanket. While driving to the basket and trying a 360-degree spinning layup, a defender struck me in the face. My bottom lip exploded, covering my face in blood. During a break in play, I rinsed my face with a water hose outside the gym, then returned to the game. That moment symbolized the unyielding spirit *Five-Star* demanded.

The camp was as much about mentorship as it was about competition. The camp's coaching staff read like an all-star team. Five Star's coaching staff featured the best assistants in the country: Rick Pitino (Syracuse), Dave Odom (Wake Forest), Mike Fratello (Villanova), Eddie Fogler (North Carolina), and Pete Gillen (VMI).

Pitino, young and intense, stood out. His style was aggressive, uncompromising. He demanded hustle over hype. Station 13, where he collaborated directly with players, became legendary for its brutal lessons and breakthroughs.

My bunkmate, Jimmy Hennessy, had the privilege of playing for Pitino's camp team. Watching Pitino coach from the sidelines was an education. He once benched a high school All-American for lack of effort and pointed to Jimmy and said, "I'll take five of him over that kid any day."

Late one evening, the camp was still and warm. The only sounds were the hum of insects and faint echoes from the woods. I knew I should have been resting, but I was out on the court, lit by a single pole light. Jimmy and I played one-on-one, drenched in sweat, no words spoken, no score kept, just movement, breath, and rhythm. The squeak of sneakers, the shuffle of feet, the sound of the ball against the pavement. It was pure, stripped down, sublime.

From the shadows came another sound, my name. Faint at first, then louder. I turned and saw the faint outline of a man approaching, smoke curling around him from a cigarette glowing in the dark.

It was Garf.

He called out again, his voice gravelly but warm. He stepped onto the court as if he had always belonged there. We greeted each other like old friends, though we had never spoken. I motioned to Jimmy to join us. Garf talked with us for an hour, no lectures, just stories, wisdom, his unique gospel of the game.

That moment, unexpected and magical, became one of the most memorable times of the summer.

Later that week, I noticed something was wrong with my left hand; it had gone numb. The camp's medical team diagnosed it as a nerve impingement in my elbow. My frustration was immediate. I could not contribute in the way I wanted to. The injury challenged not just my ability but my resilience.

When my father arrived for a visit, I saw the concern in his eyes. I had lost weight. My bottom lip was still swollen. My left hand is limited. I knew my father's visit was preparing me for my mother and sister's arrival in the days ahead. Thankfully, my mother had learned how to hold her reaction in front of my teammates, a restraint that went against every motherly instinct she had.

My camp team had to win a play-in game to qualify for a playoff spot. I scored all six of our team's points, using only my right hand, driving hard to the basket every time. We advanced to the playoffs but played flat and exited quickly. Playing with one hand did not limit my effectiveness. I played a solid floor game and excelled defensively. The injury became an opportunity to reinvent myself, to help my team however I could. That growth encouraged me.

The camp closed with an awards ceremony and an all-star game. Jimmy earned a nomination for the *Mr. Hustle* award, a tribute to his toughness. Watching him shake Pitino's hand, I understood what *Five-Star* truly valued.

Before leaving, I found Garf to thank him for the experience. He surprised me by asking about my hand, his concern genuine. Then he smiled and invited me to return the following summer.

My father stepped in, and I watched the two of them connect. Having known of their connection from afar, it was gratifying to see them interact. As I left Honesdale, I understood this was not just shaping my game. It was shaping *me*.

One Saturday morning during the youth games tryout phases, a new group of players appeared at the bottom of the stairs leading into the gym. I had grown accustomed to practicing with my teammates, so when this new group walked in, I saw it as a potential threat and felt I needed to respond.

My paranoia grew when I realized I was not playing with my usual teammates. The new players who showed up that morning were now on my side of the court, while the rest of the team stood on the sidelines watching.

The scrimmage became a blur of motion and adrenaline, culminating in a play only my father and I would understand. Running a three-on-two fast break, I surveyed the court and spotted a six-foot-seven forward sprinting down the sideline with his hand up. A soft lob pass led to a two-handed dunk by my teammate. I caught myself bouncing as the play unfolded, realizing I had never passed to a player who dunked the ball. The thrill of that play stayed with me; my father retold it to anyone within earshot when we were home. "Michael assisted on his first dunk this morning!" On the outside, I played it cool, but inside, I was ecstatic.

The United States Youth Games Boston Massachusetts Basketball Team: Gary Burke (Forward, Cathedral High School), Karl Hobbs (Guard, Jeremiah Burke High School), Gene Mewborn (Forward, Lexington High School), Tim O' Shea (Guard, Don Bosco), John Sealey (Guard / Forward, Don Bosco), Mark Green (Forward, Wellesley High School), Bubba Raymond (Forward / Center, Cathedral High School), Mike Woods (Forward / Center, Dom Savio), Nick Ward (Guard, Catholic Memorial) and Michael Semiao (Guard, Holy Family High School).

Coaches: Willis Gibson (Head Coach) and Al Brodsky (Assistant Coach and Head Coach of the Roxbury Titans)

The United States National Youth Games took place in New Haven, Connecticut, modeled after a mini-Olympics. We left City Hall in Boston after a send-off ceremony for all the athletes.

Our uniforms came in two sets: one green mesh tank with white trim, and matching shorts striped in white. The other set, white mesh with green trim and matching shorts, green striped down the sides. We also received wool warm-up suits; the jackets dark green with a broad white chest stripe framed by two darker bands and a high collar that gave the jacket a classic athletic look. The matching pants had a relaxed fit, featured a bold white stripe down each leg, accented with a thin yellow border. I describe the uniforms because we took immense pride in earning our place on that team. As young athletes, we wanted to present ourselves well, representing our city and our own accomplishments.

Still, I knew I was an outlier. Living farther away than my teammates, I often felt out of my depth, but my teammates were welcoming, making it easy to adjust.

When we arrived in New Haven, we joined a citywide parade celebrating the United States National Youth Games. During the parade, I finally grasped the scale of the event. I felt privileged just to be part of it.

The games were held on the campus of Southern Connecticut State University. We were assigned dorm rooms, daily practice schedules, and fixed mealtimes. Throughout our stay, we moved everywhere as a group. This was intentional, meant to ensure safety and to build team cohesion. We committed to attending the Boston girls' basketball games as a show of solidarity, and in return, they came to support us. The girls' team won the gold medal in their tournament.

To win our tournament, we needed five straight victories against teams from across the country. The competition promised to be tough from the start. Before our first game, we ran a brief practice to review our strategy. Without scouts analyzing our opponents, we relied solely on our basketball IQ to read each team's strengths and weaknesses. The need for instant adaptation created a heightened sense of urgency, an advanced concept for young players, but one we were ready to embrace.

Game One, Boston 72 - Detroit 60 Team Record: 1 Win 0 Losses

We were nervous when we entered the game. We all played cautiously in the first half. In the second half, we settled in, played together, and pulled away. I didn't take a single shot all game, a first for me. I kept questioning my place on this team. We have excellent players, and I need to figure out how best to contribute.

Game Two, Boston 88 - New York 69
Team Record: 2 Wins 0 Losses

Organizers moved our second game to a local high school, which irritated me. We rode a school bus. It felt like we were an afterthought as we bused across town for the game. We were curious to see New York. From the beginning, it was not close. We won easily. I managed the ball and made sure my teammates touched it enough to be effective. My floor game and my defense were excellent. I played calmly and composed throughout. I drove to the basket and scored my first two points with a twisting move.

Game Three, Boston 47 - New Jersey 40 (QTR final)
Team Record: 3 Wins 0 Losses

With the sample size of two games available, New Jersey held the ball to limit our effectiveness. We stayed composed and won a low-scoring game. It showed our versatility; we adjusted to a slow possession by possession game after two easy run-and-gun wins.

For the first time, I tried salt tablets. Encouraged by teammates, who had done this type of supplementation before. We did not really understand the risks or the benefits; we took them anyway. None of us felt side effects, but the choice stuck with me.

Game Four, Boston 92 - Baltimore 89 (SM Final)
Team Record: 4 Wins 0 Losses

It was a fast-moving and high-scoring game. Late foul trouble forced lineup changes and opened the door for a comeback. For me, one moment stands out. Handling the ball late in the game, I was fouled, and I went to the foul line for a one and one. I missed the front end of the one and one and Baltimore scored. On our next possession, Baltimore fouled me again, smart strategy. After the earlier miss, my confidence wobbled. This time I made both foul shots, sealing the win and sending us to the finals.

During our comeback, a teammate, exuberant after making a brilliant play, came over to "slapped five" with me so hard he nearly broke my hand. It throbbed through the next day. Just before the final, the pain faded.

Afterward, my father noticed my hands were too far from my body on free throws, creating an imbalance on my release. He was not wrong.

To note: following these instructions and corrections, I did not miss another free throw during the tournament.

Back at the dorm, teammates started calling me "clutch." I felt conflicted; my earlier miss from the foul line put us in a situation where we might lose the game. I vowed to make every shot count in the final.

That evening, we gathered in the communal area of our dorm floor. We tried to distract ourselves from the pressure of tomorrow's championship game by joking around and listening to music. The camaraderie was clear. We had each other's backs. In a moment of mischief, someone (me), suggested we put a sleeping teammate, who had dozed off on a loveseat, into the dorm elevator. The elevator would ride floor to floor, and the doors would open on each floor. We picked up the loveseat and moved it to the elevator without waking our teammate. However, he woke as I climbed out. He blinked, confused, waking inside the elevator.

Game Five, Boston 86 - Virginia 78 (Final) 3 OT
Team Record: 5 Wins 0 Losses

The gold medal game. As expected, the final was a grind. We could not put this team away when we had chances. We let them hang around through regulation and the first two overtimes. Teammates fouled out, and fatigue set in on all of us. I played during the middle stretch of regulation. I sat out the first overtime.

When our teammate fouled out trying to guard one of Virginia's quick guards, the coaches deliberated within earshot of the bench. I heard my name and saw their glances, and I knew I was going in. The head coach pulled me aside and said, "Manage the ball. No turnovers. Pick up their guard full court, no fouls. Can you do that, son?"

I entered the game focused on my assignment. In the third overtime, I scored ten of our last fourteen points and assisted the other two. More importantly, my defense held. Their catalyst did not score, and I did not commit a foul in that stretch.

One play stands out as we ran four corners to bleed the clock. The middle of the floor was open, our opponents hunting steals instead of guarding the paint. Later in the possession I drove toward the open space, not to score, but to shift their defense. At the top of the key, no one stepped to defend me. In my youthful arrogance, feeling disrespected, I probed further down the lane.

Mark Green streaked down the sideline, having shaken his defender. I glanced away to keep the help defense from reading me and slipped a bounce pass to Mark. He gathered himself, drove, finished through contact, and drew the foul. Our bench and supporters erupted in cheers as he made the free throw, sealing our victory and the gold medal.

We celebrated on the court, then hustled back to the dorm to prepare for the evening's awards. I rushed to pack, knowing my parents would want to head home after the ceremony. During the award ceremony, our team received the championship trophy. The individual gold medals would be sent to our homes later in the summer.

Our roster won three state championships, one runner-up, six players, All-State and All-Scholastic picks (the Boston Globe as of the year of the Junior 1978-1979) and seven college athletic scholarships.

The bond we formed at the Youth Games stayed strong throughout our high school careers. Whenever we played against each other, those teammates always greeted my family. In the 1978 MIAA State Tournament, second round, Fairhaven High School faced Jeremiah Burke High School, Karl Hobbs' team. As a sophomore, he led the Boston City League in scoring. After the game, I found my parents talking with Karl. Rivalry on the floor, connection beyond it. Those friendships remained meaningful over the next three seasons. Our success varied, but the bond was unmistakable. It was straightforward, grounded in mutual respect. For us, true respect was how hard we competed. In our world, which was the measure of character.

The rest of that summer was a whirlwind. A lengthy article appeared in our local newspaper announcing my transfer from Holy Family High School to Fairhaven High School. The piece also covered our gold medal win at the Youth Games. It was the third newspaper feature written about me in just four years of organized basketball.

One evening, my father and I went to a tournament at Monte Playground in New Bedford to support the Roxbury Titans, especially their head coach, Al Brodsky, who had been the assistant coach for our Youth Games team. Al greeted me with a hug and mentioned the local article. He felt the Boston papers barely acknowledged our win. He invited us to sit behind his bench.

That night, I had my first chance to watch Dwan Chandler play up close, another young player who had gained recognition through summer leagues, tournaments, and playing for his high school team. Dwan excelled at every stage, his constant chatter distracting opponents into mistakes.

All summer I weighed whether to stay at Holy Family. I did not want to leave, but pragmatism won. With Coach Jack Nobrega retired, Holy Family dropping to Division II, and team dynamics shifting under a new head basketball coach. My family left the decision to me.

The decision did not go public until late summer, folded into a local story celebrating the Youth Games gold medal. And my transfer from Holy Family to Fairhaven.

The article ran with one photo of me holding the gold medal. It was not a great photo. Sun in my eyes, a hard squint. What the photo really showed was stress, bags under my eyes, and an uneven smile. I remember thinking how awful I looked. Looking back, I see the weight of the decision all over my face and someone so young struggling to hold it together.

Chapter Five

I n Bristol County, Fairhaven sits on the South Coast, where the Acushnet River meets Buzzards Bay. Once called *Sconticut* by the Wampanoag people, the area carries a deep history shaped by its Indigenous roots and its maritime legacy.

Originally settled in 1659 as part of the town of Dartmouth, English settlers purchased Fairhaven's land from the Wampanoag Massasoit Sachem or Ousamequin and his son, Wamsutta. Over time, the region evolved. In 1787, Dartmouth's eastern section broke off to become New Bedford, which at the time included what we now know as Fairhaven, Acushnet, and New Bedford itself. In 1812, Fairhaven separated from New Bedford and became its own incorporated town. Later, in 1860, Fairhaven's northern section broke away to form Acushnet, completing a transformation that created four distinct communities from the original Dartmouth land.

Through these changes, Fairhaven remained closely tied to New Bedford. Both towns shared a deep connection to the sea, shaped by whaling, fishing, and a common harbor that fueled the region's prosperity.

Known locally as "The Castle on the Hill," Fairhaven High School is more than a public high school; it is a landmark. Built in 1905, it is still the only high school in the Fairhaven Public Schools district.

The site once housed Fairhaven Academy, a private secondary school built in 1798, now serving as the town's Visitors Center and Historical Society Museum. Industrialist Henry Huttleston Rogers gifted the high school's iconic structure in 1906; it was later added to the National Register of Historic Places in 1981.

One of its distinctive features was its original octagonal gymnasium, home to one of the first indoor high school basketball courts in the country. In the 1930s, an addition was built and connected to the gym through an underground passage.

The athletic profile reflected limited resources, like most small towns. The athletic department at Fairhaven High School was no exception. What the school lacked in funding, it made up for in heart and coaching. Fairhaven High School remained competitive throughout its history, dating back to the 1920s.

The town produced generations of standout athletes, including Mildred Parkinson Tunstel (Class of 1922), Edmund Andrews (Class of 1930) and Anthony "Jep" Lopes (Class of 1945). The 1950s brought stars like Bart Leach, Barry Behn, and Regina Damm. Among these, the 1950 basketball team, led by Leach, set the standard, winning back-to-back championships that became a benchmark for all future teams. In 1972, David Almeida, another outstanding athlete, played football at Boston College.

In 1963, Mr. Wilson took over as head basketball coach, replacing long-time coach Mel Entin. Just three seasons later, Mr. Wilson led Fairhaven to the first of two consecutive Capeway Conference championships (1967 and 1968), powered by a 30-game winning streak.

The 1966–67 team went 21–1 despite battling early-season injuries. Led by Lester Smith, the roster evolved under Mr. Wilson's guidance. The following year, the 1967–68 team posted a perfect 14–0 conference record. Between January 1967 and January 1969, Fairhaven High School basketball teams won 30 straight conference games before finally suffering a loss.

In 1977–78, Fairhaven High School came within a single win (*eight minutes*) of capturing the Division II state title. After claiming both the South Sectional and Eastern Massachusetts titles, the Blue Devils faced defending champion Springfield Commerce in the state final. Fairhaven led 40–38 after three quarters but fell in the final minutes, losing 67–59.

In 1978, the Massachusetts Interscholastic Athletic Association awarded Mr. Wilson the Coach of the Year. Two years later, he received the Distinguished Coaches Award. In 1995, they inducted Mr. Wilson into the Coaches Hall of Fame.

The "Starting Seven" from that legendary 1977–78 squad included: Jim Hennessy, Phil Graves, Gary Furtado, Chuck Tillett, Matt Gamache, Steve Lombardo and me, Mike Semiao. In June 2009, the Fairhaven High School Hall of Fame inducted that unforgettable team, cementing its place in school history.

Fairhaven High School, Sophomore Year, 1977-1978

Returning from Five-Star Basketball Camp later in the summer of 1977, I felt disheartened. Tensions on my Holy Family summer league team had worn on me, and I sensed challenges looming in the high school season ahead. Transferring to Fairhaven High School felt like a new beginning, and a reminder that this was my fifth school in seven years. I could not ignore the toll that kind of instability had taken.

Leaving Holy Family High School was tough. The mutual commitment I had shared with the school was meaningful. Letting go of that bond left a heaviness I could not shake. Now I was stepping into unfamiliar territory, a new town, a public school, a different culture. Holy Family has a diverse student population, which creates an energetic, complicated dynamic. Fairhaven was a town school, more insular, and I felt it at once.

Beneath my calm exterior, anxiety churned. It felt as though I might unravel completely. Signs appeared. When I looked closer, the signs were alarming. As previously noted, after our gold medal win at the National Youth Games, our local newspaper ran a piece featuring my transfer and the championship. The photo told the story I could not: stress, exhaustion, uncertainty.

My family noticed the physical signs. I had ground my teeth so badly in my sleep that I had worn down my front teeth. Alarmed, they arranged dental work and fitted me with a mouth guard. But we never addressed the root cause. We just moved forward, assuming time would fix it. Looking back, the silence only deepened my sense of isolation.

My admission to Fairhaven High School brought challenges I had not expected. One morning, rushing to class, I heard what sounded like a whimper. I stopped in the school hallway for a confirming sound. Hearing the sound again, I determined the sound came from the stairwell. I moved toward it. For me, that was out of character. Usually, I was cautious to the point of paralysis. This was brand-new territory. I still hesitated, then another whimper, louder this time, more definite. I went down the stairs, turned the corner, and saw a girl in tears, her arm gripped by a boy. She looked at me, pleading silently. Before I could react, the boy turned and snapped, "Get out of here. Mind your own business." I stepped toward them.

He lunged, grabbed my shirt, and the girl broke free and ran up the stairs. A teacher appeared, barking at the student holding me. As quickly as it began, it ended.

The boy released me, and the teacher ordered me to class. I went up the stairs to my classroom. As I shut the door, other teachers rushed toward the stairwell.

The hangover was simple: I was useless the rest of the day. That afternoon at home, my mother quietly mentioned the incident. She had already spoken with the school's administrators. She asked whether I wanted to talk about what had happened. I said no. I didn't want to make it worse or confront how that moment had clashed with everything we had believed about Fairhaven's tight-knit community. The two students disappeared from school, as if it had never happened. But I could not forget it.

Not long after, another unsettling moment shook me.

One day, as class ended, I lingered behind. A loud, startling crash behind me. I turned toward the sound. A student was convulsing on the floor. I froze, my heart pounding. Our teacher's voice cut through. I kneeled and followed his instructions, while our teacher watched the student's breathing, his eyes fixed on my classmate.

Everything happened fast. "Get the nurse," he said. I ran out of the classroom, up the stairs to my left, and through the foyer to the nurse's office. I blurted out what had happened and hurried back down the hall. She paused briefly at the head office, then followed me back. When the medical staff arrived, they sent me away while they worked. Staff cleared the hallway, setting up partitions.

The assistant principal appeared, placed a reassuring hand on my shoulder, and walked me to the office. He told me my classmate was going to be OK and not to worry.

Without pause, my mother arrived. After a brief conversation with the assistant principal, we left together, holding hands, and we drove home in silence. At home, I tried to make sense of the day, but I could not. Lying awake that night, both incidents spun through my mind. The girl's fear and relief, my classmate on the floor, our teacher's steady presence, the assistant principal's quiet kindness. I wanted to talk about it, but the words would not come.

So, I did what I always did. I buried it.

The pressure to adapt, to fit into this unfamiliar school while carrying so much unspoken weight, felt insurmountable. Those moments etched in memory became early markers of a difficult transition.

Starting over at Fairhaven High School as a sophomore in the fall of 1977, I brought more than talent with me. I carried expectations, doubts, and a complicated past.

Last season at Holy Family, I led the team in scoring, minutes played, and assists. But none of that followed me here. This was a new team, a new coach, and a blank slate. I would learn almost at once, and frustratingly, that whatever I had proven before meant little now.

The head coach, Mr. Wilson, and I had a complicated relationship from the start. There was tension, not outright, but quietly simmering. A fragile balance between what I had already done and what he wanted to see for himself.

Playing time became a mystery. In one game, I was a key contributor. In the next game, I barely left the bench. Praise came in small moments, then vanished without explanation. I never quite knew where I stood.

Outside of basketball, my coach and I did not know each other. There was no shared history, no genuine connection, just familiarity through third parties. That had been enough to bring us together, but not enough for us to understand one another.

I had visions of a better relationship. I wanted to believe we would build trust, camaraderie, even mentorship. But I did not actually know what that looked like. Not really.

For a long time, we stumbled around each other, trying to find footing. Mostly, it was me. The unfair expectations I placed on everyone, on my coach, my teammates, even myself. I wanted clarity, consistency, belonging, and I expected it to be unconditional. I naively thought I had earned that. What I got instead was a season of vague signals and surprising unease.

That discomfort stayed with me. It lingered long enough to make me question something I had not expected: was this the right place for me after all? Could I see myself staying in Fairhaven for the rest of high school?

I was not sure.

During the first day of tryouts, I felt a sharp, cold pain run down through my right leg. By the end of practice, I knew something was wrong.

My mother and father quickly diagnosed the injury as a pulled muscle. This was a preseason injury and would not technically equate to an in-season injury, but this was another first for me and my family. An auspicious start with a new team and a new coach. My father quickly arranged treatment through the orthopedic department at St. Luke's Hospital. They officially diagnosed my injury as a groin pull. For six days, I followed a strict regimen of whirlpool therapy twice daily, before school and after practice. I kept my head down, focused on recovery, and said little to anyone.

By the first Sunday morning practice, during a three-on-three half-court drill, I cut, stopped, and moved without pain for the first time in one week. During a full-court scrimmage, I hit four straight jumpers from twenty feet out, helping my team win. When my father arrived to pick me up, someone said to him, "We were wondering where the shot had been."

The comment confused my father. Later that night, he asked, "Didn't they know about your injury?"

This season began with a series of distractions for me. My injury: a pulled groin muscle is not visible. It was not like a sprained ankle where you visibly see the injury. And recovery was not something that is visible either. I did not advertise my treatment plan. I just followed what my family had organized for me, hoping the injury would heal. The misunderstanding foreshadowed the communication gap I would face all season. I learned an early lesson I should have understood sooner: I had to advocate for myself. I had not kept the coaches informed. That silence created assumptions I did not intend.

Amid the tension of the season, there were moments of levity.

One afternoon before practice, the head coach's son and I sneaked off to a nearby restaurant for French fries and vanilla frappes. We hid in the equipment room to eat, but the smell of the French fries gave us away. Through the equipment door, we could hear our coach questioning aloud, wondering what he was smelling and where it was coming from. Our coach found us instantly and scolded us as he took a sip from his son's frappe and helped himself to a handful of French fries, warning us we would regret running on full stomachs.

It became a routine. Each time we broke the rule of eating before practice, our coach would track us down each time we smuggled our pre-practice meal into the gym. Our head coach always gave us the same warning, saying we might regret this snack later, as he stood over us eating our pre-practice snacks. For all the season's challenges, these moments reminded me that even coaches had a lighter side.

Trying to understand the coach I now played for became a quiet study. Mr. Wilson focused on details as a coach and as a person. He planned our practices down to the minute, with clear goals and tightly scheduled sessions. His system was conservative, designed to control the pace, win possession by possession, and wear opponents down through discipline and execution.

Each coach I played for had his own rhythm, their own language. Over time, I understood their patterns. With more experience, I could adapt. But it took time, and I was not sure Fairhaven would give me enough time for the adaptation I wanted so much.

December 14, 1977 vs. Old Rochester Regional High School

The anticipation was palpable. I spent the entire day watching the clock, distracted by swirling thoughts about my role on the team. I knew I would not be starting. The head coach's statement:

"Mike is still learning the system; it will take time for him to adjust to our style."

This statement should temper expectations, but to me, it sounded like a quick excuse for anyone who asked why I was not starting. A simple response to a reality no one wanted to explain.

I joined the game midway through the first quarter. The moment had arrived. I caught an outlet pass on the right side of the backcourt. After two dribbles to center court, I delivered a chest pass to our co-captain in stride. He knocked down an eighteen-foot jumper, from the bench, the coach called out, "Hey, nice pass!"

The opponent dropped into a 2-3 zone. I found space at the right elbow and drilled a twenty-two-foot jumper, my first point as a Fairhaven Blue Devil. Our opponent stayed in the same 2-3 zone. This time I found a space in their zone from the left wing. I stepped into another open look from twenty feet and buried it. The defense adjusted. They closed out hard on my wing. On the next possession, I drove through the gap, took one power dribble, and floated a shot over the help defender. That sequence was the first time the crowd saw what I could offer: court vision, shot-making, adaptability. It felt like a breakthrough.

During a pivotal game versus Dartmouth High School on December 27, 1977, our Thanksgiving Day football rival and a team with imposing size, featuring two starters who stood six-foot-seven.

Late in the game, clinging to a slim lead, we shifted into our four-corners delay offense. When our co-captain picked up his fifth foul, I expected the coach to sub me in. When our coach hesitated to put me in, I was quietly freaking out. Our coach paced the sideline before finally saying my name. But to my surprise and quiet dismay, he did not assign me the role of managing the ball in the middle of the delay offense. Disappointed, embarrassed, and frustrated by the slight, I followed instructions and took a sideline position.

We won the game, but grappling with the coach's decision felt like a declaration of my untrustworthiness in managing the most crucial possessions. That night, I replayed every practice in my mind, trying to uncover what I had done wrong. What did I miss reading? That answer would prove elusive. Finding no answer, I made a quiet decision: I would control what I could, my effort, my preparation, and my presence.

Mid-season, we faced Barnstable High School. Trailing by eleven points at halftime, our coach delivered a blistering locker-room speech because of our poor execution during the first half. This was the first opportunity for me to witness our head coach display his frustration. Entering the second half, my play was much more aggressive, determined to shift the momentum. My contribution helped us come back to tie the score.

In a crucial late possession, the coach called a play and instructed me to set a down-screen on the weak side. It was not a glamorous role. People knew me for scoring, so was I now relegated to setting screens? My execution was flawless, but we missed the last-second shot.

The game went into overtime, and everything changed. Suddenly, the ball was in my hands more often. I found my rhythm, managed the tempo, and helped lead us to a hard-fought win. Even in victory, I felt conflicted. My actions were effective. I had stayed on the court. People judged me in ways that did not reflect my self-perception.

The lowest moment came after a narrow loss to New Bedford High School on January 31, 1978. In the last seconds, off a fumbling rebound, a pass toward the sideline, I retreated behind the play to give my teammate a passing lane. Now, with the ball in the backcourt with three seconds left, I struggled to get it to half court. Hurriedly, I took a shot from half-court, missed, and we lost the game.

I was the last to leave the court after the final buzzer; our head coach is waiting for me. This was unprecedented. I had never experienced this. I was completely aware of the importance of this game. And now I had to publicly explain my most recent play. Wow!

"Explain it to me," he said, standing in front of me with his hands on his hips, and voice steady. Other coaches might have missed errors or opportunities, but not him. He asked because he *expected more*. I did not back down. I explained the spacing, what I saw, when I saw it. He nodded, giving nothing away. I nodded too, acknowledging the moment. But inside, I knew I would do it again. I would take responsibility again because that is who I was.

Deflated and embarrassed, I felt like the easy scapegoat, the youngest varsity player, the transfer, the outsider. The whispers, the glances, they were not overt, but they lingered. They changed how I moved through the season.

My playing time did not change. But my confidence took a hit from which I could not recover. My father tried to help. He encouraged me to look forward, to take pride in how far I had come. He reminded me I was growing and maturing. But I struggled to hear him.

A Teammate's Point of View

After the game, the locker room held a silence that felt heavier than the loss itself. No one spoke at first, just the shuffling of person to person, heading for the showers and packing their belongings for the ride back to our gym. No one is making eye contact with each other.

You are the last to appear in the locker room, holding your trusty gold towel in your hands. We saw you processing your recent conversation with the coach. He asked, "Walk me through it."

Some coaches would have let it go. A bad read, a missed opportunity. But not with you. He was not asking you just to analyze the game. He was asking because he expected more.

You did not run from the confrontation. You met it head-on. He listened. You nodded, acknowledging the moment, but inside, you knew you would do it again. You would take responsibility again. Because that is who you were.

The rest of us saw it, even if we never said it aloud.

Lesser players would have cracked under that pressure. Others might have fought back, argued, shut down. But you did not. You absorbed it. You internalized it. And then you showed up the next day ready to do it all over again.

I do not know if the coach ever told you what he saw in you. We all saw that his expectations were not punishment, but trust. He pushed you because he believed in you.

But I think deep down, you know.

And no matter how that game ended, I still wanted you with the ball in your hands when it mattered most.

Practicing every day against one of the best players in the state pushed me to improve. I questioned whether I was a suitable competitor for him. Those encounters sharpened my skills and mindset.

Though I struggled with trust issues and inconsistent play, the season taught me invaluable lessons about resilience, adaptability, and perspective. Where preparation once protected me from the messiness of competition, I understood that even the most seasoned players had moments of doubt.

One day, near the end of practice, we scrimmaged full court. I was on the second team, playing offense at the far end of the gym, away from the coaches. Running our offense through our primary set, I found myself on the weak side waiting for the ball. The ball swung around to me, and I was ready. My jump shot was off. I missed.

From the other side of the gym, a sudden, thunderous crack broke through the noise. Our head coach slammed his clipboard onto the hardwood. Without a word, he turned and walked out of the gym.

The sound was ever-present in my mind long after practice ended.

Was that because of *me*? Had I triggered that reaction with one missed shot?

I fell into a familiar pattern I would cling to more than I was ready to admit, where sleep proved elusive. I repeatedly replayed the scene. My jump shot. His reaction. My inconsistency. The doubt I could not seem to escape. I had not been consistent all season. With our upperclassmen leading us, I hoped my play had not hurt our team. Still, I worried: would I be ready when it mattered?

The next day at practice, I was at a side basket shooting, my head down, working through reps, when I heard footsteps behind me. It was the head coach. Without saying a word, he started rebounding my shots. He fed me passes. I kept shooting. Ten minutes passed before he finally spoke. He grabbed the ball and pointed at my legs. "You're consistent on the release, but your leg positioning's throwing you off." He told me to set my feet just short of shoulder-width, keep my knees loose in the air, and pointed out how my legs came together mid-jump, robbing me of balance. I made the change. Shot after shot, something shifted.

By the time practice started, my form felt tighter. I worked on it daily, before and after every session. My shots fell consistently. From that point on, I never missed another weak-side jumper for the rest of the season.

During another rivalry game, this one against Durfee High School on January 17, 1978, one of our co-captains went down with an ankle injury. As had happened before, the coach hesitated. I saw him glance toward the bench, scanning options. This time, I was not willing to wait for Coach Wilson to decide on the substitution pattern. As Coach Wilson passed by me, I stood and walked directly to the scorer's table. "Hey! Who is your man?" he shouted. I answered with confidence and took the floor. From that moment on, the dynamic shifted. I realized I could not wait for permission. If I wanted to lead, I had to act like it. I could not rely on someone else to believe in me first.

Before one game against New Bedford High School, our varsity team waited on the sideline while the junior varsity game ran long. Out of nowhere, a voice rang out: "Hey, Semiao! Why are you wearing socks with red stripes? That is not our school color! What is wrong with you? You do not respect this school!" Standing there with my teammates, my reaction was passive, but internally, I was stunned. I had layered white socks over the red-striped pair. No one could even see them. But it did not matter. The moment felt performative, public. I stood frozen, feeling singled out. It was not the last time.

The following season, another conflict arose, this time over footwear. My plan for the season included the new line of Adidas basketball sneakers instead of the team-issued canvas Converse Chuck Taylor basketball sneakers. The night before the season opener, Mr. Wilson told my father I could not play unless I wore the assigned sneakers. These moments added up. Quietly, they eroded my sense of belonging. Every disagreement reminded me that my performance did not change my status as an outsider. I felt pushed around at every turn, over every innocuous situation.

More than once, I thought about transferring again to a Boston-area school or a program in the Catholic League. I knew it would raise eyebrows. It might seem like quitting. But the feeling lingered. I wanted to find a place where I could just *play*. Where I did not have to navigate politics or decode expectations. Where the game mattered. Just the game.

Interactions with the press only heightened my confusion. Comments about my role, or the lack of one, seemed to carry undertones I could not decipher. I often wondered what they saw when they looked at me. An asset? A liability? Or something in between? Was I truly part of this team or just passing through, dragging a shadow of past success too large to escape.

As an inexperienced player still learning to navigate the physical and emotional demands of the game, I wrestled with these uncertainties in silence. I wanted to trust my coach. I wanted to believe. But doubt gnawed at me. Whether the barriers between us were real or imagined, they shaped my experience in ways I would not fully understand until years later.

Basketball had always been my anchor. But under this new system with a coach whose signals felt cryptic, I questioned everything: my role, my identity as a player, even who I was outside the game.

Throughout the season, I often confided in my father. I vented about playing time, the expectations, the confusion. But beneath my frustration, I knew the truth; I needed to perform better. My inconsistency was maddening. Confidence came and went like the weather. There were games when I felt electric. Others, I vanished.

The contrast with the previous year was stark. At Holy Family, I was a freshman; I was the focal point. Now, I was not even the best player on my team for the first time in my life.

This team had a history. Camaraderie. Discipline. Five of the seven key contributors were seniors playing their last season together. Even the reserves had been around longer than I had. They created something I was supposed to join, but it felt unnatural.

Fairhaven's structured athletic culture intrigued me, but it also amplified my insecurities. Everyone knew his or her role. The team moved as a unit. I felt offbeat, close enough to contribute, but never there.

My performance was uneven. I never played two good games in a row. I never played a complete game. We all had flashes of brilliance, but I wanted more from myself. I expected more.

At this time, the only measuring stick that mattered was playing time. If I had stayed on the court, everything would have been fine. It felt like a personal slight. It felt like a failure. That belief was flawed, but for me, it was real, and it consumed me.

I could not understand why I played heavy minutes one game and barely touched the court the next. Coming off the bench felt alien. I had always been a starter. Now, I felt like an afterthought.

My classmates tried to be supportive, but their encouragement felt condescending. I brushed off their words, blind to the kindness behind them. Gratitude did not come easily in that headspace. I was bitter. *Didn't they know who I was? Didn't they remember what I had already done?*

My expectations were higher for myself and others. My hope was to lead. I wanted to be a starter on the basketball team. But Fairhaven's conservative style of play clashed with my instincts. The coach emphasized control, discipline, and execution. Shorten the game. Play smart. Stick to the system. My vision was unique. I saw fast breaks, high tempo, open floor, opportunities to run and score in transition. I believed our athleticism could overwhelm teams if we just turned up the pace. But the fear of making a single mistake loomed large. One bad pass, and I would find myself right back on the bench.

MIAA State Tournament 1978

To qualify for the Massachusetts state tournament, teams needed a 70%-win rate. Fairhaven's success in Division I that season with a 15-5 record secured our place. Because of enrollment calculations, we would drop a division and compete in Division II for the postseason.

Game One: Saturday, March 4, 1978, vs. Hyde Park High School at Taunton High School

Hyde Park was a powerhouse team, boasting a potent offense led by 6'7" Aubrey Stallworth and Jim Dancy. Their full-court press rattled us early, and they jumped out to a 10-3 lead. I entered the game midway through the first quarter, and from that point on, Hyde Park did not score another point in the period.

We flipped the momentum. Our second quarter was dominant, and we went into halftime with a 33–21 lead. By the third quarter, our advantage stretched to fifteen points. We closed the game strongly, winning 64–52.

Jimmy Hennessy and Phil Graves were the anchors, calm, experienced, and poised. The moment never seemed too big for them.

The game presented openings for me. Their press left holes in transition, and I thrived in that tempo. I finished with nine points and eight assists. Solid. Effective. Contributing. We advanced.

Game Two: Tuesday, March 7, 1978, vs. Jeremiah Burke High School at Braintree High School

Jeremiah Burke was another powerful Boston city league team led by Karl Hobbs and Leroy Burke. Karl was a Youth Games teammate. Despite their speed and scoring ability, we controlled the game from the start, winning 84–68. Jimmy Hennessy scored thirty points, and Steve Lombardo added twenty-one.

After the game, I found Karl speaking with my parents. We embraced, laughed, and caught up. It was a brief but meaningful moment.

Game Three: Thursday, March 9, 1978, South Semifinal vs Seekonk High School at New Bedford Vocational High School

The semifinal against Seekonk was a grind. We came out flat, but rallied in the third quarter, outscoring them nineteen to eight. Still, the game tightened late and came down to the final possessions.

Then came the moment.

I found myself open on the weak side; in the exact spot I had practiced *thousands* of times. The ball swung to me. I caught it. Rose up to shoot. Released. Short. Seekonk grabbed the rebound. Timeout.

In the huddle, I heard it: "Who do you think you are taking that shot? We could lose because of you!" The words landed like a punch. My face flushed. Tears welled up but did not fall. I had never felt this way on a basketball court.

Though my coach was harsh, I stayed in the game. And I played throughout the entire overtime period. It felt like the smallest thread of validation, but I held onto it.

Phil Graves hit the clutch shot that sealed the win. Fans rushed to the court. The chaos was euphoric, but I barely felt it. I moved through the crowd like a ghost. I could not stop thinking about the shot. About those words.

That night, I lay in bed, replaying it all. The miss, the words in the huddle, playing overtime and my team's celebration. I should have been proud of our accomplishment, but I felt ashamed. Not for missing the shot, but for letting it affect me so deeply.

Over the years, I have returned to that moment more times than I care to admit. I wondered why the coach did not pull me. Benching me then might have cost him the entire team, not just one player. Or he knew I was on the edge and losing me could have meant losing me for good. Whatever the reason, I am glad he let me stay in the game.

We won. We advanced to the South Sectional final. The town celebrated. But for me, it was a night of contradiction, victory, and vulnerability sharing the same breath.

A Teammate's Point of View

We were in a fight, and every possession mattered. The gym felt like it was closing in on us. We found it hard to breathe in that intense moment. The game was tight, and we needed to be smart. Then he took the shot.

I saw it leave his hands and held my breath. He had hit that shot a thousand times in practice. But this time, it came up short. Seekonk grabbed the rebound and called a timeout. My stomach dropped.

When we got into the huddle, frustration boiled over. Someone snapped, "Who do you think you are, taking that shot? We could lose because of you!"

It was harsh, but in the heat of the game, emotions ran wild. Fear, not anger, consumed us. We feared losing, seeing everything we had worked for slip away. And maybe scared he was not as unshakable as we thought.

But he did not crumble. He stayed in the game, and when overtime started, he was still out there, fighting. I could see it in his eyes. He would not back down. The weight of that moment was on him, but he kept playing, kept pushing.

And then Phil hit that shot. The gym erupted. We won. We were moving on.

As the celebration spilled onto the court, I glimpsed him in the chaos that surrounded our team. He looked relieved, but there was something else, something I could not place. The weight of that huddle still clung to him. Maybe the win was not enough to move on.

I wanted to say something; to tell him we trusted him, that we needed him. But the moment passed. The locker room filled with shouts and cheers, and we moved forward, chasing the next win.

Years later, I wonder if that moment stuck with him the way it stuck with me. Because that night, I saw something I had not seen before, not just a great player, but a teammate carrying more than just the weight of a game.

Game Four: Saturday, March 11, 1978, South Final vs. Rockland High School at Brockton High School

The quick turnaround between games was a gift. After two underwhelming performances, I welcomed the chance to sprint toward the next one, to put distance between myself and the criticism still ringing in my head from the last game. I needed to move forward, to reclaim my rhythm, and to help the team.

That Saturday afternoon, the importance of the game was unmistakable. When I arrived at our gym, it was a flurry of contradictions: excitement, distraction, and noise. They had expanded tournament roster rules, adding junior varsity players to our bench. They ran around the gym with the enthusiasm of court jesters, entertaining the early crowd with their antics.

I stood near the entry doors, calm, detached from the chaos. Steve Lombardo stood next to me, and we made small talk about nothing. I realized how quiet my mind was. I had not prepared to feel this still. Somehow, the solace I had been chasing all season had found me just when I was not looking for it.

The Brockton High School gym was the largest we had played in, seating five thousand, with a beautiful floor and bright lighting. The basketball court had a clean bounce, and the setting felt right. I stepped onto the court, took two shots, and felt it: *this was going to be different.*

In the locker room, I suited up with quiet purpose.

We already controlled the game by the end of the first quarter. A basket from Steve Lombardo and a long jumper I hit at the buzzer gave us a 23–19 lead. By halftime, we were up 46–33.

This was the best basketball I played all season. The second quarter belonged to me, eight points, six assists, and another buzzer-beating shot at the end of the first half. When we walked into the locker room, my teammates looked at me like I was an alien.

Heading into the third quarter, I told myself to keep my foot on the accelerator. I took two quick early shots, and the coach pulled me from the game. I did not expect the substitution, not with how I had been playing. As I walked toward the bench, I heard it. "What do you think you're doing? You are out of control! Who do you think you are?" Were those words directed at me? Did I hear them correctly? This was the second straight game where someone questioned my judgment.

I rejoined the game during cleanup time, after the game had already been decided. In my interpretation, this was a quiet punishment, my playing time reduced not because of my performance, but because of my judgment.

During the celebration, I stood near the coaching staff, feeling disoriented. The celebration swirled around me, and for a moment, I felt like a spectator of our success. I tried to keep my perspective, not to let mistrust consume me.

But the truth is, this season no player was scrutinized more than me. And it was not even close. I was not trying to play the victim. But the difference in my treatment was real. I had expected better.

We won 87–69. As a team, we did not have any signature wins during the season. We waited until the state tournament to have those signature wins. To play that well, on that stage, at this moment, it mattered. We were now just two wins away from a state championship.

After the game, a reporter from our local newspaper asked to interview me. This will be the first article in which a sixteen-year-old high school sophomore was quoted in the newspaper. What could go wrong? The natural assumption was that my quotes would appear alongside coverage of our team's win.

Instead, the next morning, I opened the paper to find a *standalone article,* a piece centered entirely on me. The article framed me as an outsider. As someone who had transferred into a tight-knit community, stepped into a winning program, and helped push the team forward.

The next day during basketball practice, I heard the whispers questioning my sincerity, my intentions, even my gratitude. It felt like another blow. I was not looking for praise or permission. But the recurring narrative, that I could do nothing right, that my motivations were suspect, was exhausting.

I kept telling myself to focus on the goal, to stay with the team, to move forward. But the gap between what I gave and what I received was widening.

Yes, I was grateful for our success. But that did not erase the conflict I felt about my place within it.

Early Monday morning, they rushed my grandfather, my mother's father, to the hospital. Doctors placed him on life support. The news shook our entire family.

As if in a dream, hurried through the tunnels of St. Luke's Hospital, trying to keep pace with my father. It felt like we were racing toward something we were not ready to face. Elevators. Corridors. Turns that blurred together. And then I was in his room, hovering like a ghost. My grandfather looked unrecognizable, his body surrounded by wires and tubes, the rhythmic hiss of the ventilator filling the room and my chest. I stood there breathing with him, silently willing him to sit up and acknowledge me.

Then my father rushed me out.

Back home, the lights were dim. The air had changed. The house was quiet in a way that made sound feel intrusive. I lay in my room staring at the ceiling, something I had done countless nights over the past three years, but this time, I was not thinking about my jump shot or my performance. I was thinking about *him*. The man who had looked after me as a child. Who kept me safe. Who treated me as someone more than just a kid.

That night, I tried to say goodbye, but it is hard to let go of your young eyes, the ones that recall those times when you were allowed to be just a kid, nothing more. Chasing his dog through the Swain School fields all hours of the night, running through the darkness with no fear, just the delirium of a child feeling loved and protected. My grandfather does not survive the night. And in a way, neither did my family. Relatives began arriving from across the country. The news of his passing spread quickly, even reaching the basketball team. The support from my teammates heartened me. From the coaching staff, nothing. Not a word. It was not a surprise. We barely communicated at all during the season. Still, the silence hurt. It served yet as another reminder of where I stood.

Real life crossed the boundary into basketball, and this time, there was no buffer. No distraction. No practice to shield me from the weight of what we were feeling. My family had always tried to protect me from moments like this.

But this one was unavoidable. We had to honor him now in the only way we knew how, through tradition, remembrance, and mourning.

I often notice how vacant and dazed people look during funeral processions, as if caught between worlds. I used to wonder: What is going through their minds? Do they feel a loss? Or is it all too big to process? Now I stood inside that prism, unsure if anyone passing by could see the boy in the suit, staring out the window, trying to understand what goodbye really meant.

Game Five: Wednesday, March 15, 1978, North-South Final vs. Marblehead High School at Brockton High School

Coming off the emotional high of winning the South Final, the days before our matchup with Marblehead felt steady and grounding. Marblehead, with a 21–3 record and a seventeen-game win streak, had just beaten Dom Savio 73–71 in their sectional final.

This game proved two things:

First, we could win in multiple ways. Up to this point in the tournament, we had averaged seventy-one points per game while holding opponents to fifty-nine, a margin of twelve. But this game was different, more of a grind, a chess match.

Second, we had toughness.

We won 55–51, our second-lowest scoring game of the season, and the second-fewest points we had allowed. It was a testament to our adaptability, and to the type of basketball we could play when the stakes demanded it.

Jimmy Hennessy was phenomenal. All tournament long, he had shown what we already knew; he was one of the best players in the state. Practicing with him every day had been one of the quiet gifts of the season.

With the win, we moved on to the state finals. The buzz was not hard to understand, not just in Fairhaven, but across southeastern Massachusetts. Early elimination befell other local teams. We were still standing. We had become the region's team.

The night of our game against Marblehead was also the second night of my grandfather's wake. With his funeral scheduled for the next day.

My grandmother's home became the central place where everyone checked in. Relatives, uncles, aunts, cousins, and neighbors filled the house. Familiar faces with unfamiliar expressions. They didn't know what to say to me. I didn't know what to say to them.

I watched my mother and grandmother, the way they carried themselves. Their grief became my guide. I had always played off their cues. This afternoon was no different. Nervous talk floated through the rooms. Uncomfortable silences pressed in between.

And yet, something inside me shifted. I chose not to make this a moment of performance, expectations, or analysis. This was not a test. It was not a purity ritual.

It was *his* life, and my memory of it. I celebrated not by trying to make sense of the loss, but by holding onto who he had been to me. There was no secret formula. No one right way to mourn. You choose how to say goodbye.

Game Six: Saturday, March 18, 1978, Massachusetts Division II State Final vs. Springfield Commerce High School at Worcester Polytechnic Institute (WPI)

As the tournament progressed, it felt as if my life no longer belonged to me. Distractions at school, in the community, were everywhere, all at once. The noise grew louder with each victory.

My grandfather's passing had reminded me of what was profoundly important. But now I felt split into thirds, grappling with grief, team responsibilities, and my own internal state. No one knew exactly how to navigate it, including me.

We traveled to Worcester the day before the game for a walkthrough at WPI's 3,000-seat gymnasium. After we settled into our hotel rooms, I called home. My mother told me she would not attend the game but wished me luck. My father would be there with my sister and uncle.

Note: My father and I had a ritual before every game. A handshake and "Have a good game." For the first time, we could not do that.

The next morning, I had breakfast with a teammate. While reading the *Boston Globe*, we found ourselves labeled heavy underdogs. Unsurprisingly, we were underdogs throughout the tournament. When we arrived at the gym, I split off from the team to find a quiet place to gather myself. A familiar step in my process.

The game opened with a statement. Springfield Commerce's All-American, Mark Hall, drove baseline and dunked over our team. Down 6–0 fast. A timeout steadied us, and we closed the quarter trailing 18–15.

I joined the game late in the second quarter. Our five senior starters were playing their final high-school game, and seniority carried weight. When I entered, we were down 26–16. By halftime, we had trimmed it to two. My play sparked the team.

In the locker room, the mood was calm. No dramatic speeches. Just resolve. We knew we were in a fight.

Midway through the third quarter, we trailed 36–28. That was when the Commerce coach made a puzzling decision. He pulled all five starters. We saw it as disrespect. And that sparked us.

Phil Graves scored 36–30. I drove the lane for a basket: 36–32. Commerce answered: 38–32. Then Steve Lombardo added a basket and two free throws: 38–36.

As a team, we did not have elaborate verbal cues, only simple ones. "24" meant full-court man-to-man. "34" was our secret weapon: a full-court zone press, rarely used.

Suddenly, we heard it from the bench: "Hey! Thirty-four!" Our coach had not given up on this game.

I responded with a steal and a layup to tie it at 38. Moments later; we trapped a Commerce player, Phil, forced a steal and scored: 40–38. We led heading into the fourth.

Commerce turned the ball over to start the last quarter and applied their own trap on the inbound. Their trap cornered me. I executed a step-through and drew a foul.

Shooting a one-and-one with a two-point lead, I knew what was at stake. Make both, and we might shift into our delay game, forcing Commerce to foul us.

I missed the front end of the one-and-one.

Commerce scored on the next possession to tie it, and we could not regain momentum. They were incredibly talented. We had spent everything just to stay with them.

Did I cost us the game? Maybe. But basketball rarely hinges on one moment. There are dozens of "what-ifs." Still, the missed foul shot haunted me.

We lost 67–59. Springfield Commerce secured its third straight state title.

During the awards ceremony, I sat on the bench, head down, trying to disappear. Then I noticed someone standing in front of me. I looked up. It was Karl Hobbs, my teammate from the National Youth Games. Karl squatted down and reached for my hand. "Nice game. Your team played well," he said. Then, he was gone.

Later, outside the locker room, I found Karl again, this time with my father, uncle, and sister. We conversed briefly. His gesture stayed with me. It spoke of character. Of leadership. And at that moment, it meant more than he could have known.

Looking back at the 1978 state tournament, my feelings were mixed. The regular season, with all its swirling dynamics, humbled me. As I had said before, sensitive, for sure. Expecting better? Definitely. But this acknowledgment was not about blame. It was about recognizing reality: I stayed afloat, and I helped my team when and where I could.

The dichotomy between my personal experience and our team's overall success was a revelation. I did not intend for my personal challenges to detract from our collective goals. I just wanted to be productive with my time, my effort, my role, whether in practice or in games.

What I could not control was the lack of communication between me and the coaching staff. I took full responsibility for my own actions and responses. But I was convinced they will never acknowledge their role in it. They should, but they would not. And I was learning to be okay with that.

Despite the complications, I was incredibly thankful for the experience. Reconciling the differences was hard, but I turned the page and did my part to celebrate what we achieved. The community was phenomenal. They gave us varsity jackets, watches, our white jerseys, commemorative pins, a celebration dinner, and even a trip to Washington D.C.

The personal support I received was heartening. The acknowledgement my junior high school teachers showed by traveling to our state tournament games was fantastic. Neighbors reacted to our state tournament run and to my individual play. Friends called constantly, wanting to share the experience. My family became the hub for managing it all. The two weeks of the tournament felt like a full-court press, every day packed with practice, games, media, and emotion.

Now, the complications of that season drifted from me. Day by day, they lose their grip. What lingered was the knowledge that I got through it. I stayed in it. I learned.

What surprises me most is how I felt about the coaching staff. I thought there would be a hangover, lingering resentment. But there was not, not really. That weight? It was on me, not them. And that was the most important lesson of all.

While we were on the Washington trip, a family friend, an uncle of our team manager, offered to take me, his nephew, and our friend, the coach's son, out to dinner one evening. The gesture itself was great.

When we returned from dinner, we ran into the coaches and their wives in the hotel lobby. Mr. Wilson seemed curious about where we had been. When he learned about the dinner, he turned to the assistant coach and asked,

"Did you know Semiao was going out to dinner tonight?"

I froze. I was certain we had gotten permission.

The look on my face must have said it all. Mrs. Wilson walked over, put her arm around me, and said,

"Wayne, leave him alone. You are scaring him."

Mr. Wilson smiled at me and said,

"Everything is fine. We knew you were going out with John."

That moment shifted something in me.

All season, my relationship with Mr. Wilson had been ambivalent at best. But seeing his reaction and that he could tease me about my worry, seeing humanity behind his seriousness opened me up to him in a way I had not expected.

Over the next two seasons, our mutual respect grew. If not for my personal trust issues, I believe our relationship could have grown even stronger.

The complexities surrounding my own ambitions and anxieties had little to do with how I felt about Mr. Wilson. In the end, I included him in my college recruitment process. When I accepted the scholarship offer from Bryant College, his involvement and support were major factors in that decision.

Weeks after the season had ended, our school and town surprised the team with a spring break trip to Washington, DC, a gesture of appreciation. Although the itinerary was well-structured and thoughtful, we stayed restless.

One afternoon, we found a basketball court behind our hotel. We broke the schedule and played for over an hour. The sound of sneakers on the pavement, the ball echoing off the backboard; it released something. Like we were letting go of all the things we had not said.

Late that night, a teammate called me to their room. Inside, a group of upperclassmen huddled around a cassette player, listening to the radio broadcast of our overtime win against Seekonk, the game where I had missed a critical shot at the end of regulation and taken heat from the coach during the timeout.

They played the moment repeatedly. Then someone said something I had not expected: "We feared losing you." What? Losing me, what? How? Not just as a teammate, but completely?

And suddenly I saw it. My struggle had not existed in isolation. My silence, my frustration, my self-doubt. They had felt it too. My battle had become theirs.

That night, I lay awake with a new thought. I could not keep letting my personal turmoil bleed into any team I play for. I owed it to them and to myself to find a better way forward.

My sophomore season at Fairhaven High School brought its share of challenges, as I have described throughout this memoir. But it also delivered key lessons that gave me confidence as I entered the spring off-season tournaments with the New Bedford Buddies. I already understood the structure of these events, which helped me mentally prepare. Because of the Waltham tournament's age breakdown, I moved up to the senior division. I welcomed the opportunity to see how I measured up against that caliber of talent.

Our team performed well, including a semifinal win over Talisman, 88–81. In the finals, we would face the Roxbury Titans, who were also competing in the junior division final that day. Each of our programs had become dominant in these off-season tournaments.

But heading into the championship, we faced a familiar challenge: getting enough committed players to show up. Only five of us made it. Three of the five players were Jimmy Hennessy, Phil Graves, and me. Despite having no bench, we battled the Titans into overtime. In the closing moments, my Youth Games teammate Bubba Raymond chased me down as I advanced the ball up the sideline. He did not mean to foul, but his hand on my hip forced me out of bounds. I turned, expecting a whistle. Instead, Bubba reached out with a big smile. "Great game, Mike."

Though disappointed by the loss, I walked away proud of my effort, proud of what it said about how far I had come.

The Lexington tournament had its own age divisions, and though I was ready for the senior group, the New Bedford Buddies coach asked me to play in the junior division, citing chemistry and cohesion with my peer group. His rationale made sense, so I agreed. We advanced to the finals, again facing the Roxbury Titans. I had a great basketball game that day. Later in the game, we held the ball, running a delayed offense. I loved to stretch the defense; I am quick enough to avoid defenders, confident enough to keep the ball in my hands. I made six free throws in the last minute, sealing our 67–65 win.

Upon learning that I had disregarded my coach's requests to pass the ball, I responded with amusement. My teenage reply had been arrogant: Why pass it? I was not sure my teammates would make their foul shots, but I knew I would not miss mine. Hearing that story years later still makes me shake my head. Teenage arrogance.

The tournament named me Most Valuable Player. Among the players waiting to get on the court were Karl Hobbs and Tim O'Shea, my teammates from the National Youth Games. Their congratulations were heartfelt and unexpected.

Our final spring tournament with the New Bedford Buddies took place in Arlington. Again, I played in the junior division, and again, we made the finals, this time beating the Roxbury Titans convincingly, 111–81. I earned a spot on the all-tournament team and received the sportsmanship award.

The respect between our team and the Titans had grown deeper through competition. After the game, I approached Coach Al Brodsky, our Youth Games assistant coach, and the Titans' head coach. A handshake would not suffice. He pulled me into a hug. We did not need words. My connection with Al and the Titans was personal, and while it occasionally frustrated my Buddies coach, it mattered to me. I would not let that bond become a distraction.

Later in the locker room, I overheard a Titans player venting about the two recent losses to my team. The Titans had beaten the Buddies in the first two tournaments of the tournament season. Bubba Raymond had expressed to his teammates and singled me out as the difference in the two consecutive losses the Titans experienced versus the Buddies. It meant everything to hear that, especially coming from someone I respected. Bubba and I hugged. "All right Mike. See you soon." I left that tournament wishing there were more games like this.

As summer approached, my father and the New Bedford Buddies head coach began discussing my future. Fairhaven's limited resources affected the athletic department. The team's outlook for the next two years was modest. My father quietly explored options: prep schools, the Catholic League, or transferring to a Boston-area school. In the end, it was my mother who made the call. She did not want me to live out of town and sleep on someone else's couch. In the end, I would stay at Fairhaven High School. My disappointment was profound. I felt ready for a bigger challenge. But I accepted the decision, knowing my next steps would require me to dig in even deeper.

Coming off our 1978 state tournament run with Fairhaven High School, and convincing performances in out-of-town tournaments, I entered the summer with confidence. The respect I had earned in basketball circles felt like validation. Unfortunately, challenges soon arose.

Invited to Five Star Basketball Camp for the second consecutive summer, I looked forward to measuring my skills against national players. Unlike the previous year, I attended alone, without the camaraderie of familiar faces. Early in the week, I injured my knee diving for a loose ball on a cement court. A poor decision in hindsight. The injury kept me sidelined for four days.

When I returned during the camp playoffs, my performance was surprisingly sharp. My camp team made the playoffs, reaching the semifinals. We played well but lost a tight game to the eventual champions. Despite the setback, I proved I could compete in the senior division, which was my goal for the summer. Contacts from the camp included Iona University, North Carolina, Southwest Louisiana, Boston University, and the University of Miami.

Back home, something felt different. As I reconnected with teammates for the upcoming summer league season, I noticed a shift. Distractions had appeared that had not existed before. I could not trace it to a single moment, but I sensed a change I could not ignore.

Hoping to build on my Five Star success, I attended the All-New England Basketball Camp in Connecticut. From the start, the week was tough. I did not know anyone, and my living arrangements left me isolated. I had to keep track of my schedule; afraid I would miss an activity.

The stress wore me down. I did not play well all week. I reverted to shy, passive behavior, and my performance suffered. Dan Doyle, the head coach at Trinity University and my camp team coach. Expressed to my father, I needed significant improvement if I hoped to play college basketball or receive a scholarship.

That critique was hard to hear, but it was fair. I had regressed, and my handling of the experience even surprised me. My father's silence during the drive home spoke volumes. Eventually, he said, "This can't happen again." His words were firm, not a cruel mix of honesty and belief in my potential. I knew he was right.

Recovering from past missteps and using the positive experiences I had gained with Holy Family High School, Fairhaven High School, and the New Bedford Buddies offseason tournament team, I entered the summer of 1978 eager to embrace a leadership role. My first step was organizing our summer league teams for both the New Bedford Recreation Summer League and the Fairhaven Summer League. I secured a sponsor, created rosters, distributed league schedules, and made sure each player received a team t-shirt. To ensure accountability, I called every player the night before each game to confirm availability and offer transportation, if needed. Often, the transportation was my car.

We would meet at a central location, and then I would drive the team to that day's court. I poured myself into the work, committed to helping us play and perform well. I believed our summer league efforts would be a clear indicator of the fall and winter seasons ahead. But even as we played well, I continued to sense something was off. I could not pinpoint the issue, but the unease lingered.

Our team qualified for the playoffs in both leagues. The New Bedford Summer League would be a bigger challenge. Its reputation for elite amateur competition in southeastern Massachusetts meant the stakes were higher and the spotlight brighter. As the playoffs progressed, the crowds grew larger, bringing a different intensity than the high school season.

We won our first-round matchup in two straight games but lost the first game of the next round. Game two drew the biggest crowd we had seen all summer. The energy was high; spectators surrounded the court, and while we played well, we lacked experience in high-pressure moments. Trust did not come naturally. When the game reached overtime, the cracks in our foundation showed.

Down by one point with twenty seconds left and possession of the ball, we set up against a 2-3 zone defense. We knew the gaps in that formation. We just had to execute. As we moved the ball around the perimeter, a pass came my way. One defender tried to close me out. I dribbled once and took a twenty-two-foot jumper. It hit the front of the rim. Game over. We lost, ending our summer league season.

I stood by my decision, but not everyone agreed. As I left the court, one teammate's family screamed at me. They rushed toward me, furious that I had taken the last shot. My father quickly stepped in, guiding me to our car without incident. We did not speak about the game or the shot the entire drive home, a rare silence between us.

I knew what I saw. The play had broken down, and with time expiring, I took the shot. Yes, I saw my teammate open in the corner. But I did not trust him. His commitment and practice habits had been lacking until recently, even though this was his senior year. It did not feel right giving that moment to someone who had not prepared for it the way I had. I trusted my ability, even if the outcome did not go our way. The voices that consumed my decision completely ignored the thirty-six points I scored to keep our team in the game. The fault lands at my feet, exactly where it should be. I accept that. What was unacceptable was a teammate's family wanting to fight me over my decision.

Later that week, I returned home from work to find a note from my mother asking me to call my head coach. When I called, he invited me to play tennis the next night. This was not something we had done before.

We met at the junior high school courts in Acushnet, a place where my father and I often played. After our match, my coach mentioned the summer league game. It was a one-sided conversation. He acknowledged my decision but suggested I should focus more on being a distributor. He did not challenge my thinking outright, but I understood the message.

We ended the night with a pledge to play tennis again. Still, his feedback timing felt manipulative. It was as if I had stepped out of line, and he needed to realign me. It did not sit well. All summer; I had led. I had organized, supported, and pushed this team forward. And yet, that effort felt ignored the moment we lost.

Despite the disappointment, I moved forward, continuing my preparation for the coming season. My inclusion as a league all-star confirmed my efforts, but the lingering feeling stayed. Something about this summer consistently feels off, and now that unease has a name.

A text from Michael J. Meade, To Not Abandon Ourselves, a noted mythologist and storyteller, finding these words relevant to my story and life; The mystic saint and writer John of the Cross wrote: "If a person wishes to be sure of the road on which they tread, they must close their eyes and walk in the dark." People attribute the phrase "the dark night of the soul," describing a descent into the self, to John of the Cross.

Abandonment is an archetypal human condition, one that shapes our deepest fears and our most ingrained defenses. From childhood, we experience moments of separation, whether literal or emotional, that leave an imprint on our sense of security. Every child experiences moments of feeling lost, left behind, or unseen, which shape their protective instincts.

Something different is about to happen now, and we are entering a deeper layer.

Before the first incident, I did not have the language for what was happening around me. Now I do.

My car had been vandalized over ten times in two years, and the police in Fairhaven knew me by name. There was some dark humor attached to the situation. Looking at it from the outside, anyone could see I was being targeted. It raised concerns about safety, not just for me, but also for those around me. Physically and symbolically, I felt isolated from my classmates. Concern stemmed from exposure to potential threats, particularly when those threats could affect others as well. I was aware of the possibility that someone could go through my friends to get to me. Unfortunately, this occurred with someone I cared about, and they became part of this drama unknowingly. A close friend and a family member, unknowingly or possibly purposefully, selfishly, put this person, their friend, into a vulnerable situation, without understanding they were pawns in a game to hurt and isolate me. And then, one night, that threat stopped being implied. It became real.

Reflecting on that period, I realized every crisis shared a common theme: abrupt isolation and a feeling of being separated precisely when connection was most essential. Abandonment was not just a feeling; it had become the air I breathed, the ground under my feet. Late that summer, it rose again in a way I never could have imagined.

That summer, I felt a strange tension at the edges of my world. Small glances, half-hearted words, and a sense of being watched clung to me after games. I pushed it aside, but it stayed with me.

After a summer league game at Cushman Park in Fairhaven, I packed up my gear, organizing myself to leave and drive home. Someone I knew asked if I could give them a ride home. Since the location was on my way, I agreed. Even then, I felt a flicker of irritation I could not name. Before I could drop this person at their destination, they asked if we could stop at a convenience store for a drink. The request annoyed me, but I nodded and pulled into the parking lot.

While waiting in my car, someone familiar approached and leaned into my driver-side window. Curiously, he asked about my summer and how the league had gone. Suddenly, without pause, a knife was at my neck, forcing me upright in my seat. My heart pounded as a series of questions filled my mind: Why me? Had I provoked this? Was I about to die?

Panicked, I shoved open the drivers-side door with full force. The attacker fell backward, landing hard on the pavement. As he moved away from me, the blade grazed my skin, drawing blood. I leaped from the car, gripping my neck, feeling warm liquid on my hand. Behind me, I heard grunts, rustling, and heavy breathing. I spun around, expecting another attack, but he was already running away.

The store owner, who had seen everything, rushed to my side. Thinking it had been a fight; he checked if I was okay. After I responded to his questions and concerns, he asked if I wanted to call the police. Before I could answer, the person I was giving a ride home, my passenger, returned and stood beside my car. His expression told me everything. I should not make this official. I thanked the store owner for his concern and drove away.

Random thoughts trampled through my head. What now? Should I tell my parents? Should I report this? My passenger interrupted my confused thoughts, asking what had just happened. I told him everything. When I finished, he asked if I had been dating anyone that summer. The question stunned me. It felt wildly out of place. Cautiously, I answered and mentioned a girl's name. He asked how often we had gone out. I told him the truth; we had gone on only one date. He nodded and then explained why the attack had happened. The reason? Jealousy. As he justified the violence, I stared, unable to process it.

When he finally said, "Thanks for the ride," reality snapped back. This was not like my usual anxiety. This was something far worse. That night, I lay awake, trying to make sense of it all. How did he know where I would be? Was this planned? Who could I trust? Was I even safe?

Exhaustion finally overtook me, and I drifted into an uneasy sleep. The suddenness of this situation created nightmares where danger, betrayal, and now the lingering fear of death surrounded me.

In the days that followed, relief mingled with a sharper kind of fear, not just for myself, but for everyone near me. I kept thinking about how easily someone else could have been caught up in that moment, how the violence that had found me could have hurt a friend, a teammate, or even a stranger. That thought stayed with me longer than the wound itself. I did not tell anyone; I folded it into the same silence that had always protected me. But from that night forward, the world felt smaller, sharper, edged with knowledge I could not unsee.

Yet the next morning, I still laced up my sneakers. I went back to practice, back to routines, but everything now carried a different weight.

In the weeks that followed, the silence around me felt heavier than ever, not just from fear, but from the familiar ache of being left to carry it alone. Even as I went back to practice, the sense of abandonment lingered like a shadow at the edge of every court I stepped onto.

PHOTOGRAPHS

Images from the Journey

Eighth Grade — Early talent taking shape.

Freshman Year — Holy Family beginnings.

Sophomore Year — Instruction and expectation.

Junior Year — Driving under pressure

Senior Year — Composure at center court.

Senior Year — Fighting through the moment.

Youth Games Gold Medal — The moment the world shifted

A childhood brush with greatness — Julius Erving

Bryant College — The cost beneath the surface

Chapter Six

I woke up confused, disoriented, and cold. The house felt quiet. Walking downstairs, I found only our dog inside. The house was empty. A note on the kitchen counter explained and reminded me of the day's activities. My parents were with my sister at one of her school events. The note also reminded me of the Sunday morning pickup games at the New Bedford Recreation gym.

As I moved in response to my commitment to playing that day, I felt a sharp pain near my ribs on the right side of my body and noticed a faint bruise in that area, and my head throbbed. Continuing to feel disoriented, I showered, dressed, and drove to the recreation gym. Everything was moving in slow motion. Once there, I could not understand why I was there. I told the Buddies head coach I was not feeling well and could not play that morning. Our conversation was brief. Was I looking to him for help but could not bring myself to ask for it? I was hoping he could see I was in distress, and he would respond. But one of my gifts was not to show vulnerability on the basketball court or in life. This performance-based presentation has now come back to hurt me.

The attempt to think clearly was a challenge, but my decision to seek my grandmother for help was more instinctive than purposeful. My body continued to speak to me as I drove to my grandmother's house. The pain in my side and the back of my head was worsening, as was the question of what happened to me. I saw that my grandmother's car was not in front of her house. Panic is slowly sinking in, because I cannot think of where she might be this Sunday morning. Then I realized my grandmother is at church services. My attempts to convince myself my grandmother would return home after the church services had failed. My thoughts feel jumbled and unclear.

It is tempting to retreat to familiar territory, but doing so can feel like a surrender. I have often wondered, do parents or grandparents recognize this pattern? Is it familiar to them when you show up at their doorstep asking for help?

When my grandmother arrived home, she found me sitting at her front door. My pain, my discomfort, she could see it on my face. Her concern was immediate, and her questions were frequent. Even if I could remember what happened, I was going to be too afraid to tell her. The memory of what happened was foggy and unreliable. Embarrassed and scared, I let her examine me. The bruise near my right rib cage had worsened, and there was a large lump on the back of my head. Scratches marked my face and right cheek. I had not even noticed the scratches until she pointed them out.

As if on autopilot, I heard, we are going to the emergency room right now. We walked together to the hospital. I could see the look of determination on her face. My grandmother always carried a businesslike demeanor in a crisis. Last winter, I watched my family navigate the passing of my grandfather, my grandmother's husband, and my mother's father. They moved through the tradition of saying goodbye with grace and resolve.

On the day of my grandfather's funeral, my mother asked me to take care of my grandmother. I never left her side. Escorting her to the church where our family celebrated each Sunday, I stood beside her on a day that was about saying goodbye to someone who had once cared for and protected me. It was a tough day, but I did my best to look after her. We left the funeral early when I sensed she was uncomfortable.

Today, she displayed the same determined look as she moved to take care of me. I gave in to the role of being her grandson because now I needed her strength.

The examination had taken on a more serious tone as it progressed. The questions pushed closer to a line my grandmother clearly did not want to cross: "Were you in a fight? Were you in a car accident? Were you drunk? What did you have to eat and drink?" The X-rays came back negative for both my ribs and head injury. The blood test results were not available at once. They were looking for toxins I might have ingested.

When we returned to my grandmother's home, I saw that someone had moved my car. My concern must have been visible, because my grandmother quickly explained that someone was detailing the car and would return it later. If I needed another reminder of how serious this was, that moment provided it.

Resting in the bedroom where I had spent nights as a child brought back memories of when things had felt simple, easy, and safe. The smells, the sounds, even the feel of the bed linens were familiar. But those comforts only reminded me of how vulnerable I had become. It was clear now; I had brought my problems to my grandmother's doorstep. It felt like a retreat, a regression. The assumption that growing up meant having the ability to figure out and process what life handed you felt fleeting.

Last basketball season, I faced challenges that needed problem-solving. With guidance from my father and family, I had worked through those issues. I had not always succeeded or met my expectations, but I believed I had become better prepared for challenges on the basketball court. However, this case was unique. This was not a missed shot or tough practice.

After a brief nap, I woke up in the late afternoon. Through the window, I saw my grandmother outside speaking with another man. Upon joining them, they questioned me further and told me about their car inspection findings. There was a scrape on the rear bumper, vomit in the backseat, and a towel soaked with it. The rest of the car appeared intact. They mentioned they would evaluate the vomit to decide whether any toxins were present. The mention of the word "toxins" during this investigation unnerved me to the point of paralysis.

Then, as quickly as it had begun, the conversation ended. The man walked to his car and drove away, leaving my grandmother and me standing quietly on the sidewalk. After a moment, she said she would talk to my mother and explain what had happened.

I turned to her, confused. "How can you explain what happened," I asked silently, "when I can't even explain it myself?"

Before I left to go home, I thanked my grandmother for her help, and she hugged me and told me we would figure things out and not worry. Those words were comforting, but only for a moment. The uncertainty surrounding my well-being still lingered because I could not answer the fundamental question of what had happened.

Over the next few nights, I struggled to sleep. When I did, fragmented memories returned. My body had healed slowly, but my mind was restless and hesitant to explore the truth. In time, I recalled driving to a location, feeling suddenly ill, sensing movement around me, and hearing voices. With these memories, I pulled away from schoolmates, isolating myself. I kept my head down during the day, silently battling the overwhelming urge to run.

One afternoon, about five days later, I could manage my workouts as my body slowly healed, and my mother approached me. She asked how I was feeling and mentioned that my grandmother had spoken to her about my situation. It felt as though I had thrust this situation into my grandmother's hands, hoping she could fix what I could not face myself. How could I tell my mother about this situation when I could not bring myself to tell my mother about the incident in the convenience store parking lot? I knew how that would affect and hurt her, and the idea of exposing my vulnerability frightened me.

We talked about what we knew: the injuries, the lab tests, and what little I could remember. As we spoke, I saw a shift in my mother. She became more than a parent; she became the professional caregiver, evaluating me with her eyes, always watching. I learned from my lab tests that showed a mix of alcohol and drugs in my system. She explained how dangerous the combination was. The conversation then moved to my appetite, sleep, studies, and workouts. I admitted to struggling with all of it: inconsistent sleep, poor focus, and a lack of motivation.

My mother warned me about the toxicity of the drugs I had ingested and how lethal they could be when mixed with alcohol. The weight of that information stunned me. As we sat in silence, she finally asked what I had dreaded: "Michael, based on this information, someone had intentions of harming you. Do you have any idea who that may be?"

I shook my head, unable to speak. She reached over and squeezed my hand, assuring me it was okay to talk. But I did not. I could not. Determined to process this as an adult, unwilling to admit I could not manage it. I had spent the past year fighting myself on the basketball court. Now, that struggle seemed trivial in comparison. My mother did not push. She simply reminded me she was there if I needed her, and that this would stay between us.

Feeling out of control terrified me. The inability to solve this mystery plagued me, and though my energy and focus eventually returned, I was no longer the same. Mistrust clouded my optimism about the upcoming basketball season. I immersed myself in training and playing at local gyms, trying to keep my mind busy.

Weeks later, my mother would intervene when she noticed me pushing too hard, trying to redirect the obsessive part of my personality. One example was when she learned the annual Cheerleaders Dance was coming up. Without telling me, she arranged a date, transportation, and dinner reservations. Though I resisted, I eventually gave in. The distraction was welcome, with basketball season just weeks away.

Looking back, I can see how this episode cemented a deeper mistrust, a sense that harm could find me anywhere, without warning, and that safety was never guaranteed. Even as I returned to training, to school, and to the rituals of basketball life, part of me stayed in that fog of disorientation, building walls no one else could see. It became another layer of abandonment, another place where I learned to endure in silence.

No matter who hurt, harmed, or tried to destroy you, keep being a good person.

Unexpected events occur, and I wanted to remember them. This was one of those times. It was the fall of 1979. The day was perfect, with warm sunshine and early fall-like temperatures not hinting at the approaching winter. I pulled into our driveway after school. My mother usually parked her car in the first spot in our driveway; today was no exception.

As I walked toward her car, I noticed the driver's side door was ajar. Looking inside, I saw her purse on the passenger seat. Strange, since my mother never left her purse on the seat while driving and would leave nothing in the car when she arrived home. As I pulled away from the driver's side door, I noticed a smear of blood on it. Alarmed, I pivoted my focus toward the back door of the house and called out to my mother.

There was no response.

I hurried up the walkway. Reaching the porch, I saw another smear of blood on the doorknob of the back door. I rushed inside and entered the kitchen. Another blood smear marked the counter to my right. Hearing the shower running in the bathroom, I focused on that sound. I walked down the hall, stood outside the door, and called my mother. Relief flooded through me when I heard her voice. "I'll be right out," she said.

As I turned back toward the hallway, I noticed a pile of clothes on the floor, my mother's nursing uniform splattered with blood. I sat on the floor near them, flooded with questions. When my mother appeared, wearing shorts and a T-shirt with her hair still wet, she looked like a different version of herself, younger, vulnerable.

I stood up, unsure of what to do. Instinctively, I reached out to comfort her. But she touched me first, checking me as if to confirm I was real.

"Are you okay?" she asked more than once.

Just moments earlier, I had worried about her, but now, something in my mother's demeanor shifted the focus to me. My unease turned inward. She finally broke the silence.

"I want to go somewhere," she said. "Anywhere."

Minutes later, we were walking, then running, through the wooded trails behind our house. The silence between us was steady and intentional. We ran through the next town before turning back. When we returned home, we prepared dinner together. The silence continued until my mother finally spoke.

That afternoon, my mother had been the first person on the scene of a motorcycle accident. The victim was a young man, barely in his twenties. He had crashed, leaving himself hanging upside down, and tangled around a guardrail. My mother rushed to his side, only to realize there was nothing she could do.

He drifted in and out of consciousness. All she could do was comfort him while waiting for the ambulance. As she told the story, her voice cracked, and I could see the weight of it all crashing down on her.

I listened, unable to ease her pain, knowing my presence was necessary. I had learned early on that sometimes just listening was enough.

Days and weeks passed. Then one day, I looked outside and saw my mother again, truly herself, standing in the garden with my grandmother. I walked over to them, and both embraced me in silence.

Their presence had always impressed me. From an early age, I had felt the strength and confidence they radiated. I wished I could absorb it for myself, to hold myself together the way they always seemed to.

The gift they gave me was my sensitivity, my ability to see, to feel, and to understand. But with that came the fear of not being able to sustain myself in their eyes.

They asked me to retrieve the gardening supplies from the garage. As I walked away, I turned back to see them. My mother caught my eye and smiled; a soft, familiar smile that told me she was okay.

At home, basketball practice began. The season brought structure to my life and a kind of mental cocoon, allowing me to focus on daily work with the team and escape the surrounding drama. The coaching staff seemed unaware of the situation involving the team. I hoped, as I had before, that the season would offer protection. In theory, this sounded promising, but I had seen coaches lean on the excuse of "kids will be kids." I saw it as a convenient line, and disingenuous.

Back to basketball, and the upcoming season. As a team, we practiced and met the goals set for us. I realized early in practice that I did not have anyone to compete against. My coach recognized this and apologized within the first two days.

Assigning two junior-varsity players to chase me around the gym proved ineffective. The situation sparked a new level of communication between us. I tried to take the challenge in stride, but it was difficult. I had taken for granted the value of having a skilled player to match up with each day in practice. That luxury was now gone after the '78 class graduated. For the next two seasons, I would have no one to practice against who could truly challenge me.

One day during preseason practice, we were scrimmaging full court. A teammate picked up a loose ball and pushed it down the floor on a two-on-one fast break. The play broke down and ended with the ball sailing out of bounds. We did not even get a shot off. A whistle blew. Our coach was clearly upset. Then he said loudly and clearly for everyone to hear, "From this play forward, we will only run a fast break unless Semiao has the ball in his hands. Is that clear?"

Standing on the other side of the court, I heard it plainly. The decision surprised and pleased me. But I also knew what would follow. The resentment. I could hear it already: "Who does he think he is?" "He's not that good."

Our team had lost seven seniors from the state finalist squad. None of the current players had logged meaningful varsity minutes. An example of this occurred when our coach tried to implement our full-court zone trap, thirty-four. Executed correctly, it created turnovers and fast-break chances. But we quickly discovered we did not have the quickness to execute even the first step: the trap in the corner.

We learned to play every position in 1978 under our coach's guidance. That group had experience and versatility. This team did not. Expectations needed to shift. Comparing this squad to the '78 team was unfair. Their chemistry, experience, and record were unmatched in southeastern Massachusetts.

We scheduled three preseason scrimmages against Coyle Cassidy High School, Silver Lake High School and Rockland High School, both on the road. I had connections to both programs, either through our head coach or through my experience with the New Bedford Buddies. The Rockland scrimmage surprised me; we had beaten them the previous year in the state tournament in the South Final.

We played well and won both scrimmages. I averaged twenty-six points in both scrimmages, and the Rockland's head coach, Bob Fisher, said, "We won't face a better guard all season." I was proud of how I had moved forward from the summer's hardships.

Preseason articles promoting my play and expectations circulated in the region and across the state. I expected recognition. I had worked hard. The Boston Globe article, "The Year of the Junior," featured me alongside other standouts, six of whom had been on the Youth Games team. I also appeared as an All-State preseason choice in the national newspaper Basketball Weekly. The attention, while deserved, stirred tension within the team. Players reacted. In the days before our first game, the whispers and jealousy rippled just under the surface.

In our season opener, our opponent played a box-and-one defense. I was the "one." The plan was to take the ball out of my hands. That strategy worked; but we still won the game. But our coaching staff had no solution for the defense, and the team did not seem concerned. The next day this sentiment surfaced: "We don't need him to be the leading scorer; we might not need him at all."

Having heard this conversation, I stayed in the gym until the locker room was clear and then grabbed my clothes and left without a shower. This response did not surprise me. Everyone freely expressed themselves so openly, without pausing or arguing. As if this was the team's dialog.

In the next game, just before tipoff, as the national anthem played, my head coach stood behind me and leaned closely. He whispered he wanted me to lead and to be a better teammate than I had been so far that season. The number of firsts I had experienced since enrolling at Fairhaven High School felt incalculable. And yet again, I felt off-balance, never good enough.

My coach's words frustrated me. The lack of a solid strategy to counteract a defense designed to remove or limit my effectiveness already preoccupied me. Did my disappointment appear selfish? If so, the coach's pre-game remarks made sense. But why wait until seconds before we stepped onto the court to bring it up?

The season itself turned out to be a disappointment for our team. In our fourth game, our captain sustained a hand injury that sidelined him for a large part of the season. We finished with a record of twelve wins and eight losses, which was not enough to qualify for the state tournament. Without our captain, opposing teams capitalized, employing gimmick defenses, box-and-one, triangle-and-two, which took our best players out of the game. These schemes specifically targeted me. My frustration continued to deepen as I realized we had no simple response to these defenses, not this season or the next.

Even though we won the first four and last six games of the season, we went two and eight during the stretch without our captain, and that cost us.

The anxiety I experienced began manifesting in new ways, creating a heightened sense of caution in every situation. The pattern of animosity that surrounded me was nothing new. This pattern had been developing since sixth grade. As the expectations grew, so did the scrutiny.

Someone once asked me, "Did you face any blowback when you came to Fairhaven High School for potentially taking playing time from someone else?"

My answer was, and still is, no. My feeling was, if someone wanted that time, they had every chance to compete for it. For me, it had always been about preparation and being ready to perform. No one stepped forward to the challenge for minutes when I arrived. Let me repeat that: no one.

The resentment I faced stemmed from those who believed they had waited their turn, who thought that time, not effort or improvement, would earn them a spot. Resenting my initiative. The unfortunate mantra that followed became clear and, unfortunately, familiar: "We'd rather lose without him than win with him."

As the season continued, the drama on and off the court washed away any hope I had of simply focusing on practices and games. When our captain went down, the coach appointed a co-captain to fill in, and he named me. The reaction? Indifference at best, resentment at worst. A core group of upperclassmen lacked trust and confidence in my abilities.

But like so many moments in those years, the incident disappeared into silence; school resumed, games continued, and on the surface, nothing had changed, yet inside, everything had shifted again.

By that winter, frustration with our losing record had curdled into something darker. Glances lasted longer. Jokes sounded sharper. I had sensed I was more than a player to blame; I was a target.

When the team was not winning, the blame landed squarely on my shoulders. I understood. It came with the territory. What I did not expect was the animosity from the broader school community. One student who had been harassing me and my family decided he wanted to fight me. Yes, fight me.

One day, while searching for a book in my locker, he came from behind and shoved me face-first into the metal locker. He had clearly been waiting. I stood up, and we exchanged words. I told him I would not fight him. He punched me in the chest, knocking me off balance and tearing my shirt. As I regained my footing, he landed another punch on my shoulder. I shoved him away, and he fell backward.

Thinking it was over, I turned to grab a T-shirt, but he rushed me again. I ducked one punch, but another landed hard in my ribs, exactly where I had suffered an injury in October. I grabbed him and threw him across the locker room. He landed at the feet of a school administrator, who looked at me and calmly said, "Get back to class. I will manage this."

They took no further action. No questions asked. No one said anything else.

I did not tell my parents, my sister, or my friends. I buried it and moved on. In health class, we learned about bullying and harassment, but no one taught us what to do when it found you. I became the scapegoat for losses I could not control, carrying both the bruises and the silence alone. My first instinct was to run, transfer schools, quit the team, escape, but where could I go? I had convinced everyone, including myself, that I was in control. But I was not. The pressure from classwork, basketball, and social expectations were collapsing around me. I tried to ignore the pain, not to look weak. Internally, I broke.

Still, the next day I stepped onto the court as if nothing had happened.

There are moments in a story that demand more than narrative. They demand pause. Reflection. A reckoning with questions that linger long after the chapter ends. This is one of those moments.

Why did I stay?

Why did I keep returning to the court, the classroom, the locker room, when I was clearly in harm's way?

There is no simple answer to this question.

The complexity behind my choice or my inability to leave is not just a matter of personal will. They stem from a place of survival, of perceived duty. It was not about protecting myself. It became about protecting my family, preserving tradition, and supporting the illusion of stability. I feared that stepping away would unravel everything I thought I was supposed to hold together.

Someone recently asked if parts of my story were triggering. I did not expect to confront these memories again, not with the weight they now carry. But revisiting them during this final editing phase has stirred deeper emotional undercurrents than I expected even now, decades later.

My response to pain was to disappear into practice. That became my shield. Drill harder. Focus deeper. Outwork the fear. But practice did not always save me. Sometimes, it pushed others away. Sometimes, it pushed me away from myself. The relationships I irreparably damaged, and those who were collateral damage in a war I did not know I was fighting.

The tension between harm and identity preservation is real. When you are inside it, it becomes your reality. The pain, the silence, the self-betrayal as normalization. They root deep. And even when they poison your clarity, you hold on, because letting go feels like letting go of yourself.

You did not stay because you did not care. You stayed because something in your wiring believed that leaving meant losing everything that defined you.

That is the truth I could not say back then. When an injury or illness struck, I did not just feel pain; I felt a threat to my very existence. I froze. Not physically, but emotionally. Mentally. How do you explain that paralysis to anyone?

Set the scene: one of the best basketball players in the state. Expected to lead. And yet, flat. Empty. You show up because you are supposed to. But inside? You are not ready. You are not OK, and neither are the surrounding people. They do not see it. Because you are still standing.

And that is the tragedy. But there's also grace.

In the end, I survived. Not triumphantly, but truthfully. With humility. With scars and gratitude. I have learned to honor the boy who endured, who faltered, but kept going. My survival is not a celebration of toughness; it is a quiet acknowledgment of growth.

This is not perfect. All of this is messy.

The Keepers: When the Silence Breaks

By the end of that season, something in me had gone quiet. The noise of the games, cheers, and headlines faded when I was alone. In its place came a space I had not known how to name, part exhaustion, part retreat, part survival. I did not yet understand that I was building a place inside myself where truths could surface before I could speak them aloud. What follows is not an event in the way a box score records one; it is when my inner world became visible enough for me to see it, and to give it form.

That silence became a kind of space, an opening where my inner voice, older, wiser, and unspoken, surfaced. In that stillness, I sensed what I could not yet name: not just exhaustion, but emotional injury. Not just isolation, but the fracture of trust.

And that is when I imagined them. Not ghosts, not visions, but the form my mind gave to truths I could not yet speak. They felt undeniably real because the pain behind them was. They did not interrupt the story; they revealed it.

I called them the Keepers.

One early spring afternoon, I stood alone in my driveway, working through my practice routines. The air was crisp, and the sunlight appeared too bright, as if trying to expose something hidden.

In that brightness, my mind summoned them, figures at the bottom of the driveway, familiar yet enigmatic. They were not actually there, not in the way a neighbor or passerby might be. They were how my mind gave shape to what I could not say aloud. Imagining them there brought an unusual sense of calm, a knowing smile forming before I even registered why. I knew them, yet I did not.

A question surfaced inside me: Is anyone home? Without hesitation, I answered, "No one is home." In my imagination, I let them follow me inside, turning my house into a secluded space cut off from time. Their voices, my own inner dialogue dressed as companions, carried a weight I could not yet place.

They spoke of my success, All-Scholastic, All-State, national recognition but the words felt hollow. "Not the success you wanted," one of them remarked. It was not a question. It was a truth I had yet to admit. They told me things I feared but could not face. "Rather fail without me than succeed with me." That my isolation was not accidental but orchestrated. They came for me. The sudden jolt I felt when those words snapped me out of my daze: "Michael, DO YOU UNDERSTAND!" Like a thunderclap echoing through a valley, rolling until it washes over you. You shudder in response. My breath is quick, gasping for air. I suddenly fell but kept upright in my mind.

I listened until the words blurred. My body went rigid. This was not just a story. This was my story. When I blinked back into focus, the house was quiet, and I was alone again, standing with a truth that was too painful to grasp.

Through the troubling days that followed, The Keepers reached far beyond my life. I pictured them as guardians who had whispered to athletes, poets, and leaders across time, unseen hands who guided those who walked alone.

Whether any of that was real did not matter. At seventeen years old, it was how I made sense of my isolation and ambition, how I convinced myself that the silence I carried was not emptiness but belonged to a larger story.

In time, the figures faded, but the language they gave me remained. The Keepers were never supposed to stay as separate beings. Looking back now, I see them not as ghosts or visions, but as the first honest conversation I had with myself. They allowed me to survive what I could not yet articulate, to keep moving forward even when I felt erased. When I returned to the driveway, to practice, to school hallways and bus rides, I carried their words inside me not as prophecy, but as a promise that I could endure.

The spring basketball tournaments with the New Bedford Buddies were a week away. They would offer a distraction to bury this story beneath the noise of competition. For now, that would have to be enough. Unfortunately, my play left me. The complications from this past season with my high school team resulted in challenges I preferred to avoid confronting. I struggled throughout the off-season tournament season, where I had hoped for a reprieve from the noise that continued to surround me.

My play, and lack of effectiveness, fractured my relationship with the Buddies head coach. As with all my relationships, my tendency was, unfortunately, to apply a purity test to each situation and relationship. The defense mechanisms I have developed followed the psychological definition of "splitting." Where individuals perceive themselves, others, or situations in all-or-nothing terms, either as entirely good or entirely bad, without ever recognizing the complexities and nuances in between. It made sense to me now, years later, where the fallout from those past seasons ended up crashing at my feet.

There was one exception during this period, and it was the New Bedford Recreation Tournament. We faced the Roxbury Titans in the semifinals. Thinking I was prepared for the intensity the Titans would bring to this game left me naked. The gym was standing room only. I would normally have thrived in this type of atmosphere, but my play was less than inspiring. In this game, my major contribution was scoring twenty-six points, making ten of twelve field goals and six free throws. That was all I had. My attempts to contribute to other phases of the game were missing. We scrambled at the end, applying a fouling sequence that forced them to make foul shots. It was an ingenious strategy, but we still came up short.

My father reintroduced me to the game of tennis. It became my outlet, saving me from the awful results my team and I were experiencing. I finished the spring off-season tournaments without winning a championship, placing runner-up in three of the five tournaments we played. Not awful, but our standards and expectations were much higher. I stepped away for a period to regroup. My father and I picked up our tennis racquets and played three times a week, indoors and outdoors. These welcome distractions had an immediate benefit. Professional instruction and tournament play followed. With my mind focused on something else, allowing myself to fail felt liberating. Not having any expectations guided me through the end of the spring and into the summer.

As my tennis acumen increased, so did my interest in measuring myself against competition. My unflinching competitive spirit returned. It turned out I could hit well, but I lacked strategy. I learned to read my opponents' weaknesses, use my athletic ability to win points, play within myself, and, most importantly, not beat myself. I came away from the competitions encouraged, granted a tryout for a local tennis team, received new tennis rackets, and renewed my commitment to the game I once loved.

With sports came the inevitability of injuries. Those injuries fit into categories, where the more serious ones receive professional assessments, while others require treatment and rest; most were annoyances I learned to tolerate. Up to that point in my athletic life, I had been fortunate to experience limited downtime.

The following foreshadowing events affected me throughout my adult life. From an early age, while playing tennis and receiving professional instruction, I experienced pain in my right leg, my buttock and hamstring after matches or practice sessions. Interestingly, I did not feel this pain during activity, only afterward. Trying to ease the discomfort, I developed my own stretching techniques. I kept the pain to myself. After rigorous stretching, the pain would disappear overnight, and I would wake up pain-free. This cycle continued, with the pain present only after physical exertion and resolving by the next morning.

The summer of 1979 marked a turning point in my basketball career. After careful deliberation with my family, we decided I would not return *to Five Star* Basketball Camp. This was not a simple decision. Competing at that level required mental resilience, which, disappointingly, I did not have after the challenges of my high school season. Instead, I went back to the *All-New England* Basketball Camp in Connecticut, which I had attended the previous summer. Though unsure of this choice, rooming with someone familiar provided comfort. My experiences at camps, often attended without a familiar face, had left a deep impact on me.

Attending basketball camp away from home, oddly enough, lifted the weight of expectation I had been carrying. Away from familiar pressures, I played my best basketball in over a year. Over five days, my play was consistent and strong. My team won the camp championship. I was the camp MVP, and I won the MVP award in the camp counselor game. For the first time in a long time, I felt like I had found myself on the basketball court.

The adjustments I made when attending the camp during the summer of 1979 were subtle. I was more attentive during the week, focusing on instructions from coaches, tuning in to camp lectures. Finally, my disappointment earlier in the summer motivated me. That week, I was on top of my game from the first minute I stepped onto the campgrounds. The overall maturity I showed during the week made all the difference.

Dan Doyle, the head coach at Trinity University, the previous summer had a frank and honest conversation with my dad about my performance and areas for improvement. Returning that summer, his acknowledgment of my maturity, leadership, and improved play was unexpected but gratifying. However, I valued outcomes beyond awards or accolades. I was rediscovering the joy of the game and the respect of my teammates, something I had been desperately searching for without fully realizing it.

Returning from basketball camp, my summer league play began in New Bedford, Fairhaven, and Taunton. Returning from camp, I suffered a back injury on my left side that did not respond to treatment for weeks. The pain was debilitating, limiting my play, and diminishing my confidence. Eddie Rodrigues, a former player who was refereeing one of my summer league games, noticed my struggles one cool July night. A brief conversation with him, where he expressed concern and support, reminded me people were paying attention and rooting for my success.

The origin of the injury was unclear, and I worried it might become chronic. Rest, stretching, and heat-and-ice treatments provided little relief, and my performance suffered. I fell out of shape, and my basketball timing and confidence seemed to vanish. Each morning, I woke up hoping to be pain free, only to face disappointment. I was concerned about a series of matters about my back injury. The lack of a clear path to treat the injury scared me. In my desperate moments, my thought was that my athletic life was suddenly over. The pain I was experiencing every day was not diminishing. The thought of stripping away who or what I had become was incalculable. Those feelings you believed people had placed on you would be gone, the walls of protection you have built would no longer be necessary. Unthinkable. Start over? How?

Weeks later, my father, always thinking creatively, found a chiropractor. This was new ground for my family, since I was not even sure we knew what chiropractic care was. Acknowledging I was in desperate straits, I took the appointment my father made for me. After a complete examination, the diagnosis was an inflamed disc in my lower back causing misalignment. This was the source of my pain. After my first chiropractic adjustment, I was pain free for the first time in weeks. I returned to basketball, managing the injury with regular check-ups throughout the summer. The physical setback taught me to listen to my body and prioritize recovery.

My team was playing at Monte Playground the following week. This opportunity reminded me of the trajectory ahead of me. First, I had to play a configuration of the New Bedford High School team, and second, I had never played at Monte Playground.

Monte Playground had an unparalleled reputation for generational competition. Those courts had traits identified with them almost analogous. Ethereal proportions of legacy survived and felt as if you could reach out and touch it.

My discussion with my father the afternoon before the game was about my long-term health. Understanding his point and the stated consequences, I agreed not to play if five players were available. My dad agreed.

Entering Monte Playground, one hears the sounds reverberate through the park. Four players were available for my team. The stars had aligned. I walked down the stairs from the basketball courts to retrieve my basketball gear. With my metamorphosis complete, I recognized I was missing basketball shorts and protection for this game. I was wearing cut-off jean shorts. This display counteracted my considered reasoning. I stopped on the pavement below the basketball courts, uncertain whether to continue. My dad's statement was in my head. Was it worth endangering my health for a summer league game? Probing for an answer or a sign, I ascended the stairs to the basketball courts. The virtue of competition, and placing myself on the edge, drew me forward.

I played and dominated in every aspect of the game. Playing with five players, undersized, I took control, and we won a close game. When the game concluded, I spoke with Mr. Wilson, who was aware of my injury and had considered it during our discussion. Emotions felt raw. The decision to invest in a summer league game and its qualifications concerned me. I recognized that this exercise was not continuous, but tasting it, uncovering it, and presenting it for all to see was exhilarating.

In explaining my decisions to my dad, I accepted the impractical view. When the conversation finished, he asked, "How was the game? How did you play?" I told him we had won, and that I had played well.

Drawing myself down, accepting my identification with the competitive structure cultivated for me, I craved and coveted more. I was uncertain how to pull it out of myself. The night drifted into morning. I woke reinforced by the opportunities. I accepted it, wishing to grab it.

The following afternoon, my dad had lunch downtown in New Bedford. An assortment of conversations about my game the previous night occurred during lunch. Back at home, my dad asked why I had not mentioned how well I had played.

Despite the early challenges, I completed the summer league schedule without further injury. By balancing exercise with rest and therapy, I could regain my form.

My team won the Taunton and Fairhaven summer league championships. Despite tougher competition in the New Bedford league and my team's second-round playoff loss, I still earned an all-star choice. Reflecting on the summer, I felt a sense of accomplishment, especially considering I had played through injury.

Throughout my basketball career, speculation about which school I would attend next followed me. Every season, local newspapers publish articles about potential prep school opportunities or transfers. While these stories often lacked substance, they reflected the curiosity surrounding my next move.

Each summer, my parents and I had candid discussions about my future as a student-athlete. While unsettling, those conversations were necessary. I understood the importance of considering all options, even if it meant moving to a new school. The unpredictability of those discussions mirrored the larger uncertainties I faced in my basketball career.

Chapter Seven

Fairhaven High School, Senior Year, 1979-1980

During the fall of 1979, the *Colonel Daniel Marr Boys Club* of Dorchester, Massachusetts, held its Fifth Annual Basketball Preview Tournament. The New Bedford Buddies were one of four invited teams. Each roster featured nationally and statewide recognized players. The Buddies' first game was against a powerhouse squad that included Patrick Ewing, Martin Clark, Karl Hobbs, and Tim O'Shea. We could not match their size inside and lost a high-scoring, close game. They scheduled the third-place game for 11:00 a.m. the next morning.

Despite the quick turnaround, we played hard and won convincingly, securing third place. They named me one of the five All-Tournament selections. During the second half of our game, I noticed college coaches arriving early for the championship game. During the second half, I noticed my father looking amazingly comfortable with the coaches that were then on site. My father had relationships with Rick Pitino, John Calipari, and Vic Colucci. He developed those relationships during his time in Honesdale, Pennsylvania, when I was at *Five Star* Basketball Camp. Later that day, I found out my father had been networking with those coaches, seeking advice and gauging interest in college opportunities for me. As of that weekend, I had not committed to any school.

My performance in the two-day tournament encouraged me. I kept excellent form and adjusted to the style of play in each game. In the first game, I focused on scoring. In the second game, I assumed the role of floor general, controlling the tempo and distributing the ball. My performance pleased me, though the team's result was disappointing.

A side note: the animosity between my coach and the coach of Ewing's team affected the tournament draw. The tournament draw ensured we would not be facing each other in the final. We were the better matchup, and our presence might have disrupted the showcase planned for Ewing's team.

This was the last time I played in this gym, a place that had been a proving ground since eighth grade. Pickup games, sanctioned events, and the chance to assess my skills against elite competition had defined that space. Yet the gym's exterior, covered in graffiti, always reminded me of the racial and socioeconomic tension embedded in the area. My father often pointed out how fortunate I was to live the life I had, and I never took that for granted. Sports opened my eyes and sometimes slapped me in the face. What I experienced in moments was the daily reality for others.

One afternoon I had a study period and requested to substitute it with gym class. Wanting to blow off steam, I asked to run the track. Once outside, I noticed our football team's punter was practicing. I approached and asked if he wanted help shagging punts. With a shrug, he agreed.

I wore only a T-shirt, shorts, socks, and sneakers, which was inappropriate attire for the task. I lacked traction and padding. What I did not expect was the height, speed, and sound of the punts. The footballs descended with a whip-like snap, and I caught a third of them. Most bounced off my hands or forearms, leaving them bruised and red.

Just as I debated whether to stop, I heard someone yelling my name. Looking up, I recognized the head football coach moving quickly in our direction. As he got closer, his shouting grew louder. "Stop!"

He stormed up to me and asked what I was doing.

"Shagging punts," I replied with a straight face.

That answer only made him angrier. He examined my bruised forearms and said, "What were you thinking? What if you broke a finger or a hand? Wayne Wilson would have my ass!" Then, pointing toward the school, he ordered us back to class.

Later in the school year, my parents ran into the head football coach at a local restaurant. When he shared the story with them, they all laughed at my audacity. My intentions were pure, and that was how they interpreted it.

Moments like that, where I threw myself into something without thinking, were becoming more common. I once thought I could outrun consequences on a basketball court. But in the weeks that followed, I learned there were other battles I couldn't outrun. My body was about to make that clear.

It started with a persistent skin rash; thought to be a reaction to a new fabric softener my mother had used weeks earlier. What seemed like a simple explanation became a month-long ordeal as the rash spread across my underarms, arms, and chest. Despite the discomfort and embarrassment, I kept silent, managing the symptoms with chamomile lotion. My mother noticed stains on my sheets and clothes, leading to a dermatologist's visit. A week of treatment cleared the rash, but the experience left me humbled and reminded me to speak up, a lesson my mother reinforced during multiple quiet conversations.

While at home, I struggled to assert my independence while navigating strict rules about curfews, phone calls, and relationships. The resulting tension created an almost unbearable atmosphere. Basketball provided an outlet; playing for the New Bedford Buddies and traveling for games became my escape. The late nights and disrupted routines took their toll on my sleep, diet, and academics, further straining my relationship with my parents.

One afternoon, while doing chores in our yard, I noticed a rash spreading across my groin area. Feeling overwhelmed, I confided in my mother. My mother, hoping to mitigate the situation, had me stop my chores. In the next breath, I was showering and changing my clothes. From my room, I overheard a loud conversation taking place between my parents, my mother's voice; "You need to fix this." Minutes later, I was in the car with my father heading to the hospital. In the emergency room, the familiar phrase, "Look at me," prompted my weary eyes to lift toward him. "You know everything will be all right." His words transported me back to my childhood, a time when his presence meant unquestioned security. The diagnosis of acute hives and a B12 shot brought immediate relief, and for the first time in months, I slept. This incident, though, made me reconsider my pursuit of independence.

Anxiety had a way of making itself known in my body before my mind even recognized it. While others could mask their stress, mine surfaced so I could not hide welts rising across my skin, a physical betrayal of the turmoil I fought to control. Chronic hives became my uninvited companion, appearing whenever my mind decided I had pushed too far.

I tried to rationalize it, blaming the food I ate, the tightness of a shirt collar, the pressure of a waistband. But deep down, I knew it was something more. My mind was reacting to something I could not name, an internal war manifesting as a visible, undeniable mark. The more I tried to ignore it, the worse it became. How do face failure each day? My emotional state said that the existence of those welts covering your body was a failure; you had failed. What do you do about that feeling? I did not have an answer. I covered my body, attended school, took part in basketball practice and games, and hoped people wouldn't see me as a failure.

The number of failures I had recognized significantly affected my resilience. Yes, I was hard on myself, and these projections may have put me or led me to this point. I did not know how to recognize stress formerly. Not addressing the image, my image, which I had worked so hard to preserve. My ego was all about how one looked or was about what I wanted people to see. I hated it; it made me feel vulnerable. Appearance had always been a shield, a way to protect myself from judgment. And now, my mind and body were turning against me, disrupting the illusion of invincibility I thought I had built.

A cruel trick played on my nervous system. It was as if my mind had unlocked a hidden weakness, one I could not out-think or outmaneuver. If I could control their appearance, why couldn't I stop them? The frustration fed my anxiety, creating a cycle I could not break. Each outbreak convinced me I was losing control, showing my body would always remind me of its limits, despite my efforts.

The first byproduct of managing visible skin conditions was that you kept everyone at arm's length away from you. Because of past traumas, I sank inward even more. I was afraid to engage with my classmates, teachers, or teammates. I was always waiting for the next outbreak. In the end, thankfully, I never had to deal with that level of embarrassment.

As basketball practice began, my head coach named me team captain, a role I expected and welcomed. Preseason scouting reports cited my experience as the linchpin of our success. My focus, however, remained steadfast: qualifying for the state tournament. This goal overshadowed all else.

The preseason article in our local newspaper before the 1979-1980 season included this from our head coach: "As far as all-around ability, he's the best around." While I appreciated those words, I always wished for this recognition earlier in our relationship. This was part of my personality, always wanting more.

It was always about the shots I missed, not the ones I made. The striving for perfection, though not realistic, circled my mind as I got older, always wondering if you could play perfectly. What would that feel like? Would it matter in the end? Last season, our captain's injury altered my relationship with my coach. Suddenly, communication was straightforward and purposeful. As with all relationships, it was not perfect, and it took a conscious effort on both of our parts to make it work.

Preseason recognition came in abundance. Regional and national publications included me on the All-Scholastic and All-American lists. *Street &*

Smith's magazine was a highlight. These accolades felt like a payoff for years of sacrifice and hard work. Along with this recognition came unexpected reunions: former coaches, old classmates, and even people I had not spoken to in years reached out to reconnect. Despite the years and changes, these conversations felt seamless, as though no time had passed.

During preseason practice, an innocuous play left my right forearm swollen and painful. By the next day, the pain intensified, and a doctor put a plastic cast on my arm for a week. The cast became a talking point at school, attracting unsolicited attention from students and teachers. Flashing back to my sophomore year where a miscommunication surrounding an injury led to distrust and a fragmented relationship with the coaching staff. I at once informed my coach of my limited ability and my timeline with this injury.

In one drill, I improvised a left-handed jump shot, a skill honed through countless driveway hours. To my teammates' surprise, I made the shot. The head coach, however, ended the drill, wary of encouraging others to emulate the play. Later, he asked me not to shoot left-handed, a frustrating but understandable request.

Practice often felt stifling. For the second season, my coach assigned two junior varsity players to guard me. This was to simulate a single competent defender. Their job was to shadow me everywhere on the court. My coach continued to be wary of my advanced skills. Restricting creative plays, like behind-the-back or tap passes. He concluded the drill by saying, "If I don't permit him to do it, no one else should either." The expectation to "play down" was frustrating, but I understood it.

The season began with elevated expectations but also new challenges. In the first game, I scored a career-high thirty-three points, silencing any doubts about my readiness. The local newspaper featured me the next day, dedicating an entire page to my performance, an interview I had given weeks earlier and a full-page caricature. While the attention was flattering, it brought added pressure.

As the season moved forward, each day required meticulous planning to avoid visible reactions. Despite my efforts, a strenuous day at school led to a substantial outbreak prior to our home opener, which left me self-conscious and distracted. During the game, as if I did not need any further distractions, my back seized up for the first time in weeks. While my teammates carried us to victory, I limped home to recover.

An early chiropractic visit on Saturday morning relieved the stress and alignment problems. The visit to the chiropractor suddenly evolved quickly into weekly scheduled visits, hoping to stay ahead of any further serious issues.

The following week brought our first loss of the season and a new low for me. I had to wear a T-shirt under my uniform to hide the rash that I was suddenly experiencing. The visible reminder of my struggles continued to twist my mind. My father's unexpected presence in the locker room after the game conveyed his concern. While he tried to reassure me, I felt hyper and unable to articulate my feelings. The weight of my performance, my injury, and my health bore down on me.

The next day, Saturday morning, I found myself back at the dermatologist's office, discussing yet another medication possibility to manage my worsening hives. The consistent side effects of the medication I had been taking were drowsiness, lack of appetite, and irritability. All of that contributed to my inability to play with clarity. Also, the difficulty of scheduling medication doses had become increasingly troublesome to manage. My recent struggles during a game underscored the urgency of finding a better solution. My anxieties, unchecked, had reached a point where it felt like I had to shout to be heard, even as I battled this internal turmoil.

I knew the prescribed medication offered limited relief. When I first learned about this medication and that it would "control the hives," my mind was screaming, "CONTROL?!" Not once during the series of exams would I hear the word eliminate. I was not interested in controlling anything. But this is where everything landed: manage, control, and mitigate damage.

The new medication brought much-needed consistency to my life. Body checks, once constant, became less stressful as outbreaks diminished. I no longer needed to wear a T-shirt under my uniform, and the drowsiness faded. I experienced only one episode for the rest of the basketball season. Overall, the new medication worked. Yet, the emotional and physical toll of the previous weeks lingered, coloring my experience for the balance of my senior year.

A stretch of games from January 4th through January 29th. Eight games. I played my best basketball. Dominant. More importantly, I played freely without pause. Unfortunately, my psychological struggles remained.

With that, a conversation rang through my mind. My coach emphasized teamwork over individual dominance. "Do you want to lead the league in scoring or take this team to the state tournament?" he asked. The answer was obvious: the team came first. As noted, there were games when I had to take control. Reminding anyone who had doubts, my dominance in those moments highlighted both my skill and capability.

During a game against Dartmouth High School at their gym, I reached a new level of perspective about my chronic hives. Throughout the day at school, I felt out of sorts. My familiar burdens surprised me; I could not push through. Why couldn't I work through this? Was this situation really any different from all the others?

My psychological response goes back to fight, flight or freeze mode. The adrenal glands release stress hormones like adrenaline and cortisol, which increase heart rate and breathing. The "freeze" response involves a general shutdown of non-essential functions and heightened awareness of potential threat, in this case, perceived failure or negative judgement.

Each day, I already needed careful management of my medication, food intake, and rest. This time, however, numbness gripped my play, and I stayed frozen. That never happened before, nor would it happen again.

My father, for the second time that season, visited me in the locker room after the game, something he had never done in earlier seasons. That concerned me. He was showing his hand, and though I knew it came from a place of love and concern, the gesture made the situation feel more serious than I wanted to admit.

With the last home game of the season and the school administrators planned a ceremony to honor our retiring head coach. As captain, I had collected contributions for a gift and prepared a speech. Fairhaven High School did not traditionally host senior nights, so the event came as a surprise. The unexpected tribute disrupted our pregame routine, leaving us unfocused.

Our opponent used a triangle-and-two defense. This was not a surprise. The history of that school versus our school and specifically me was to play a gimmick defense. This defense limited my effectiveness during the game. I got into foul trouble and sat out the third quarter. Early in the fourth quarter, my coach put me back in the game with four fouls. I discovered I could make plays and potentially put us in a position to win the game. After a timeout, with four seconds left, I hit a 20-foot jump shot to win the game.

After the game, I approached the opposing coach (as I customarily did) and extended my hand to offer "a nice game." He looked at me and yelled, "Fuck you, Semiao." Stunned, I turned back toward him, unsure if I had heard him correctly. A player from the opposing team and his father stepped in, urging me to walk away. My father, now by my side, placed an arm around my waist and guided me to the locker room. The surreal encounter faded into the background as I showered and left the gym.

The next day at practice, my coach asked me about the incident. I confirmed it. Later that week, the school principal inquired as well. Months later, school and league officials met and suspended the opposing coach. The situation gained attention, but not the kind I wanted. I was not seeking an apology. I just wanted to move on. Unexpectedly, the incident took on a life of its own.

I cannot pinpoint the moment everything shifted, only that it did.

The incident did not involve a dramatic explosion or a definitive breaking point. It was more like the slow withdrawal of something I did not know I depended on. A quiet retreat.

One day, the ground beneath me no longer felt solid, and the walls that once felt like home felt foreign.

I still went to practice. Still got up and did the work. But I started carrying something else, something I could not name, that felt heavier by the day. A kind of emotional static surrounded me. Conversations at home became clipped, or overly polite. Doors closed more softly, but they stayed closed.

Around me, relationships I trusted fractured. There were shifts in loyalty, changes in tone, and looks that felt different from they had before. I felt like people were seeing me differently. Others left, turned away, or simply vanished.

There are moments in life when the truth becomes too heavy for the people who once held it with you. And when that happens, you either speak into the void... or you carry it like a stone. My personality carried it.

It is only now, with distance and language which I did not have then, that I can admit this: I stayed silent, not because I did not trust them. I stayed silent because I could not bear to be the one who brought the house of cards down.

So, I held it. All of it.

And it was too much for someone my age. But it felt like the only way to survive *and* to protect what still felt whole.

The world did not slow down for what I was holding. Senior year pushed forward. The games resumed. College conversations surfaced. People around me spoke of plans as if everything were immutable.

But I had already crossed an invisible line.

Something in me had shifted, not in a way that anyone could see. I felt in every conversation, every decision, every silence I let linger just a little longer than before.

I had learned to live with a kind of dual awareness: what I showed and what I knew. And as I stepped back into the rhythms of school, basketball, and expectations, I carried both.

It is always both.

MIAA State Tournament 1980
Game One: vs Archbishop Williams at
Braintree High School

In my senior year, my one goal was to lead my team to the state tournament. This mattered because I wanted to prove I could lead us there. When we qualified, I realized how important it was to me. During the season, our head coach, Mr. Wilson, announced his retirement, making the tournament even more significant.

The late-season performance of our team was inconsistent. During the regular season, my deferential role felt right. But in the tournament, I knew the ball had to go through my hands more often for our team to be truly effective.

Our opponent started with a 2-3 zone defense. From the start, I played aggressively. I refused to defer at that moment. I scored twelve points in the first quarter and finished with nineteen points and eleven assists. Setting an aggressive tone helped us dominate, winning 64-42.

◇ ◆ ◇

"Point to the Passer" has been a tradition for the University of North Carolina basketball program. Since the Dean Smith era, coaches have instructed players who score to acknowledge their teammates who aided them by pointing at them and expressing gratitude.

In the second half of our first-round game, we ran a motion offense. This allowed me to use my off-the-ball skills. Since transferring to Fairhaven High School, my role has been to run the team. Opportunities to play off the ball were rare.

I made a sharp cut to the basket, and our center found me with a perfect pass. I scored with a powerful drive. To show appreciation, I pointed at him, recognizing his play. We connected on two more similar plays that quarter. Each time, I returned the same gesture.

The next day at school, a teacher asked me about the game. He was curious about my gesture. I found his interest both frustrating and tedious. Explaining nuanced communication in high-level sports is difficult for someone unfamiliar with it.

The explanation I offered came from the same perspective as Dean Smith. Among the subtle and thoughtful strategies Coach Smith introduced was the practice of pointing to the passer, a thank you to teammates for their willingness to share the ball.

Game Two: vs Nauset High School at New Bedford Vocational High School

Playing our second state tournament game at New Bedford Vocational School's gym felt like a home game. This gym brought mixed emotions to me. My teams had excellent results on this court, never losing in the four games our school played there. The unfortunate shadow that exists for me on this court goes back to the 1978 state tournament's south sectional final when we defeated Seekonk in overtime. I never forgot how our head coach's words devastated me at the end of that game. That was then, and this was now.

Nauset came into this game with a 19-1 record. They could not play with us, or with me. Another strong effort by our team, winning 53-33. I finished with a game-high fourteen points. Not my best game. One would have thought that playing in a familiar gym would have been beneficial, not a distraction. But it was. Thankfully, my performance did not affect the team moving on to the next round.

Game Three: vs South Boston at Brockton High School, South Sectional Quarterfinals

As expected, the competition intensified as we advanced in the state tournament. This time, we did not have enough to compete with a talented and hungry team. We made a late run, but our top scorer and I carried more plays than usual. Our inexperienced players struggled under pressure. Another season of varsity play would have helped them, but that is not how it worked out. It was a known fact that our school lacked the depth of larger programs.

I was proud of our effort and performance that season. Despite my personal conflicts, I saw where we succeeded. There were a series of issues that haunted me. I always hoped that my personal struggles did not take away from our accomplishments. Knowing the senior leadership on this team was going to create a vacuum of talent the next season. I always hoped the younger players would develop early so that they could gain experience for their upcoming seasons. This would not happen.

At season's end, I made every all-star team in the state. I earned an All-Scholastic award for the third year, and I was an All-State choice for the second year. Publications like *Basketball Weekly* and *Street & Smith* recognized me. Fairhaven High School honored me with the Principal's Award, and I also signed a letter of intent to attend Bryant College.

Back in seventh grade, high schools and colleges began recruiting me. As I have said, all of this was new to me and my parents. We went ahead as if we were prepared for this, but we were not. We would learn about the recruiting process together. Over the years, local, regional, and national interests grew. Hindered by my physical location in southeastern Massachusetts, we realized off-season tournaments and basketball camps were the best opportunities to bring more attention to my abilities.

The daily and weekly recruiting process, while ego-boosting, felt surreal. It was noteworthy and important to understand the authenticity of who and what you were. Not losing yourself in conversations that might include exaggerated promises. Navigating through this constructed reality could easily lead to confusion and disorientation. Even though the circumstances were often uncertain, I understood my identity and where I could best use my abilities. This was among the valuable lessons I received from my father. Do not fall for false promises or ads; stay honest, and excellent results will come. These words and sentiments carried me a long way, even when I felt myself drifting away.

As a family, we did not decide on my next steps until after the first of the year in 1980. The eventual choice of Bryant College was based on strong academics and participation in the competitive Northeast-10 Conference. The basketball program was among the top ten nationally ranked teams for the 1979-1980 season.

Here is a sample of the recruiting interest I received from the time I was in seventh grade through high school. Over three hundred letters of interest arrived from colleges over six years:

- Stonehill College: the requirements included a year of prep school, followed by admission as a walk-on basketball player and a three-season scholarship.
- Providence College: a more complicated process, but it mirrored what Stonehill College proposed. This opportunity evaporated when Head Coach Dave Gavitt resigned. I had always dreamed of playing at Providence College.
- Holy Cross: there was a path forward for me if I had stayed at Holy Family High School. The Holy Cross basketball program was introduced to me during my freshman year while at Holy Family.
- Iona University: during the summer of 1978, after attending *Five Star* Basketball Camp, my father received a call from Iona University's head coach, Jim Valvano. The program was trying to transition to become a major Division I school. The interest flattered me, but I was unsure if I could play at that level. Any potential offers disappeared when Valvano left for North Carolina State in 1980.
- Trinity College: a Division III school with no athletic scholarships. I received sincere consideration after I won most valuable player (MVP) award at the *All-New England* Basketball Camp during the summer of 1979.
- Naval Academy: multiple phone calls and a recruiting visit to our home during my junior year of high school. My parents met with the representative, and discussions about my attending the Naval Academy continued throughout my senior season. My grades were not strong enough for admission.
- The University of Pennsylvania: between my sophomore and junior years in high school, Penn's recruitment was the most consistent of any other school. My academic record fell short of admission standards.
- Tabor Academy expressed interest over two years, 1979 and 1980. They offered to invest in my education for three years, beginning with a prep year and pushing my college admission out to at least 1983. After

weighing up every aspect of the opportunity, my family and I decided I would stay at Fairhaven High School.

- Bryant College was a late addition to the recruitment process, which took place during my senior year. A visit from Bryant College's head coach, Leon Drury, following our game versus Dartmouth High School. These discussions led to an official visit to Bryant College's campus.

In the spring of 1980, my father and I visited Bryant College to make it official and sign a National Letter of Intent (NLI) to attend Bryant College. We are meeting at the president's office. The Bryant head coach Leon Drury, assistant coach Mike McQuinn and sports information director John Gillooly joined us.

William T. O'Hara, the president of Bryant College, was telling all of us about a *60 Minutes* segment on Bobby Knight, the head basketball coach at the University of Indiana. The president was quite impressed with Coach Knight and his philosophy regarding student athletes.

After my high school season, local newspapers announced my scholarship to Bryant College. One was from the *Standard Times* and featured my head coach, Mr. Wilson, and me in an interview and photo. I reflected on our growth together; how our relationship began and where it ended was remarkable.

The other article appeared in a local weekly, *The Advocate*, where our assistant coach, Gil Viera, served as editor-in-chief. This article had a different tone, more celebratory.

The attention I received from local papers marked a peak in my public journey. On the outside, it seemed like everything was falling into place. Yet privately, something else was unraveling. As the accolades arrived, so too did a strange and silent reckoning. While others celebrated the outcome, I confronted the cost.

As the basketball season ended, my acute hives, and chronic back injury disappeared. Yes, the back symptoms and my skin virus disappeared. With the symptoms gone, I realized how my anxiety had taken control of my life. When the physical symptoms vanished, I felt temporary relief. Then, I focused on understanding what had happened. I searched for explanations and solutions, trying to make sense of everything. The anxiety remained, leaving me feeling alone in the moment. I assumed that once my physical symptoms stopped, I would be fine. When that did not happen, as an eighteen-year-old, what are your options? Deep introspective thoughts? Not likely. Professional analysis, definitely not. You turn the page, walk through the next door, find the next distraction that will occupy your mind. That is what I did. Réoussite ou échec, I could not judge.

My attempts to understand my feelings became the most difficult to manage. Honesty was in short supply. Again, I faced my inability to cope with and confront what had been plaguing me. The constant pressure I put on myself to solve this problem put me in a difficult position. My mother's advice, her mantra of "be kind to yourself," left me wanting more. Somehow, this thought sat with me. Did I position myself as a willing victim? Did I somehow bring this upon myself unwittingly? Now, with the physical symptoms gone, I had to grapple with the emotional pain, which was an entirely different matter.

The spring of 1980 brought another season with the New Bedford Buddies. Complexities suddenly surrounded me because the Bryant head coach was arranging for me to play with a team competing in the Open Division. With my preparation less than ideal, and since the end of the basketball season, I had not picked up a basketball in weeks. Instead, I focused on tennis, preparing for the upcoming Fairhaven High School tennis season. Returning to the basketball court felt daunting, reminding me of recent struggles and pain.

My performance in the first game was dismal. Our coach benched me out of frustration, and afterward, my father gave me two options: quit or fix my game. The next day, as one would expect, I spent six hours in my driveway, rediscovering the rhythm of the game. My improvement was noticeable in later games, though my shooting remained inconsistent.

Playing in the open and senior divisions demanded a level of basketball commitment I had not expected. Sometimes, I played two games a night. This was draining.

Overthinking every aspect of the schedule sets the stage for failure. This pattern of self-sabotage had become familiar. Still, I helped lead my team in the senior division to the finals, forcing overtime with a 25-foot jump shot. We would lose the championship game. Despite my inconsistency, my overall play earned all-tournament honors. With that, I caught glimpses of my former self.

My team in the Open Division won the championship. I excelled in this division only because the players we competed against did not know me. My youthful arrogance reappeared when I took offense that the opponents did not show any respect towards my game. The lack of familiarity, which is a role I had thrived in the past, where you could drift for an entire game and just take and make open shots.

The Waltham Tournament was next on the calendar of off-season tournaments with the New Bedford Buddies. They held the tournament at the Waltham Boys Club. This tournament was especially significant for me. I played here as a freshman, experiencing my earliest basketball success. This time, however, things felt different. I struggled through the first game, controlling the pace more out of necessity than strategy. My coach praised me for dictating the tempo, but I knew I was masking my lack of stamina.

In the second game, a defensive play surprised me. Running back to defend a three-on-two fast break, I planted myself to take a charge. The impact knocked the wind out of me. This play shook me physically and emotionally, and I realized how unprepared I was. My mind flashed back to a similar play years earlier when I had avoided contact with this type of play. This time, I absorbed the full hit, exposing my fragility.

Though I finished the game and contributed to the win, my ability left me wanting. In our next game, we lost in the quarterfinals. The emotional toll of my growing indifference to the game was mounting. Basketball, once a source of joy and identity, now felt like an obligation.

Even with its nostalgic connection, the New Bedford Recreation Department Tournament could not rekindle my enthusiasm. My team played flat, as I did. Despite a brief third-quarter rally, we lost. The Bryant College head coach was in attendance, but my uninspired performance did not reflect my potential. I lacked the energy to explain myself or even care about the outcome.

Afterward, I made the tough decision to withdraw from the remaining tournaments. My parents, always supportive, seemed relieved rather than disappointed. Once again, I could not articulate the depth of my internal struggles.

The end of my high school basketball career left me grappling with the emptiness of unfulfilled expectations. The physical and emotional toll of the season had drained me, leaving me unprepared to transition to the next phase of my athletic life. Opportunities like the Boston Shootout and international competition with my former Youth Games teammates passed me by. I lacked the will to seize those chances, even though I recognized their importance.

The emotional confrontations I faced throughout the season, both internal and external, culminated in this moment of reflection. I had spent years pursuing the dream of an athletic scholarship, sacrificing, and enduring countless challenges. Now that the goal was within reach, I felt hollow, unable to reconcile the cost of the journey with its rewards.

This past season was emotionally challenging, marked by trauma and attempts at recovery. My greatest takeaway was my resilience. Fear gripped me, and I wanted to flee, leaving behind everything I had worked for. It was not perfect. In my mind, I always believed tomorrow would be a better day.

Then there are those situations where strangers, acquaintances, neighbors, or friends somehow find you:

- Working out with the New Bedford High School football team during the summer of 1976, just before my admission to Holy Family. My father hoped to create a more confident athlete through these workouts. Imagine a fifteen-year-old working out with a Division One football program, lifting weights, doing agility drills, distance running, and sprints.
- This story: a father and son who approached me. It was after what would be my last game for Holy Family during the winter of 1977, and they asked for an autograph. Wow!
- Or when I saw my dentist in the summer of 1977, a family friend, having my teeth filed down because of grinding my front teeth. Listening to him talk about seeing me play and how impressed he was with my poise as a young player.
- This happened on a Saturday evening in early fall 1977. I had just begun my transition to Fairhaven High School. The New Bedford Buddies head coach asked me to bring my Boston Youth Games uniform and gold medal to the gym. The coach said he wanted the players who were coming up through his teams to see what success looked like through hard work and dedication. He would then discuss our relationship. There was also a request made that I speak and give my perspective. I was nervous about speaking. The faces in front of me were unfamiliar, but they looked at me as if they knew me. They recognized me only from watching me play and reading about me in the newspaper. I later questioned their impressions. What did they see? How did they feel when I spoke? I answered their questions, and more importantly, I connected with this group of players. During this brief lecture, or whatever it was, I found unexpected comfort. I felt no hesitation or fear. I spent two hours walking them through drills on shooting, ball-

handling, and endurance. It was a wonderful experience for me. I hoped it was for the junior players as well.

- And in this story, I did not return on the team bus after beating Hyde Park in the first round of the state tournament in the winter of 1978. Instead, I went home with my father and the New Bedford Buddies' head coach. When my father parked our car in the driveway and we were walking towards our home, we heard a noise from behind us. Turning, we both saw our neighbor running toward us from across the street, waving his arms. His children often sat on our lawn to watch my practice sessions in the driveway. As he reached us, breathless, he excitedly recounted listening to my game on the radio. My performance and the praise I received from the broadcasters amazed him. He talked about telling his friends he lived across the street from the kid with the newspaper article, the one who broke the junior high school scoring record and then led a local high school in scoring as a freshman. Our neighbor went on and on. He told his friends he would watch me practice (weird, sure) and how I never missed a shot. Until then, our communication had only been glances and waves. My father found the outburst humorous and interesting. I felt uncomfortable; past difficult relationships had tainted my reaction to attention on my abilities and accomplishments.

- In the summer of 1978, my father and I attended a homecoming event in Fairhaven. As we walked through the center of town, people greeted me. My father, always quick to tease, said, "He forgot he was with the mayor of Fairhaven." Instantly after my father's comment, someone greeted my father by name. This person looked right through my father and directly at me. It was an unsettling maneuver. As I would learn, this man was the father of one of the junior players I had spoken to last fall. His son attended my talk at the New Bedford Recreation gym. This person congratulated me on my success and mentioned our team's trip to the state finals. He spoke about how impressed his son was with me. I thanked him, and our conversation shifted to his son's future in basketball. This father wanted his son to play at Fairhaven High School, just as he had. That made me uncomfortable. Legacy conversations always unsettled me. I would question their honesty and motivation with this type of conversation.

Hoping to bring my father into this conversation felt right. He had always strategized for me. Yet, this time, he let me stand on my own. While I spoke, my father faded into the background. When I stopped trying to search for my father, I suddenly realized more parents gathered around me, mostly fathers. You would have to wonder what it looked like as these fathers stood around listening as a seventeen-year-old gave advice. My immediate response to the group of fathers was: "Encourage and support your children. Find good coaching. Be there for them. Help them find their way." I also recommended using the town's existing programs. When I finished my statement, I realized how quiet it was. All eyes were on me.

Then the conversation shifted to my future. The heat of the summer made the exchange feel even longer. I wanted to leave. Thankfully, the wives grew impatient and pulled their husbands away. They all thanked me, wished me luck, and said they enjoyed watching me play. An interesting dynamic between me and the people who were surrounding me was that, to a person, they all wanted to physically touch me. Either with a handshake or with a brief hug. To say this was overwhelming for me does not accurately describe my feelings. My father, never showing excitement, walked me toward our car. As we left, he whispered a reminder. My chores had to be done before sundown. I could not play basketball until my chores were completed. Reality had returned, and all was right in the universe.

- This story occurred prior to the 1979-1980 season, my senior year at Fairhaven High School. During the fall of 1979, the *Boston Sunday Globe* reported its scouting report for the high school basketball season. I saw the article mentioned me, which was great. Home alone, I headed out for an afternoon run. Our home phone rang. I debated whether to answer the call and just go for my run. I answered the phone with reservations. Not recognizing the voice at the other end of the call initially. It was one of my classmates from Holy Family, calling to congratulate me on the mention in the *Boston Sunday Globe*. We talked for over an hour, talking about everything, and the conversation was so easy. When we finally said goodbye, I could not think about my exercise program; my focus was on what I suddenly realized, what I was missing in my life. Genuine and organic friendships. I knew why I did not have any friendships in my life, but that did not make it any easier to understand what I was feeling.

- My junior year, 1978-1979, was tumultuous, dangerous and, in my eyes, a failure. A point of interest during our first game at home vs. Old Rochester High School (ORR). As noted, ORR always wanted to take the ball out of my hands at any cost. During this game, they applied a full-court press, hoping to do just that. Unfortunately for them, forcing our team to execute our full-court press offense would not end well for them. On consecutive plays while breaking their full-court press, I was called for traveling. Confused by this, I let the plays go and focused on the game. I learned later that my father had spoken to the referees after the game, looking for an explanation. During this conversation, my father playfully said, and I quote, "Just because you have not seen this move before, you shouldn't penalize the player for it." Over the summer, I developed a hesitation dribble move where I held the ball and let the ball appear to bounce high, and then power dribbled to execute a double tap (Maravich) crossover dribble to fake my opponent. The referees surprised me by calling traveling violations during this game. I had not been called for this infraction in the two summer leagues I played in while executing this move.

- Another story: during my senior year in high school, after the first-round game in the state tournament during the winter of 1980, I walked through the Braintree High School gym after playing our game. "Hey, Semiao!" someone called. I stopped and turned toward the voice. An older man approached me, smiling. As he got closer, I struggled to recognize him. He extended his hand and expressed how great it was to meet me. We shook hands, and I smiled. He introduced himself. He had watched me play five times over two seasons with the New Bedford Buddies. Five times? Interesting. He seemed eager to share more. Then, I heard Coach Drury's name. He said he had recommended me to Coach Drury. Knowing Bryant College needed a point guard. I was at a loss for words. I thanked him for his support and walked away. On the bus ride home, his words stayed with me. My father's words: "Always play hard. You never know who is watching. Leave a powerful impression every time you step on the court."

- One afternoon during the winter of 1980, my sister, who had transferred to Fairhaven High School from Bishop Stang (a private Catholic high school in North Dartmouth) was playing a basketball game against Bishop Stang. The Fairhaven girls game preceded our practice. My connection to Bishop Stang began in eighth grade when we searched for a varsity opportunity. Bishop Stang did not allow freshmen to play varsity. They prioritized freshman and junior varsity development. Bill Hart, the head basketball coach for the girls' basketball team at Bishop Stang, was a respected and supportive presence. While my team warmed up, running a three-man weave, Coach Hart appeared on the sideline talking with Mr. Wilson. Mr. Wilson waved me over. Coach Hart greeted me with a firm handshake and a warm smile. The words I remembered most were: "Congratulations, thrilled for you, and well deserved." That moment transported me back. After one of my sister's games when she was a freshman at Bishop Stang, I had shot baskets at the conclusion of her game. I was feeling down after a mediocre performance the night before. Coach Hart appeared, rebounding for me and offering encouragement. His support was unexpected but reflective of who he was. His words that morning filled me with warmth and inspired me to practice self-compassion.

- Playing against a rival school on a Friday night during the winter of 1980, the crowd under the basket stood five people deep. We lost a tough, close game. While changing after the game, someone entered the locker room and said my father wanted to see me. I put on my warm-up jacket, left my game shorts on, and put on my unlaced sneakers sockless, then walked out to the gym. Across the gym, I saw my mother and father speaking with someone. The gym lights had been turned off, and only the nightlights remained on. I could not make out who they were talking to. As I approached, I recognized my math tutor from last summer. He was a teacher at the school we had just played against. Seeing him again was unexpected. He greeted me with a firm handshake and a big hug. My tutor explained that he had discussed the rivalry with his colleagues and mentioned me to them. His peers spoke highly of my ability. Out of character, he came to the game that night out of curiosity and specifically to watch me play. I later learned he had only attended the annual Thanksgiving football game. He rarely watched other sporting events, preferring to support from a distance. The conversation shifted to the game and our team's performance. My father stood beside me; his arm wrapped around my waist. This was a familiar stance, one that felt comforting. Though I said little, I felt an unexpected sense of peace. Amid life's chaos, this tutor took time out of his life to come and watch me play.

- One afternoon during the summer of 1980 at a local convenience store, I ran into my first basketball coach, Mr. Viera. I had not seen him for years. After leaving Ford Junior High School, unfortunately, I lost touch with my classmates and everyone surrounding that time. During random events, somehow, we would find each other, if only briefly. Mr. Viera and I talked for an hour. Learning that people followed my career from afar created a deep appreciation and curiosity. My cynicism made me question why someone would care and speak of it without hesitation. In my mind, I should have been kinder and gentler with myself. Being in a different mental space gave me an odd perspective.

These acknowledgements are still with me. Never would I have thought that anyone would come watch me play. Of all the things I expected during this time of my life, this was an unexpected sense of joy for me. Other athletes may have experienced similar moments of support, but these were mine. These interactions are impossible to predict, yet they reveal the unseen impact of presence and ability. They are byproducts of effort, time, and sacrifice, not the goal, but meaningful just the same.

I often wondered if I stopped playing basketball, would my problems disappear? Would people still seek my advice? Would I take that deal? It is a complex question. Taking the deal meant losing the complexities of identity, feeling, and self-expression. For eight years, I lived in a world of expectations. I thrived, but I struggled. Others shaped this reality, yet I had to acknowledge my blindness. My ego held power over me, influencing my thoughts and actions. Before my final high school game, I would have refused the deal. But during the season, in moments of desperation, I might have accepted it. If someone had asked, "What if you overcame everything?" What if walking away solved your problems? I do not know how I would have answered. I know this for sure: my younger self would have refused.

Epilogue Still Standing

When I first began writing this memoir, I thought it would be a simple collection of basketball stories. I did not expect it would uncover the hidden parts of myself I had long kept at a distance.

People praised the boy I used to be, talented, determined, but he also feared failure and truly being seen. He built walls to survive. Over time, those walls kept him isolated.

Now, standing at the edge of one chapter ending and another beginning, I see the weight of what I carried. Survival became normal. Achievement became armor. But beneath it all, fractures quietly formed.

I acted the part: strong, composed, and successful. Inside, I was unraveling. Self-worth tangled with winning, grades, and expectations. Every misstep felt like a collapse.

There were moments I wanted to scream, *"I'm not okay,"* but the words never came. Instead, my body spoke through chronic hives, a recurrent back injury. We did not know how to talk about emotional pain back then. Silence became its own language.

For years, I believed I could engineer success. Control every play. Hide every fear. But the moments that shaped me most were the ones I could not plan or protect myself from.

Authoring this story has been a way of seeing that boy again. Not to judge him, but to understand him. To honor his struggle. To forgive him.

Life after basketball taught me that genuine success comes from authentic connections and being seen as you are.

If you see yourself in these pages, know this: healing is possible. The person you were does not define the person you can become.

I do not have all the answers. But I have stopped trying to outrun the questions. I have learned to sit with them. To honor the truth of what I carried and what I survived.

Because in the end, I did not disappear. I am still here. Still standing.

For those who carry silent burdens, you are not alone.

Author's Note - About the Keepers

When I was a teenager; I did not have the language for what I was experiencing. I knew only the pressure, the isolation, and the sense that my world could vanish if I faltered. In that silence, I created an inner space I came to call The Keepers. They were not literal figures. They were how I gave shape to truths I could not yet speak aloud, a way of keeping myself safe when everything felt exposed.

Including The Keepers in Courts of Reflection is my way of showing what it felt like from the inside. They are not meant to confuse the reader, but to reveal the psychological architecture of survival. Where a straightforward narrative might reduce a life to scores and timelines, The Keepers honors the inner world that ran alongside the outer one.

This book is not just about the games I played. It is about the unseen work of endurance and how, sometimes, we need to create a language to survive long enough to tell our story.

Final Notes: A Message to Families and Mentors

If you are supporting a young athlete, a child, a sibling, or a student, what you see on the surface may only tell half the story. Behind the routines and repetition might be a young person working through fear, insecurity, or the quiet belief that their worth depends on performance.

Praise can feel conditional. Encouragement, if too narrowly focused on outcomes, can deepen the fear of failure. Sometimes, a child needs to hear, "I see how hard you're trying," more than "You've got this." They may need space to fail without it shaking your confidence in them.

I knew that my family loved me. I never doubted that. But I also know how hard it is to decode silence. When a child does not speak, it is easy to assume they are fine, especially if they are achieving. But silence can mean pressure. It can mean loneliness.

One of the most powerful gifts you can offer is not a solution; it is presence. It is asking a question without rushing to fix it. It helps a young person understand they are more than what they produce. That matters, even when they struggle.

Reflective practice is not just for athletes. It is for families too. "Asking not just how someone is performing, but how they are doing." "It means making room for the inner world, the one often hidden behind discipline and drive."

When I look back now, I do not wish for fewer drills or fewer expectations. I wish for more understanding of what I had been carrying. If this chapter of my life offers anything, I hope it offers a window and a reminder that the strongest young people often carry the most unspoken weight.

Neat endings do not conclude this story. But it carries hope in its honesty. And for anyone carrying unseen pain or trying to protect a young person from being consumed by it, I offer this: our scars can become our strength. Our silence does not have to last forever.

Thank you for reading.

Final Dedication - To the boy

Before I close, there is someone I need to speak to, the boy who carried it all. Sometimes, I questioned whether I should have acted, spoken out, sought help, or sought attention. But what I know now is that I did what I had to do to survive.

I lacked the resources to understand everything. But I do now. And for the boy I once was, the one who gave everything, who held everything in, and who never stopped moving forward, this letter is for you.

You did not imagine it. The pressure, the silence, the feeling that no one really saw what you were going through, it was all real. You were not weak from feeling overwhelmed. You were strong in ways no one understood, including you.

I know you thought success would fix it all. Being the best would make everything around you more solid, more certain. But even in victory, you were still holding back tears, still wondering why everything felt so fragile underneath.

There will be times when you consider leaving the game. Walking away from trust, and from your own voice. But I need you to hold on just a little longer.

Because what feels like a loss right now … space is opening for greater honesty and wholeness.

You will leave behind things that once defined you. People you loved, roles you played, even parts of yourself you thought were permanent. And it will hurt. But on the other side of that hurt, something beautiful will grow.

You will learn to make peace with what has left. You will learn to appreciate what has stayed. And one day, you will look back with gentleness, not because it was easy, but because you finally see it clearly.

So, keep going. Keep breathing. And remember: the right things will always connect.

With love, You

Sources and Acknowledgements

The opening epigraph, "Perhaps everything terrible is, in its deepest being, something that needs our love", is from Rainer Maria Rilke, Letters to a Young Poet., translated by Stephen Mitchell (Vintage International, 1986). Its spirit of compassion and transformation frames much of the reflection that follows in this memoir.

AUTHORSHIP AND MEMORY—LITERARY REFERENCES

Joan Didion, "We tell ourselves stories to live," from The White Album (1979)

James Patterson, Sams Letters to Jennifer (2004): "I want to tell you stories…the way I remember them, anyway."

Fyodor Dostoevsky, Crime and Punishment (1866): "Your worst sin is that you have destroyed and betrayed yourself for nothing."

Fyodor Dostoevsky, Netochka Nezvanova (1849): "You sensed you should follow a different path…you began to hate everything around you."

Jerry West, My Charmed, Tormented Life, his reference to Didion's line underscored the memoir's core question: why we tell the stories we do, and what truth we hope to reclaim through them.

Michael J. Meade, To Not Abandon Ourselves: The mystic Saint John of the Cross wrote: "If a person wishes to be sure of the road on which they tread, they must close their eyes and walk in the dark." The idea of "the dark night of the soul" echoes throughout this work, symbolizing descent, transformation, and return.

REGIONAL AND HISTORICAL CONTEXT

Southeastern Massachusetts: historical background adapted from public records and Wikipedia (accessed 2025).

Acushnet, Massachusetts: historical background adapted from the Town of Acushnet public record and Wikipedia (accessed 2025).

Fairhaven, Massachusetts: historical background adapted from the Town of Fairhaven public record and Wikipedia (accessed 2025).

Fairhaven High School: institutional details drawn from Wikipedia, "Fairhaven High School and Academy" (accessed 2025).

Holy Family High School (New Bedford, Massachusetts): historical details drawn from Wikipedia (accessed 2025).

Jack Nobrega and Wayne Wilson: their careers and legacies documented in articles by Buddy Thomas in the Standard Times and SouthCoast Today (1970s–2010s)

CLINICAL AND PSYCHOLOGICAL REFERENCES

Sports performance anxiety, sensory activation, and arousal regulation connect to the experiences described where physical contact or impact could "wake" the player, restoring focus and calm.

- Clinically, this may reflect sensory grounding, a process where a physical stimulus refocuses the mind.
- It mirrors the inverted-U theory in sports psychology: optimal performance occurs at a specific level of arousal, not too low (lethargic), not too high (overanxious).

The trembling before games represented a physical manifestation of performance anxiety, part of the "fight or flight" response triggered by adrenaline release.

The "quiet mind" experienced during peak performance aligns with what psychologists call "flow state" or "being in the zone", a state of deep focus and immersive awareness where time slows, coordination sharpens, and movement feels effortless.

Psychologists also refer to the hedonic treadmill: the relentless pursuit of external goals that raise the bar but never satisfy.

Ancient traditions warned that external validation could never bring lasting peace, a truth the athlete in this memoir discovers through experience, not theory.

ACKNOWLEDGEMENTS

To my family, who have guided me through life and healing. They know how much I love them. The unspoken word "unconditional" is where all this lands.

My friends who have given their time, space and love, thank you.

Last, thank you to everyone for trusting me to tell this story, my story.

About the Author

M ichael K. Semiao, who is a former standout basketball player from Southeastern Massachusetts, whose early success and personal struggles inspired this memoir. Now a healthcare executive and founder of MKS Associates. He lives in North Andover, Massachusetts, with his wife, Rita.